100 THINGS CUBS FANS
SHOULD KNOW & DO
BEFORE THEY DIE

Jimmy Greenfield

TRIUMPH
BOOKS

The Library of Congress Cataloging has catalogued the first edition as follows:

Greenfield, Jimmy, 1967–
    100 things Cubs fans should know & do before they die / Jimmy Greenfield.
        p. cm.
    Includes bibliographical references.
    ISBN 978-1-60078-662-4 (pbk.)
    1. Chicago Cubs (Baseball team)—History. 2. Chicago Cubs (Baseball team)—Miscellanea. I. Title. II. Title: One hundred things Cubs fans should know & do before they die.
    GV875.C6G76 2012
    796.357'640977311—dc23

                            2011049411

This book is available in quantity at special discounts for your group or organization. For further information, contact:
    Triumph Books LLC
    814 North Franklin Street
    Chicago, Illinois 60610
    (312) 337-0747
    www.triumphbooks.com

Printed in U.S.A.
ISBN: 978-1-62937-462-8
Design by Patricia Frey
All photos courtesy of AP Images unless otherwise noted

For my wife, Jill, and my sons, Casey and Eli, who have made my life complete.

*But I'd still like to see the Cubs win the World Series **(again)** before I die.*

Contents

Introduction

True or false: It's great to be a Cubs fan.

If you had to ponder the answer or laughed it off with a smirk and a knee-jerk "false" then you're certainly not a diehard—or you're possibly wearing a Cardinals hat at the moment. And you somehow aren't aware of what transpired during the fall of 2016.

If it was clear as a summer's day at Wrigley Field that loving the Cubs is no more difficult than loving your family, then you don't need me to remind you of something you've likely known your whole life: It is great, and has always been great, to be a Cubs fan.

Note that I didn't ask if it can be painful, discouraging, or traumatic. Because it can be, has been, and, in all likelihood, will be again. But if the Cubs' well-documented history of tormenting their supporters was all that mattered then this book would have been called 12 Things Cubs Fans Should Know & Do Before They Die.

As far back as I can remember, the Cubs have been a part of my life, though I don't remember exactly how it all began. Unlike some people who can reach into their past and vividly recall first walking into Wrigley Field or who introduced them to the Cubs, I've retained no such memory.

My dad, an avid sports fan but no fanatic, regularly took me to Blackhawks and Bears games and gets the credit, as well as the occasional blame, for those teams being part of my life.

But the Cubs? I honestly don't know how I latched onto them. I'm sure some of it was falling in love with baseball at an early age, or the circumstance of being placed in my school's morning kindergarten class, then choosing to spend my afternoons with Jack Brickhouse upon returning home.

My mom says I learned to read by looking up the baseball standings in the newspaper, but given the Cubs' general state of disarray during the mid-1970s that doesn't explain why I didn't subsequently turn on them. However it happened, it happened. I grew to love the Cubs, warts and all. But there was never a day I wished I'd have been born a Cardinals fan, Yankees fan, or, God forbid, a White Sox fan.

When the first edition of this book was published, the Cubs were mere months into Theo Epstein's tenure as the Cubs' president of baseball operations. I thought about taking out one of the "100 Things" and replacing it with an item on Theo's hiring and what it may bring, but the truth there is we just didn't know. Now we know that Theo may one day have a statue erected outside Wrigley Field, and nobody would be shocked.

What we also know is the Cubs have had a long and extraordinary past, checkered though it may be. I haven't spared sharing the most painful moments, trades, or seasons. But as you read this book I have no doubt you'll find there has always been far more to the Cubs than the stale narrative about their losing ways.

And that it truly is great, and has always been great, to be a Cubs fan.

1 It Happened

"When the Cubs win the World Series—and they will win it one day, though I'm not at liberty to tell you when—nobody will be calm. There will be crying and shaking and TV reporters will try to ruin much of it by sticking their microphones in the faces of crazed fans who will only want to hug their friends or call their mom or visit their grandpa at his grave to tell him what just happened.

And I can tell you this, as well: the Cubs players who eventually win the World Series will be remembered as gods. They will be gods because they will have the power to make Cubs fans, if not forget the past, at least change the way in which they remember it."

—The last two paragraphs I wrote from the previous first chapter of this book, titled "Watch the Cubs Win the World Series."

We watched the Cubs win the World Series. Now what?

Cubs fans got what they desperately wanted and, much like the proverbial dog that finally caught the rabbit but then didn't know what to do with it, now have to figure out how to handle this new reality. Because—and I can't emphasize this enough so I'll use italics—*this is strange.*

It's strange to finally be on the other side after years of wondering what it would feel like to watch the Cubs win the World Series. I vividly remember the 1984 season, when the Cubs went to the playoffs for the first time in my lifetime, and thinking simply getting to the playoffs was bizarre. Winning the World Series just never seemed possible. So, yes, this is very strange. It's wonderful and cathartic and nothing in the world of sports will ever bring me greater joy, but it does necessitate a rethinking of what it means to be a Cubs fan.

A little less than a minute before the Cubs won the World Series, my 10-year-old son pushed the video record button on our iPad to capture what we hoped would soon be a celebration to remember. The mood in our family room was tense. Words were being chosen carefully, there was little physical movement by any of us, and I distinctly remember wondering if it would help if I switched the remote control from one part of the room to another.

In short, I was losing my mind. And then it happened.

Cubs reliever Mike Montgomery got Cleveland's Michael Martinez to weakly dribble an 0–1 pitch toward third base, Kris Bryant fielded the slow but routine grounder, and Anthony Rizzo stood tall as Bryant's true throw found its way into the back of his waiting mitt. In the immediacy of our celebration my son screamed out, "Finally!" which led to many chuckles from people I showed the video to, who pointed out the irony of a 10-year-old feeling as though he'd waited a long time for the Cubs to win the World Series.

But it wasn't about the wait for my son; in his short time on this earth he'd become a "long-suffering" Cubs fan. There was no other way to be; it didn't matter how old you were. And those days are now over. From now on, every new Cubs fan will inherit the joy of 2016 as well as some of the pain of the 108 years that preceded it.

That's what's different for all of us. Because it happened. It really happened.

25 Things to Know About Wrigley Field

Wrigley Field isn't going anywhere—the $575 million in renovations is seeing to that—so while you need to see a game there before you die don't worry that it'll disappear before you do. The Cubs moving to another ballpark is as unthinkable as the first family moving out of the White House. It's just not going to happen. Without Wrigley Field, the Cubs wouldn't be the Cubs, they'd be the White Sox, and that's an alternate reality too sad to comprehend.

All you really need to enjoy Wrigley is a ticket to sit anywhere in the ballpark and at least one of your five senses. It might help just a little bit to know these 25 things:

1. The land Wrigley Field was built on was previously occupied by a seminary. The park was commissioned by Charles Weeghman for his Federal League team, the Chicago ChiFeds, also known as the Chicago Whales.

2. When you go, don't pay for parking. If you're driving to the game, park on the street near Irving Park Road and take the Red Line to the game. It's cheaper, faster, and is perfectly safe.

3. Wrigley Field was designed by architect Zachary T. Davis, who also designed the original Comiskey Park.

4. The Cubs offer several different types of tours of Wrigley Field, ranging from $25 per person tours that will take you to see the clubhouse, press box, and possibly a chance to step on the field to $50,000 per group mega-events that include the chance to take batting practice.

5. It took 50 days to build Wrigley Field. Ground was broken on March 4, 1914, in a public ceremony, and the first game

was played on April 23, 1914. The ChiFeds beat Kansas City 9–1.

6. With the addition of Ron Santo's statue, there are four statues of important figures in Cubs history surrounding the park. Although they have been relocated during Wrigley's renovations, Santo's is usually at the corner of Addison and Sheffield, as is Billy Williams' statue. Ernie Banks has a statue on Clark Street near the main ticket window, and Harry Caray's statue is at Sheffield and Waveland after initially being a block south.

7. The ballpark was named Weeghman Park until 1920 when it was renamed Cubs Park following the sale of the club to William Wrigley. In 1926, it became known as Wrigley Field.

8. The original seating capacity was 14,000, although contemporary newspaper reports indicated more than 21,000 fans attended the first game.

9. The original dimensions were 310' to left field, 440' to center, and 345' to right.

10. Weeghman bought the Cubs in 1916 after the Whales folded and moved the team from the West Side Grounds to Weeghman Park. The Cubs played their first game at Wrigley Field on April 20, 1916, defeating Cincinnati 7–6 in 11 innings.

11. The first no-hitter at Wrigley Field was thrown on May 2, 1917, by Cincinnati's Fred Toney. This was the famous game where the Cubs' Hippo Vaughn also didn't allow a hit for nine innings before faltering in the 10th.

12. Wrigley Field has hosted three All-Star games—1947, 1962, and 1990. The American League won all three games. Andy Pafko and Ernie Banks are the only Cubs to get a hit in an All-Star Game played at Wrigley Field. Ryne Sandberg, Andre Dawson, and Shawon Dunston went a combined 0-for-7 in 1990. Milt Pappas saved the 1962 game, but he did it for the AL as a member of the Baltimore Orioles.

13. The Cubs have a record of 3–13 in World Series games played at Wrigley Field. They won Game 5 of the 1935 World Series, Game 6 of the 1945 Fall Classic, and Game 5 in 2016.

14. Despite making it to the 1918 World Series, the Cubs didn't play their home games at Wrigley Field. The series was moved to Comiskey Park to take advantage of their larger seating capacity.

15. Wrigley Field was home to the Chicago Bears from 1921 until 1970. Only Giants Stadium, due to the New York Giants and New York Jets double occupancy, and Green Bay's Lambeau Field have hosted more NFL games.

16. The highest attendance ever was on June 27, 1930, when 51,556 fans packed Wrigley Field to see the Cubs play the Brooklyn Dodgers. At least 30,476 women entered free for Ladies Day.

17. 3,300,200 fans came out in 2008, the highest single-season attendance at Wrigley Field. They surpassed 2 million for the first time in 1984 when attendance reached 2,107,655.

18. The first major renovation took place prior to the 1923 season when the single-deck grandstand was rebuilt and seats were added to the bleachers. Capacity increased to around 30,000.

19. In 1925 the left-field line was 319', resulting in a ton of home runs being hit. In response to public outcry, the Cubs took out roughly 1,500 ground-level bleachers to increase the home-run distance to 370'.

20. The Cubs started construction on an upper deck for the grandstand following the 1926 season, but only the third-base side was ready by Opening Day 1927. Still, the new capacity of around 40,000 enabled Wrigley Field to draw 1,159,168 fans, the first time a National League team surpassed 1 million in attendance.

21. For the first 46 years of its existence, the Cubs clubhouse was located on the mezzanine level on the third-base side. In 1960,

a new bi-level clubhouse was built with an entryway in the left-field corner. This lasted until 1983 when the current clubhouse connected to the dugout was constructed.

22. The basket hanging over the front of the bleachers was installed in 1970 to prevent fans from jumping out and onto the field. The first game with the basket was played on May 7, 1970.

23. Alcohol wasn't served at Wrigley Field until 1933, following the end of prohibition. The first beer was actually low-alcohol beer commonly called "3.2" beer.

24. It's a staple for ballparks to have an organ these days, but it wasn't until April 26, 1941, that the first one was installed in a major league ballpark—at Wrigley Field. The current organist is Gary Pressey, a job he's held since 1987.

25. To learn 1,000 more things about the ballpark, do yourself a favor and get a copy of *Wrigley Field: The Unauthorized Biography*. It's a fantastic book with wonderful anecdotes, stories, and fascinating tidbits uncovered by author Stuart Shea.

1969

There's a running gag in the classic Mel Brooks comedy *Young Frankenstein* in which every time the name "Blücher" is spoken, a team of horses lets out a loud, terrified whinny. It's very funny.

The same can be said of Cubs fans whenever the year 1969 is mentioned, although there's absolutely nothing funny about that. There is a visceral, even primal reaction to this most famous and disturbing of Cubs seasons, which has defined the team for generations and still haunts every player, coach, executive, fan, vendor, and usher who witnessed the team's epic collapse. Even the ivy can't forget.

Ron Santo poses for a photo in April 1969. (AP Photo/Robert H. Houston)

The only thing that could beat the despair of 1969 out of Cubdom would be a World Series ring, and as Durocher, Santo, Banks, Williams, Hundley, Jenkins, Beckert, Kessinger, and the rest of the boys learned that's not an easy thing to do when you've got decades of losing to face down. It also doesn't help that black cats occasionally dart out in front of you.

There was a great deal of excitement and hope when the 1969 season got underway. The Cubs had posted consecutive seasons above .500 for the first time since 1945–46, and fans, media, and the players were convinced next year was here. And on Opening Day it sure seemed like it was.

A Wrigley Field crowd of 40,796, including 27,000 who started lining up at dawn to buy tickets that day, saw Willie Smith's dramatic two-run walk-off homer in the bottom of the 11th inning give the Cubs a 7–6 win over Philadelphia.

Smith's homer touched off an insane scene on the field, in the stands, and inside the clubhouse that set the tone for what became an insane season. Years later, in Rick Talley's essential book *The Cubs of '69*, legendary Cubs third baseman Ron Santo recalled that moment. "We knew right there," Santo said, "that this was the season we were going to win."

And for five glorious months, they did win. A lot. The record book shows the Cubs were above .500 in each of the first five months of 1969 and began September with a 4½-game lead over the New York Mets. The season ended with a historic collapse, but there was far more to it than that. The Cubs seemed to pack more fun, intrigue, and controversy into the 1969 season than the previous 25 years combined.

Smith's Opening Day homer kicked off an 11–1 start and they were still well above .500 in late April when they made their first visit to Shea Stadium to face the New York Mets—a franchise even more hapless during their brief eight-year history than the Cubs—for a four-game series.

Before the Superstation
The Cubs have been such a marketing juggernaut for more than three decades, it's hard to believe it wasn't always that way. Attendance at Wrigley Field didn't top 1 million for 15 straight seasons from 1953 through 1967, and in 1969 not even all the games were televised.

A blurb in the July 1 edition of the *Chicago Tribune*, while the Cubs were on a road trip to Montreal, reported that fans could only listen to Vince Lloyd and Lou Boudreau on WGN Radio.

"[WGN] has a contract to televise only 144 of the Cubs' 162 games," the *Tribune* reported. "And today's contest along with Thursday's afternoon game between the same two teams is among the 18 games which will not be shown."

The Cubs took the first three but lost the finale—the second game of a doubleheader—3–0 on Cleon Jones' three-run ninth-inning homer. It was no big deal, the Cubs were still 14–6 and the Mets were a lowly 7–11. Their paths would cross again.

Back at home, a group calling themselves Bleacher Bums were starting to garner some attention. They were a motley crew of kids and old-timers who began and ended their day at Ray's Bleachers at the corner of Waveland and Sheffield but spent the rest of their time sitting in the bleachers tormenting opposing outfielders.

While the Bums made waves, the players started to cash in on their fame by making paid personal appearances, endorsing anything they could affix their signature to and—17 years before "The Super Bowl Shuffle"—recorded an album called *Cubs Power*. They became, literally, rock stars. Ernie Banks even started writing a regular column for the *Chicago Tribune*.

They kept on winning, but signs of their fate started to show by mid-summer. On June 30 in Montreal, Banks hit an apparent home run that umpire Tony Venzon ruled went through a hole in the fence. Durocher, of course, went berserk. Years later, Expos outfielder Rusty Staub confirmed the ball had cleared the fence. The Cubs lost the game 5–2.

By the time they went to Shea Stadium for a three-game series in early July, the Mets were the only other team above .500 in the National League East. In the opener on July 8 an incident occurred that would mar Ron Santo's reputation for years.

Don Young, who was 23 at the time, probably shouldn't have been in the majors. He was a year removed from Class A ball and only with the big league club because Durocher had no better option in center field. Still, Young was a good fielder and that's why he was in center field in the ninth inning with the Cubs leading the Mets 3–1.

Ken Boswell led off with a pop fly to center, but Young got a bad start and what looked like a catchable ball turned into a double. One out later, Young got his glove on a fly ball over his head but dropped it. The Mets still trailed by a pair of runs but after a double, intentional walk, and a ground out, Ed Kranepool hit a two-out walk-off single to beat the stunned Cubs 4–3.

Back in the clubhouse, Durocher ripped into Young, calling him a "disgrace" and saying his "three-year-old could have caught those balls." Santo wasn't as harsh but no less forgiving, telling Jerome Holtzman of the *Sun-Times*, "He was thinking of himself, not the team…when he hits it's a dividend, but when he fails on defense he's lost—and today he took us down with him."

Managers will do that, and everyone expected that kind of talk from Durocher. But Santo was the team captain, and it was unheard of to throw teammates under the bus. The reaction was swift, and early the next day Santo apologized publicly and personally to Young.

The Cubs went 18–11 in August but the Mets had started to soar, and when the teams met on September 8 in New York the Cubs had lost four straight, and their lead—which had been as high as nine games on August 16—was down to 2½.

The first pitch from Cubs starter Bill Hands went right at Tommie Agee's head. It was a purpose pitch, Hands would later say, but it only gave purpose to the Mets. Jerry Koosman retaliated by plunking Santo in the second inning, and the Cubs responded by doing nothing. "That's when we should have gotten into a fight," relief pitcher Hank Aguirre told Talley years later. "It really hurt me deeply that Santo just walked to first base, and nobody did anything…Leo or Santo or somebody from the dugout should have started a fight."

Things got worse. In what was probably the biggest play of the year, Agee scored the go-ahead run in the sixth when umpire Satch Davidson ruled Hundley missed a sweeping tag. The run held up for a Mets victory, and the following day they won again to cut the lead to a half-game. It was on this day that a black cat was dropped onto the Shea Stadium field and it raced around in front of the Cubs' dugout.

From September 3 to September 15, the Cubs lost 11-of-12 games, including eight in a row at one point, and the team went from being five games up on the Mets to 4½ games back. It was over, and the slow pain from that epic collapse started to sink in. It's still ingrained in the DNA of many Cubs fans.

There are a million theories about why the team folded, but Ernie Banks, who never played in a World Series, may have said it best. "Well, a lot people say we needed more rest, the bench, the black cat in New York, all of that stuff," Banks told Talley. "But it wasn't pressure or outside activities or anything like that. It was fear. When you haven't won, it's scary, and that's life. Dealing with the uncertainties, the unknown. It's fearful when you get there, facing the unknown.

"And that's what I think happened to us in 1969."

4 Listen to Ryne Sandberg's Hall of Fame Speech

By the time Ryne Sandberg was elected to Baseball's Hall of Fame in 2005, the game of baseball was changing in ways that disgusted him. Or rather, as Sandberg saw it, the players were changing. Hard work had been replaced by easy fixes and the old adage that you keep your eyes open and your mouth shut was not only quaint but laughable for the latest me-first brand of ballplayers.

Sandberg watched as the steroid era had rendered home run records meaningless and the way baseball's ruling class—both players and owners—conveniently overlooked it for years was and remains a travesty. Respect for the game was fading.

A smooth almost flawless fielder, Sandberg was neither muscle-bound nor talkative. His 282 career homers—277 as a second baseman, the most ever until Jeff Kent surpassed him—did most of his talking for him, and when he did speak to the press it was reluctantly.

Named after New York Yankees pitcher Ryne Duren, Sandberg grew up in Spokane, Washington, and bypassed a football scholarship to Washington State to sign with the Philadelphia Phillies as a 20th-round draft pick. His rise through the minor leagues was steady if not spectacular, and he made his major league debut with the Phillies late in the 1981 season.

When Sandberg was sent to the Cubs in the off-season he wasn't one of the principals in the trade that dealt Ivan DeJesus to Philadelphia and Larry Bowa to the North Siders. He wasn't a mere throw-in, however. Cubs General Manager Dallas Green insisted on including Sandberg, and the Phils, to their regret, acquiesced.

Sandberg spent his rookie season as the Cubs' third baseman, hitting .271 with seven homers after starting the season 1-for-32.

The arrival of Ron Cey in 1983 pushed Sandberg to second base where he excelled, winning a Gold Glove during his first season at the position.

In 1984 Sandberg had one of the great coming-out years in baseball history, hitting .314 with 19 homers and 84 RBIs to lead the Cubs to their first playoff appearance in 39 years. He became the first Cubs player to be named National League MVP since Ernie Banks in 1959.

Over the following eight seasons, Sandberg kept building his Hall of Fame credentials. He averaged 25 homers, 81 RBIs, and 27 stolen bases during that span, and in 1990 he hit 40 homers to become the first second baseman to lead the NL since Rogers Hornsby in 1925.

Despite those gaudy numbers, Sandberg's near-flawless defense was perhaps more impressive. In 1991, he set a major league record

Ryne Sandberg slugs a triple during a game on Wednesday, August 29, 1984, against the Cincinnati Reds. (AP Photo/Jon Swart)

13

for second baseman (since broken by Luis Castillo) by going 123 games without an error, and he continued to pile up Gold Gloves, winning the award every year until Pittsburgh's Jose Lind beat him out in 1992.

In 1994, Sandberg was earning $7.1 million a year with a couple seasons left on his contract when he stunned the Cubs by retiring in mid-season. He was mired in a 1-for-29 slump and hitting just .238 at the time but said retirement had been on his mind since spring training.

"I lost the edge that it takes to play—the drive, the motivation, the killer instinct, all those things that had been a part of me before," Sandberg told gathered media during his retirement news conference. "I kept thinking it would come back one day, but it never did. It took me 2½ months to realize that."

Eight days after retiring, Sandberg's wife, Cindy, filed for divorce. Their marital problems became the subject of wild rumors, but in his 1995 biography, *Second to Home,* Sandberg emphatically denied his divorce had anything to do with his decision to leave baseball.

Sixteen months later, with a renewed desire to play baseball as well as a new wife, Margaret, Ryno announced his comeback. He clubbed 25 homers in 1996, but he wasn't quite the same player and finished the season hitting .244. After hitting just 12 homers in 1997, a year the Cubs lost their first 14 games, Sandberg ended his playing days for good.

Sandberg's second retirement was in stark contrast to his first but more in line with his reticent personality. So on July 31, 2005, after getting elected to the Hall of Fame on his third try, there was little reason to suspect Sandberg would give baseball the spanking it deserved when he walked to the podium to give his induction speech.

But make no mistake, that's exactly what happened. The theme of his speech was respecting the game, and Ryno used the word "respect" no less than 19 times during the course of it.

"The reason I am here, they tell me, is that I played the game a certain way, that I played the game the way it was supposed to be played. I don't know about that, but I do know this: I had too much respect for the game to play it any other way, and if there was a single reason I am here today, it is because of one word, respect."

He graciously thanked dozens of former teammates, coaches, friends, and family members but never mentioned Sammy Sosa, at least not by name. The *Washington Post* wrote, "Sandberg's surprisingly biting speech mentioned neither steroids nor Sosa explicitly, but it was obvious of what and of whom he was speaking."

"A lot of people say this honor validates my career," Sandberg told the crowd. "But I didn't work hard for validation. I didn't play the game right because I saw a reward at the end of the tunnel. I played it right because that's what you're supposed to do, play it right and with respect. If this validates anything, it's that learning how to bunt and hit and run and turning two is more important than knowing where to find the little red light at the dugout camera."

Sandberg later added, "[Harry Caray] used to say how nice it is that a guy who can hit 40 homers or steal 50 bases drive in a hundred runs is the best bunter on the team. Nice? That was my job. When did it become okay for someone to hit home runs and forget how to play the rest of the game?"

Bobby Dernier, one of the teammates Sandberg singled out for teaching him the right way to play baseball, told the *Chicago Tribune* in 1995, "I first met him as a rookie in 1978 in Helena, Montana. He was 18 and he didn't say anything for two months. I thought he was a Spanish player."

It took nearly 30 years, but Sandberg found his voice. Be sure to listen to it.

5 Sit in the Bartman Seat

Go ahead, you're not going to get in any trouble. Walk down Wrigley Field's left-field line and look for Section 4, Row 8, Seat 113. After you find it, sit down and let your mind wander.

Think about what it must have been like on October 14, 2003, when the Cubs were five outs from reaching the World Series and 40,000 crazed fans watched a foul ball off the bat of Florida's Luis Castillo carry this way. Imagine how a few of them, including a huge Cubs fan named Steve Bartman, instinctively reached toward the sky. Imagine it was you who touched that ball.

Look a few feet away to the outfield grass and picture a livid Cubs left fielder Moises Alou directing his anger toward you, giving every fan in Wrigley Field license to do the same. And then, as Mark Prior fell apart, Alex Gonzalez booted a ball and the Marlins buried the Cubs, imagine that's what every fan in Wrigley Field did.

It takes your breath away to think about the hell Bartman went through that night and in the immediate aftermath. One moment he's a tense Cubs fan on the edge of his seat, the next he's getting death threats, has become the butt of jokes on late night TV, and is blamed for the Cubs not reaching the World Series.

There's an urge to examine how complicit Bartman was in the Cubs' collapse in Game 6, but to even explore that is an acknowledgment he shares more than cursory blame. Yes, he got his hand on the ball among many others reaching for it but, as has been pointed out countless times, the Cubs blew it on the field.

Prior ended up walking Castillo then gave up an RBI single to Ivan Rodriguez. A sharp but routine grounder was muffed by Gonzalez, who has escaped goathood all these years thanks to

Bartman. If any single play was responsible for the Game 6 collapse it was Gonzalez' error on what could have been an inning-ending double play.

Instead, the Marlins had the bases loaded with only one out and the next batter, Derrek Lee, hit a two-run double on Prior's 119th pitch to tie the game at 3–3. Only then did Cubs manager Dusty Baker, who some believe ruined Prior in 2003 by letting him throw too many pitches that year, take him out of the game.

Cubs reliever Kyle Farnsworth gave up Jeff Conine's sacrifice fly and Mike Mordecai's horrifying bases-loaded double that put the game out of reach. By that time, Bartman had long ago departed Section 4, Row 8, Seat 113, and was in protective custody with Wrigley Field security.

Steve Bartman's Statement

The following was released by Steve Bartman on Wednesday, October 15, 2003:

"There are few words to describe how awful I feel and what I have experienced within these last 24 hours.

I've been a Cub fan all my life and fully understand the relationship between my actions and the outcome of the game. I had my eyes glued on the approaching ball the entire time and was so caught up in the moment that I did not even see Moises Alou, much less that he may have had a play.

Had I thought for one second that the ball was playable or had I seen Alou approaching I would have done whatever I could to get out of the way and give Alou a chance to make the catch.

To Moises Alou, the Chicago Cubs organization, Ron Santo, Ernie Banks, and Cub fans everywhere I am so truly sorry from the bottom of this Cubs fan's broken heart.

I ask that Cub fans everywhere redirect the negative energy that has been vented toward my family, my friends, and myself into the usual positive support for our beloved team on their way to being National League champs."

A good deal of Cubs fans became unhinged that night, making loud and public threats toward Bartman and embarrassing themselves in the process. Over time, public opinion has swayed in his favor and while his name is still synonymous with the incident he'd be more likely to receive cheers than boos if he were to make a public appearance at Wrigley Field.

There have been efforts over time to talk to Bartman, and I've been part of that group. In the spring of 2004, I was assigned by my editor to find and interview Bartman. By this time he had made it perfectly clear he had no intention of talking to anyone. But just a few months had passed, not years, and I thought maybe there was a chance. So I went down to his parent's home in a suburb north of Chicago and rang the doorbell.

A woman I assumed to be his mother came to the door, and I introduced myself. She pursed her lips and without any hint of a smile let it be known I wasn't going to be the exception to the no-interview rule. "Put it to sleep," she told me. "We've had enough."

Bless Steve Bartman for keeping quiet all these years. If there was a way to put the genie back in the bottle and give him his name back that would be the right thing to do. But that's impossible.

Nobody will ever know what it's like to be in his shoes. But you can at least try by sitting in his seat.

The Homer in the Gloamin'

At 5:37 PM on September 28, 1938, with darkness falling over a Wrigley Field that wouldn't be afforded the benefit of lights for another 50 years, Gabby Hartnett swung through the evening haze to hit the most famous home run in Cubs history.

It's not possible to overstate how dramatic Hartnett's homer was, whether looking at its importance to the National League pennant race at the time or its everlasting place in Cubs lore.

To set the table for this tale, we'll go back a little more than two months to July 20, 1938, when the Cubs trailed the Pittsburgh Pirates by 5½ games and owner Phil "P.K." Wrigley decided manager Charlie Grimm would have to step down. Wrigley wanted shortstop Billy Jurges to be Grimm's replacement, but Jurges turned down the job. Instead, Jurges came back with a recommendation of Hartnett, a 37-year-old catcher in his 17th season with the Cubs.

After first checking with Grimm, Wrigley handed over the Cubs to Hartnett. The team remained uncomfortably far behind the Pirates, and on August 15, Hartnett broke his thumb on a foul tip. He didn't return until September 8 when the Cubs still trailed by five games.

The lead had been pared to 1½ games on September 27 when the Pirates, alone in first place since July 18, arrived at Wrigley Field for a three-game series. There was no mystery; this series would decide the pennant. The Cubs took the opener 2–1 behind the pitching of Dizzy Dean, and first place was just one win away.

At the time, the Cubs often scheduled weekday games for 3:00 PM and without long breaks for television or an endless march of relief pitchers slowing the pace down it was still possible for the contests to reach their inevitable conclusions without lights. It wasn't rare for a game to finish in less than two hours. Indeed, the Cubs win in the opener took just 98 minutes to complete.

On September 28, however, the Cubs went to the bullpen early and used six relievers along the way. They needed a pair of runs in the bottom of the eighth to knot the score at five, and when the ninth arrived with the sun setting, both managers were informed it would be the last inning.

At this point in baseball history a tie game didn't result in a suspended game to be completed later. If the Pirates and Cubs ended at a tie, the game would have to be replayed in its entirety as part of a doubleheader the following day.

This created urgency on both sides, but Charlie Root set down the Pirates in the top of the ninth, and Pittsburgh's Mace Brown quickly retired Phil Cavarretta and Carl Reynolds in the bottom of the frame. Then up strode Gabby Hartnett.

Hartnett was so tough, Hall of Fame pitcher Carl Hubbell once said he could turn a bat into sawdust with his bare hands. But toughness doesn't matter a whole lot if you're fighting a ghost, and with the "gloamin'" settling in, Hartnett whiffed on Brown's first pitch and barely got a piece of the second, both curveballs.

On the 0–2 pitch, Brown tried to get another curveball past Hartnett.

"I swung with everything I had, and then I got that feeling— the kind of feeling you get when the blood rushes to your head and you get dizzy," Hartnett recalled. "A lot of people told me they didn't know the ball was in the bleachers. Well, I did. I knew the minute I hit it.

"When I got to second base I couldn't see third because the players and fans were there. I don't think I walked another step. I was almost carried the rest of the way. But when I got to home plate I saw [home plate umpire] George Barr taking a good look. He was making sure I touched the platter."

Fans poured onto the field as bedlam broke out at Wrigley Field, and Hartnett had to be surrounded by a circle of ushers and several other men to ensure his safety.

In its game story the following day, the *Chicago Tribune* wrote, "After the skipper finally had struggled to the plate things got worse. The ushers, who had fanned out to form that protective barrier around the infield, forgot their constantly rehearsed maneuver and rushed to save Hartnett's life.

"They tugged and they shoved and finally they started swinging their fists before the players could carry their boss into the safety afforded by the tunnel behind the Cubs dugout. There was new hysteria after Gabby reached the catwalk which leads to the club house. But by this time the gendarmes were organized. Gabby got to the bath house without being stripped by souvenir maniacs."

The game had put the Cubs a mere half game in front of the Pirates, but their backs had been broken and for all intents and purposes the pennant had been decided. The Cubs pounded out a 10–1 win the following day to complete a series sweep and two days later clinched it with a 10–3 win over the St. Louis Cardinals.

Hartnett and his teammates were still celebrating in the clubhouse when a knock on the door came. A letter carrier had scooped up the ball Hartnett had deposited into the left-field bleachers and came to deliver it to his hero.

That baseball and the bat used to hit the "Homer in the Gloamin'" now rest in the Chicago History Museum.

7 Mr. Cub

Ernie Banks was as positive and joyful a man as has ever graced the Friendly Confines, a nickname fittingly given to Wrigley Field by Banks himself. His signature baseball-affirming mantra "Let's Play Two" succinctly captures a childlike spirit, which Banks has never strayed from since first joining the Cubs more than 60 years ago.

A graceful shortstop until his knees betrayed him, Banks' powerful bat whipped around faster than you can say 512 home runs. Nobody ever played in more games or wore the uniform with more pride.

Deservedly, Banks is and forever will be Mr. Cub.

Hall of Famer Ernie Banks poses in front of his newly unveiled statue in front of Wrigley Field during ceremonies on Monday, March 31, 2008. (AP Photo/ Charles Rex Arbogast)

Yet the one thing that's missing from Banks' Hall of Fame career—a postseason appearance—can't be overlooked when set against the public perception that the Cubs were a bunch of lovable losers, a devastating description that still haunts the franchise.

Banks played in 2,528 games for the Cubs, the vast majority of them losses, and not once was he ejected. While steam could almost be seen coming from Ron Santo's ears after a loss, Banks never stopped smiling.

In a profile of Banks in the October 1967 issue of *Ebony*, writer David Llorens relayed how after the Cubs had lost seven in a row a "star player stormed into the clubhouse the morning after and went into a tirade."

"Don't let the past influence the present," Banks cheerfully told him.

"What the hell's wrong with you?" the player responded. "You like losing?"

Banks just walked away, muttered something about it being a nice day out—even though it was raining—and said it was time to go "beat the Pirates."

Ernest Banks was born January 31, 1931, and raised in racially charged Dallas when segregation was a way of life. He spent his youth playing every sport except the one that would be his calling. A scout spotted him playing softball and Banks was persuaded to try his hand at baseball, eventually joining the Kansas City Monarchs of the Negro League.

When Banks joined the Cubs as a wiry 22-year-old in 1953 to become the team's first African American player—six years after Jackie Robinson broke the color barrier—the team hadn't finished above .500 for six seasons. The run mercifully ended in 1963 with an 82–80 record.

Through those lean years—in Banks' first nine full major league seasons the Cubs finished below .500 each year and went an astonishing 587–806—he became the face of the franchise while putting up numbers for a shortstop that were previously unthinkable.

During a six-year run from 1955–60, Banks averaged 41 homers and 116 RBIs, numbers every bit as dominant as those of Hank Aaron, Willie Mays, or Mickey Mantle, the other top sluggers of the era. He was named the National League's MVP in 1958 and 1959 to become the first NL player to win the award in consecutive seasons.

Banks played 424 straight games to start his career, a record that was only recently broken by the New York Yankees' Hideki Matsui. From 1956–61 Banks had another streak—this time 717 consecutive games—until his knees forced him to start taking days off and necessitated a move to first base.

The First (Acting) African American Manager

When Frank Robinson was hired as a player-manager of the Cleveland Indians in 1975, he broke an important color barrier by becoming Major League Baseball's first African American manager.

But he wasn't really the first. Ernie Banks beat him to the punch by nearly two seasons.

On May 8, 1973, Banks was a coach with the Cubs when manager Whitey Lockman was ejected in the 11th inning at San Diego. The two coaches who would have taken over for Lockman were Larry Jansen and Pete Reiser. According to George Langford of the *Chicago Tribune*, Jansen missed the game due to his wife's illness and Reiser had got hurt in a recent melee against San Francisco.

The only two coaches left on the bench were Banks and Hank Aguirre, who incidentally were born on the exact same day. Banks took over, and in the top of the 12th inning Joe Pepitone's run-scoring double broke the tie and the Cubs went on to win 3–2.

Acting managers don't get credit for a win, and as a result Banks doesn't have a managerial record. That doesn't change the fact that the first time a black man managed in the major leagues, the win actually went to a man named Whitey.

Even though Banks is best known for being a shortstop, he played more games at first base (1,259) than at short (1,125) and didn't play any at short during the final 10 seasons of his career. It didn't really matter where Banks played; he never complained. In 1957, third baseman Gene Baker, Banks' roommate and best friend on the team, was traded to Pittsburgh. The Cubs tried desperately to find a replacement, and they did: Ernie Banks.

Banks played 58 games at third base that season, the most of any player on the team. He committed just three errors and despite moving all over the infield still hit .285 with 43 homers and 102 RBIs.

As the Cubs became a contender in the late 1960s, their dependence on Banks decreased. Irascible Cubs manager Leo Durocher was, to say the least, not a fan of Banks. After Durocher took over the club in 1966 he tried to trade Banks several times and only played him because he felt he had no choice.

In his autobiography, *Nice Guys Finish Last*, Durocher wrote of Banks, "He couldn't run, he couldn't field; toward the end, he couldn't even hit. There are some players who instinctively do the right things on the base paths. Ernie had an unfailing instinct for doing the wrong thing. But I had to play him. Had to play the man or there would have been a revolution in the street."

Banks was not the same hitter he had been but during the failed campaign of 1969, when Durocher deserted the team on at least two occasions during the season, Banks showed up every day and hit 23 homers with 106 RBIs.

There was never a time, not even when Durocher was riding him, that Banks became cynical about the Cubs or baseball. During the 1969 season, a couple months before the collapse, Banks wrote a column for the *Chicago Tribune* and professed his love for the game and Wrigley Field.

"When I come to the ballpark, I leave all the world's troubles and mine behind," he wrote. "I enjoy baseball so much and the enthusiasm of the fans that I'd be happy to stay nights in Wrigley Field if they'd roll out a cot for me near first base."

The man just loved to play. In 1962 Banks was hit in the head by a Moe Drabowsky pitch and was hospitalized for two nights. Four days after the beaning, with a batting helmet on for the first time in his career and a throbbing headache, Bank returned to the Cubs' lineup and went 4-for-5 with three homers and a double.

By the time Banks retired in 1971, he was the Cubs' all-time leader in games played (2,528), at-bats (9,421), total bases (4,706), and extra-base hits (1,009), and he ranked second in hits (2,583) and RBIs (1,636). His 512 homers were also the most ever until Sammy Sosa, with 545 in a Cubs uniform, eclipsed him.

After retiring, Banks briefly served as a Cubs coach and minor-league instructor. Since 1976 he has been a goodwill ambassador for the team, except for a brief period in 1984 during the Dallas Green regime when he was inexplicably fired. A public uproar ensured that Banks' absence didn't last long.

The softball player who left Texas and grew up to become the greatest player in Cubs history died on January 23, 2015, at the age of 83. Cubs fans will never forget his annual slogans—"Santo's in heaven, so we're going to win in '11!"—that were as sure a sign as any that Opening Day was near.

8 The Most Dominant Game Ever Pitched

If someone tells you they were at Wrigley Field to watch 20-year-old Kerry Wood throw a one-hitter and strike out 20 Houston Astros in his fifth major league start, you might want to ask for proof.

Chances are they weren't there. Few people were. Only 15,758 were in the park on May 6, 1998, to see perhaps the most dominant pitching performance in the history of Major League Baseball, certainly the most dominant by a boy who barely needed to shave yet.

And who would have been clamoring to be at Wrigley Field on a chilly, rainy Wednesday afternoon in May? Sure, Wood was a former first-round pick out of Texas who had developed into an exciting prospect, striking out 329 hitters in 54 minor league starts.

But just 12 days earlier, in his third major league start, Wood looked like a lost boy while getting only five outs and giving up seven earned runs in a 12–4 loss to the Los Angeles Dodgers. There would be time for greatness to arrive. Nobody had any idea it would arrive so soon.

The game began with Wood striking out the side, which was somewhat tempered by the fact that Houston pitcher Shane Reynolds did the same to the Cubs in the bottom of the first. So maybe it was just the cold.

But Wood fanned the first five hitters he faced, and if not for an infield hit by Ricky Gutierrez that Cubs third baseman Kevin Orie couldn't handle to lead off the third inning, Wood would have been working on a no-hitter.

After six innings, Wood had 12 strikeouts. That's a tremendous day for anyone, but to challenge Roger Clemens' mark of 20 strikeouts in a game he would have to strike out practically every hitter he faced for the remainder of the game. That's just what he did. With an array of fastballs, curveballs, and sliders, Wood struck out the side in the seventh and eighth innings and then in the top of the ninth fanned his seventh straight hitter to get within one of the record.

Houston's Craig Biggio managed to make contact and grounded out to short to end Wood's bid to break the mark. But the next batter, Derek Bell, didn't have a chance. He missed wildly on a sweeping curve to become Wood's 20th strikeout victim.

The Forgotten 20-Year-Old

When Kerry Wood tied the major league record for strikeouts in a game he broke the Cubs' record of 15, a mark held by Rick Sutcliffe, Burt Hooton, and a name that doesn't ring as many bells: Dick Drott.

On May 26, 1957, Drott struck out 15 Milwaukee Braves, including Hank Aaron three times. Like Wood, Drott had a wicked fastball and a big curve that buckled the knees. They also shared the distinction of being 20-year-old rookies when they set their strikeout marks. Wood was making his fifth career start, Drott his seventh.

The other thing they would have in common was arm trouble. Wood came back from Tommy John surgery in his second season to become an above-average starter for several years before more injuries forced a move to the bullpen.

Drott's arm problems also surfaced in his second season following a 15–11 rookie campaign. However, he never really recovered. Drott went 7–11 in 1958 and then missed most of the 1959 season. He returned to go 0–6 in 1960 and 1–4 in 1961, alternating between starting and relieving.

He was selected by Houston in the 1962 expansion draft and retired after the 1963 season when he went 2–12. Drott passed away in 1985 at the age of 49.

After the game, Astros first baseman Jeff Bagwell, who struck out in each of his three at-bats, wasn't just impressed that Wood had filthy stuff but that he had filthy stuff when he wasn't supposed to.

"He threw breaking balls behind in the count for strikes," Bagwell told the *Chicago Tribune*. "You can never expect that, and I won't expect that the next time we face him. You can't expect anyone to keep doing that. If he does, then he may never lose."

So how good was this performance? According to Game Score, a metric created by legendary baseball statistical peoneer Bill James, Wood's was the most dominant nine-inning game ever pitched. Wood didn't walk a batter and only allowed two base runners—Gutierrez on his third-inning single and Craig Biggio, who was hit by a pitch in the sixth. Only two Astros even hit the ball out of the infield. Clemens didn't walk a batter in either of his 20-strikeout games but gave up three and five hits, respectively.

The final out brought on the look and feel of a no-hitter with Cubs catcher Sandy Martinez, first baseman Mark Grace, and the rest of the team swarming the mound to acknowledge what Wood had just accomplished.

When you watch that moment it's not hard to be struck by the look on Wood's face. There's an absence of emotion, as if he can't understand why everyone's so excited. And that's because he didn't know he had broken the record until he did a postgame interview.

"After the first inning I knew I had three, but I lost track after that," Wood said after the game. "I wasn't real worried about getting strikeouts. I knew it was getting up there. I was just glad we were able to get a win out of it."

More than a win came out of Wrigley Field that day. There was an insatiable amount of joy, not only for what had just happened on the field but for what Cubs fans hoped and imagined was still to come.

9 The 39-Year Itch Is Scratched

Everything changed for the Cubs in 1984. And with the exception of a few gut-wrenching games in San Diego, the changes were for the better, at least on the field. The debate over the benefits of Wrigleyville as a national tourist attraction still rages, but this was the season that started it all.

This was the season the Lovable Losers, who hadn't made a postseason appearance since 1945, transformed themselves almost overnight to become a phenomenon helped by Harry Caray's popularity on the WGN superstation, the nationally televised "Sandberg Game," and a tight race against their 1969 nemesis, the New York Mets.

This was the season Sandberg started his run to the Hall of Fame, every move Jim Frey and Dallas Green made was golden, and every start that Rick Sutcliffe made—well, almost every—was right on the money.

This was the season that Steve Goodman's classic "Go, Cubs, Go" pushed aside "It's a Beautiful Day for a Ballgame" as the team's anthem.

This was the season the 39-year itch was finally, mercifully, scratched.

The Cubs had lost 91 games the previous year and, with the exception of an 81–81 record in 1977, had suffered along with their fans through their 11th straight sub-.500 season. Their last

For Starters, 1985 Was Also Painful

In 1985, the Cubs brought back the entire starting rotation that led them to the 1984 division title—and one by one the entire starting rotation got hurt.

Rick Sutcliffe went down first, tearing his right hamstring in May, and a couple days later Steve Trout landed on the disabled list with a sore elbow. By August, Dennis Eckersley was on the DL with a sore shoulder, and Dick Ruthven joined him the same day when a line drive broke his left toe.

On August 17, Scott Sanderson's chronic bad back laid him up, and the entire starting rotation was on the disabled list at the same time. Sutcliffe alone was on the DL three times, and during the course of the season the original five-man rotation missed a combined 60 starts.

The lineup was also hit as outfielders Gary Matthews and Bobby Dernier missed a significant number of games. After a 35–19 start, the Cubs lost 13 games in a row and finished in fourth place in the National League East with a 77–84 record.

postseason appearance was in 1945, and as spring training got underway in 1984, there wasn't much hope anything would be different.

Not that the outcomes of Cactus Leagues games are indicative of regular-season success, but the Cubs were an embarrassment. They lost 11 straight at one point, finished 7–20, and endured a nasty brawl between 23-year-old outfielder Mel Hall and veteran pitcher Dick Ruthven.

In other words, it seemed to be the same old Cubs. But this wasn't your grandfather's team, and it certainly wasn't former owner P.K. Wrigley's. Under the Tribune Co., which bought the team from the Wrigley family in 1981, the franchise actually had a baseball plan in place that was being led by executive vice president and general manager Dallas Green.

The first two years at the helm had been spent shedding dead weight and searching for what Green called "gamers," players who didn't need to be told to run out ground balls or put the team before their own stats.

During the off-season, Green acquired starting pitcher Scott Sanderson from Montreal in a three-team deal, a solid trade that would pay dividends. But his biggest move was firing Lee Elia and bringing in as skipper Jim Frey, who had led the Kansas City Royals to the 1980 World Series.

Still, the talent on the field from the previous season wasn't that much different as Opening Day approached. That changed on March 26 when Green dealt aging reliever Bill Campbell and minor league outfielder Mike Diaz to Philadelphia for outfielders Gary Matthews, Bobby Dernier, and pitcher Porfi Altamirano.

It was a brilliant trade, with the Cubs getting two key starters for spare parts. Matthews immediately took over left field and became the veteran leader they needed while the speedy Dernier, who the Phillies were going to send to the minors, claimed the center-field job.

Not only did the deal remake the outfield, it also led to two in-season trades that dramatically altered the Cubs' season. When Matthews and Dernier arrived, Hall remained a utility outfielder and promising rookie outfielder Joe Carter stayed in the minors. It also forced disgruntled Cubs veteran Bill Buckner to the bench.

Less than three months later, none of them were in the Cubs organization.

The first two games of the season—both victories—were started by Dick Ruthven and Chuck Rainey, bottom-of-the-rotation pitchers at this point in their careers. Aside from Sanderson, the only dependable starter they had was fun-loving left-hander Steve Trout. The Cubs needed pitching to contend.

On May 25, Buckner was traded to Boston for Dennis Eckersley, a fiery 29-year-old who won 20 games in 1978 but had endured some rough years and during the first few months of the season was just 4–4 with a 5.01 earned-run average.

Less than three weeks later, on June 13, Hall and Carter along with minor leaguers Darryl Banks and Don Schulze were traded to Cleveland for backup catcher Ron Hassey, reliever George Frazier, and a red-headed giant by the name of Rick Sutcliffe.

Sutcliffe was an All-Star with the Indians in 1983 and had been the National League's Rookie of the Year in 1979, but he was in the midst of a down season caused in part by a painful root canal. He was 4–5 with a 5.15 ERA in 15 starts for Cleveland.

When the Cubs traded for Sutcliffe, they were 34–25 and 1½ games up on the New York Mets in the NL East race. Sutcliffe's first start didn't come until June 19 when they were stuck in a four-game losing streak and had fallen out of first.

As he would do all season—seven of his victories came after losses—Sutcliffe rejuvenated the Cubs. He allowed one earned run and struck out nine over eight innings in a 4–3 win over Pittsburgh to right the ship.

Four days later, Sandberg hit a pair of homers off Bruce Sutter in a 12–11 win over St. Louis—the mythical "Sandberg Game"—and the city was overcome by Cubs mania.

Sandberg deservedly won praise for his offense, but he didn't lead the Cubs in homers or RBIs. The offense was distributed almost perfectly with six players—Keith Moreland (80 RBIs), Matthews (82), Sandberg (84), Jody Davis (94), Leon Durham (96), and Ron Cey (97)—driving in at least 80 runs.

The Cubs took over first place for good on August 1. As in 1969, the Mets were their fiercest competition but this time there would be no collapse. A four-game sweep over their rivals at Wrigley Field in early August increased their lead to 4½ games, and after August 24 the Cubs never led by fewer than five games.

The clincher came on September 24 at Pittsburgh's Three Rivers Stadium, fittingly a complete-game shutout by Sutcliffe, whose 14th straight win touched off a wild night as fans poured out of the bars to surround Wrigley Field in celebration.

That was the end of a glorious regular season. The playoffs were a different story, the epic collapse against San Diego only serving to burn the 1984 season deeper into the mind of every Cubs fan.

10 "We Either Do or We Don't, But We Are Going to Be Loose"

In an era when air travel still wasn't commonplace, it wasn't the least bit rare for a ballclub to spend several weeks at home and if the baseball gods were smiling, maybe fatten up their record a bit. This is what the 1935 Cubs had in mind, and sorely needed, as they returned to Wrigley Field for a 20-game homestand in third place, trailing St. Louis and the New York Giants. An up-and-down season was on the upswing—a 24–3 stretch in July had seen to that—but the Cubs still trailed the Cardinals by 1½ games and the Giants by a half-game in the National League pennant race.

Cubs manager Charlie Grimm made the decision to ride his four-man rotation—Larry French, Charlie Root, Lon Warneke, and Bill Lee—and hope the Cubs would still be in contention when they closed the season with five games in St. Louis.

The first two games against Cincinnati didn't portend much when the Cubs split a doubleheader against the Reds, but the morning after an off day Grimm called a clubhouse meeting and found just the right words to light a fuse.

"We're home for the last long stand and we either do or we don't," Grimm said. "But we are going to be loose."

Augie Galan was pretty loose that afternoon as he hit two home runs, including a grand slam and drove in six runs, and French went all nine innings in an 8–2 win over Philadelphia. The next day Root went the distance in an 11-inning 3–2 win, and Warneke followed that with his own extra-inning complete game, another 3–2 triumph over the Phillies. Lee's 4–0 shutout the next day completed the sweep of the Phillies.

That was pretty much how it went for the next three weeks as the Cubs marched to the World Series with an incredible 21 straight wins. Only the 1916 New York Giants have ever won more consecutive games, but they finished a distance fourth that season. No team in baseball history has ever turned it on like the Cubs did so late in the season with so much on the line.

The starting pitchers, which also included Roy Henshaw for two spot starts, were so good they only needed the bullpen in three games, and in one of those it was Warneke who came on in relief. In all but one of the 21 wins the Cubs gave up three or fewer runs. When Root had an off day and allowed nine runs against Brooklyn, he still got a "W" as center fielder Freddie Lindstrom drove in five runs in an 18–14 victory.

The offense that season was led by a pair of veterans in catcher Gabby Hartnett and outfielder Chuck Klein, who led the Cubs with 21 homers. Hartnett's .344 average and 91 RBIs earned him the NL MVP award, which he won despite missing nearly two weeks in August with torn ligaments in his ankle.

The 1935 club also benefited from 18-year-old Phil Cavarretta, who drove in 82 runs after taking over first base from veteran Charlie Grimm. The affable Grimm clearly enjoyed the attention his clubhouse speech got, which was as legendary in its time as Lee Elia's rant was 47 years later. Following the 16th consecutive win, Grimm told the *Chicago Tribune*, "After I give the boys this slogan about being loose, I keep a sharp eye for symptoms of unlooseness, and as victory is piled upon victory I see the boys are getting looser and looser and better and better."

The Cardinals didn't go down without a fight. They won 8-of-10 as the Cubs started their streak and didn't give up first place until September 14. The pennant hadn't been decided when the Cubs arrived in St. Louis on September 25, but Warneke's 1–0 shutout that day put them up four with four to play, and two days later Lee beat Dizzy Dean in the first game of a doubleheader to clinch the pennant.

The Cubs also took the nightcap to win their 21st straight, not to mention their 100th game of the season, a milestone they did not reach again until winning 103 in 2016.

11 Lou Brock and Greg Maddux: The Ones Who Got Away

Every team has players they gave up on for whom a crystal ball surely would have come in handy. But not every team gave up Lou Brock for a sore-armed pitcher or let Greg Maddux—arguably the greatest pitcher of his generation—walk away in his prime for nothing.

Lou Brock

In the history of the Cubs, no name has been more maligned than that of Ernie Broglio, at least until Steve Bartman came along. As with Bartman, it's unfair to look askance at Broglio since he didn't pull the trigger on the June 15, 1964, deal that sent Brock, Jack Spring, and Paul Toth to St. Louis for Broglio, Doug Clemens, and Bobby Shantz.

Broglio, a right-handed starter, was neither old nor a mere prospect when he came to the Cubs. He had gone 21–9 in 1960 and the year prior to the trade won 18 games with a stellar 2.99 ERA. He was, however, finished. The first sign of a problem came in his second start with the Cubs when he retired the first batter— and nobody else. He gave up four singles, a double, a homer, and walked a man before being mercifully pulled.

Nobody knew he would only go 7–19 over three seasons with the Cubs before his major league career ended due to arm problems, and keep in mind that Cubs general manager John Holland wasn't the only one excited about the deal. The headline in the *Chicago Daily News* the morning after the trade declared, "Now we have two contenders!" and one in the *Chicago Tribune* read, "Santo Jubilant About Trade for Broglio."

"With our pitching staff," said excitable Cubs third baseman Ron Santo, then 25, "now we can win the pennant."

What did happen was the Cubs finished in eighth place and the Cardinals, with Brock hitting .348 and stealing 33 bases in 103 games, won the pennant and defeated the New York Yankees in the World Series.

Should the Cubs have known what they had in Brock? Unequivocally, yes. Brock was signed by the Cubs and came through their farm system, reaching the majors in 1961 at the age of 22. He was not a prototypical lead-off man due to his high strikeout rate, but his blazing speed was always present.

Brock stole 50 bases in 72 attempts during parts of four seasons with the Cubs, a 69.4 percent success rate. Not as good as the 75.7 percent success rate (888 stolen bases in 1,173 chances) he had with the Cardinals, but not too far off.

The strikeouts continued with the Cardinals, as well; he averaged 112 whiffs in his first eight seasons in St. Louis. The big difference was that the Cardinals didn't care. They played in a huge ballpark at the time—Busch Stadium—and told him to run, run, run. And that's what he did, all the way to the Hall of Fame.

Greg Maddux

Unlike Lou Brock, Greg Maddux had some great years with the Cubs. He went 19–12 to help them to the NL East title in 1989, won 20 games and a Cy Young Award in 1992, and returned in 2004 to win 38 more games in a Cubs uniform at the tail end of his

Joltin' Joe Should Have Been a Cub

Think about how different Cubs history, not to mention baseball history, might have been if Joe DiMaggio had played his Hall of Fame career at Wrigley Field. It almost happened.

The Cubs had obtained Augie Galan from the minor league San Francisco Seals in 1933 and, as Warren Brown wrote in his seminal 1946 book, *The Chicago Cubs*, were content to deal with the Cubs when it came to DiMaggio, a rising star.

The only problem was that Joltin' Joe had hurt his knee and the Cubs weren't sure he was still healthy. So according to Brown, the Seals made the Cubs an offer.

"Take DiMaggio on trial," a Seals representative told the Cubs. "Give us so many players and so much cash. Keep DiMaggio until July and give him a thorough looking over. If you are not satisfied that he can make the grade, the deal's off."

The Cubs said no. A short time later, the Yankees said yes.

career. But he'll always be most remembered by Cubs fans for what he did in an Atlanta Braves uniform and how Larry Himes thought three allegedly above-average players were equal to one superstar.

Maddux was baseball's top free agent during the winter of 1992, a situation that should never have come to pass. A year earlier, Maddux's agent, Scott Boras, and the Tribune Co. had agreed on a five-year, $25 million contract before the Cubs corporate owners yanked it off the table.

Greg Maddux throws against the Cincinnati Reds in the first inning of a baseball game on Friday, June 9, 2006, in Cincinnati. Four-time Cy Young Award winner Greg Maddux was traded from the Chicago Cubs to the Los Angeles Dodgers on Monday, July 31, 2006, for infielder Cesar Izturis.
(AP Photo/Al Behrman)

The deal would have been a bargain as Maddux responded by winning his first Cy Young and sparking a bidding war for his services. The main pursuers were the Cubs, Braves, and New York Yankees, who at the time could only outbid teams by millions instead of tens of millions.

The Yankees, who hadn't finished above .500 in four seasons and were not a perennial playoff team, weren't Maddux's first choice and he ultimately turned down a five-year, $34 million offer from them. Boras turned his attention to the Braves and Cubs.

Himes, to his credit, offered Boras a five-year, $27.5 million deal before free agency began, and Boras rejected it. Shortly after, Himes announced he was on the prowl for other pitchers. The problem, which Boras recognized and Himes didn't, was that Maddux was a rare pitcher.

"The Cub franchise is in dire straits without Greg Maddux," he told the *Chicago Tribune*. "There is no one in this existing free-agent market that can replace him."

As offers were being knocked about, Himes announced on December 1 that he had signed right-hander Jose Guzman to a four-year deal worth $14.35 million, money that had been earmarked for Maddux. Eight days later, Maddux signed with the Braves. But not before Boras called the Cubs one last time. It was too late, Himes told him. The Cubs had just signed closer Randy Myers to a three-year, $10.7 million deal and the last of the Maddux dollars had been spoken for.

So to sum up, Himes elected to go with Guzman, Myers, and Dan Plesac over Maddux.

"If this had been a trade," Himes told *Tribune* columnist Bernie Lincicome in the spring of 1992, "I would have had to take it."

Hindsight's a funny thing, but sometimes it's all we've got. And hindsight tells us that Maddux went 89–33 with a 2.13 ERA during the course of his first contract with the Braves, and the three players who got his money did, shall we say, far worse.

Guzman actually pitched a one-hitter in his first start as a Cub but finished the season a mediocre 12–10 and started only four games in 1994 before a shoulder injury ended his career. Plesac had a 4.68 ERA in 111 relief appearances, gaudy stats that only several hundred, if not thousands, of other players have produced during the course of a career.

Only Myers, who saved 112 games, lived up to his contract. Himes, who was removed as the Cubs' GM less than two years after letting Maddux go, did not.

12 Take the Immortal Mike Royko's Annual Cubs Quiz

"This is not an easy quiz, even for the most loyal fan. I wrote the test and every year I miss half the answers."
—Mike Royko, April 9, 1969, *Chicago Daily News*

For many years, the start of a new baseball season in Chicago brought boundless hope, renewed dreams, and legendary newspaper columnist Mike Royko's annual Cubs quiz. Royko's Cubs quiz first appeared during the 1960s when he rose to fame at the *Chicago Daily News*. The questions were ridiculous, the answers more so, and they often comically referred to players as being "immortal."

As in, "What did the immortal Wayne K. Otto hit?" The answer: "Nothing. But Hack Wilson once hit him. He was a sportswriter, so he probably deserved it."

Royko would sarcastically tout his quiz as being just as important as Opening Day. In 1969, he wrote, "Today is the big day for Cubs fans. That magic moment has finally arrived. Yes, today is the day they get to take my annual Cub fan quiz."

Royko was born on September 19, 1932, just a few months after Cubs owner Phil Wrigley inherited the team. Royko loved the Cubs as much as anybody and poked as much fun at them as anybody. They were an easy target, sure, but Royko could have made the 1927 Yankees whimper with his biting wit.

For Royko, being a Cubs fan was a tortured existence and many of his wonderful columns were not really about the Cubs so much as how painful it was to live and die by them. In 1980, after he had

The Ex-Cub Factor

Mike Royko didn't discover the ex-Cub factor, but his many columns about the uncanny way in which the factor could predict the World Series loser made it famous. The man who discovered it was longtime Cubs fan and writer Ron Berler, who first introduced his theory in the *Boston Herald* on October 15, 1981, whimsically explaining the notion that having three or more ex-Cubs will kill a team's chances of winning the World Series.

In that first article, Berler wrote how former Cubs have the chronic condition of "Cubness" in them, and any team with too much of it will suffer. For example, in 1981 the Yankees had five ex-Cubs—Oscar Gamble, Bobby Murcer, Dave LaRoche, Rick Reuschel, and Barry Foote—and Berler's prediction that they could not win the World Series came to pass. They lost to the Los Angeles Dodgers in six games.

When Berler first put forth his theory, there was one exception to the rule: The 1960 Pittsburgh Pirates had ex-Cubs Smoky Burgess, Gene Baker, and Don Hoak. However, Berler surmised, because Hoak was virulently and publicly anti-Cub he had somehow escaped his "Cubness."

Incredibly, the ex-Cubs factor has twice been overcome in recent years. The 2001 Arizona Diamondbacks—with Luis Gonzalez, Mark Grace, Miguel Batista, and Mike Morgan—still managed to defeat the Yankees who had no ex-Cubs. It was also overcome in 2008 when the Philadelphia Phillies beat the Tampa Bay Rays despite having ex-Cubs Tom Gordon, Matt Stairs, Scott Eyre, and Jamie Moyer on the roster.

Who knows? Maybe the time is coming when having three or more ex-Cubs will be an indicator of World Series success instead of failure.

moved to the *Chicago Sun-Times*, Royko announced he was becoming, of all things, a White Sox fan. It didn't take, and the following year another column announced his allegiances had returned to the North Side.

The last column Royko ever wrote appeared in the *Chicago Tribune* on March 21, 1997, and fittingly it was devoted to the Cubs, specifically Phil Wrigley and the curse of the Billy Goat. The column was a historical look at Wrigley's failings, which, he wrote, included not signing African American ballplayers until long after Jackie Robinson's debut.

"So what might have been, wasn't. It had nothing to do with a goat's curse. Not unless the goat wore a gabardine suit and sat behind a desk in an executive suite. Yes, I know, so don't grab your phone: The corporation that owns this paper has owned the Cubs since 1981. So why, you ask, haven't they made it to the World Series?

"Because they haven't been good enough. But I do know that if they thought a three-legged green creature from another planet could hit home runs or throw a 95 mph fastball, they'd sign it.

"And we'd cheer."

A few weeks later, after Royko passed away on April 29, 1997, his wake was held at Wrigley Field.

Here are five questions from Royko's 1976 Cubs quiz, some of which were used many times over the years. If you're compelled to look up more of his wonderful quizzes, and there really can be no greater use of your time, Chicago's Harold Washington Library keeps the archives of the *Chicago Daily News*, *Chicago Sun-Times*, and *Chicago Tribune*, the three newspapers for which Royko wrote his indispensable columns.

Q. In 1969, when the Cubs blew the pennant to the New York Mets (Curse their souls!), Ron Santo got mad and screamed at the Cub center fielder because he goofed up. Who was this unfortunate young man?

A. He was the immortal Don Young, and if I ever meet him, I'm going to scream at him, too.

Q. The Cubs have had three home run champions since 1940. Which one spit the most?
A. The immortal Bill Nicholson used to spit the most. He could spit 20' with the wind. One day, he accidentally spit on the immortal but tiny Peanuts Lowrey, and the game had to be held up while the trainer applied artificial respiration.

Q. In 1958, the Cubs had a rookie who crossed himself every time he came to bat. Who was he, and can you come within 10 points of his batting average?
A. The immortal Tony Taylor used to cross himself all the time. That year, he hit .235 and did not convert many atheists in the bleachers.

Q. Who was tinier, Peanuts Lowrey or Dim-Dom Dallessandro?
A. The immortal Dim-Dom Dallessandro was even tinier than the immortal Peanuts Lowrey, but he had enough sense to hide when the immortal Bill Nicholson was spitting.

Q. In 1972, the Cubs got a pitcher named Bob Locker from the Oakland A's. Who did they give away to acquire this all-time mortal?
A. For the immortal Locker, the Cubs gave away Bill North, who has since been seen in numerous World Series games. Why do we remain Cubs fans? Are we all crazy?

13 Visit the Jack Brickhouse Statue on Michigan Avenue

The school bells rang and for kids all over Chicagoland the mad dash home to catch as much of the Cubs game as possible was on. Waiting faithfully at the finish line, as always, was Jack Brickhouse.

With a cherubic face and infectious enthusiasm that never seemed to dim, Brickhouse was exactly what the team that couldn't win to save itself needed. Critics sometimes denounced him as being too nice and too much of a homer but so what? He was.

"I don't want to be a stick-in-the-mud, but when you go overboard you don't hurt just the athlete," Brickhouse wrote in his third biography, *A Voice for All Seasons*. "You hurt his wife going to the grocery store and his kid going to school. Why? What does that prove?"

There was a timeless decency to Brickhouse, who received the Ford C. Frick Award from the Baseball Hall of Fame in 1983, that remained with him throughout his life. He was a mainstay at charity events, always quick to offer advice and encouragement to young journalists, and when the Cubs finally broke their color barrier in 1953 with Ernie Banks and Gene Baker, he gave them air time just like he would anybody else.

"Usually, the other guys would kind of back off a little bit," Banks told the *Chicago Tribune* in 1998 shortly after Brickhouse died. "But Jack was always there. He interviewed us on the postgame shows and the pregame shows. He was right there to nurture us along. We talked about that a lot."

John Beasley Brickhouse was born in Peoria, Illinois, on January 24, 1916. After getting his start on a Peoria radio station, Brickhouse made his way to Chicago and by the 1940s he was a rising star for WGN Radio. When WGN-TV televised their first

Cubs game on April 16, 1948, the first thing viewers saw was Brickhouse.

And so it went uninterrupted for 34 seasons, a stretch of Cubs baseball that some might have found interminable. Brickhouse suffered, to be sure, but he remained the kindly uncle whose home run calls ("That's pretty well hit! Back, back! Hey, Hey!") enthralled even the most cynical fans.

He could always find a little good in everything and everybody. Well, almost everybody. Brickhouse and prickly Leo Durocher, who managed the Cubs for 6½ seasons from 1966 until he was fired midway through the 1972 season, never got along, which wasn't unusual for Durocher. For Brickhouse, it was practically unheard of.

"I tried, but I failed," he once told longtime Chicago baseball columnist Jerome Holtzman. "I just can't get to like the guy."

One man Brickhouse liked quite a bit was Harry Caray, who replaced Brickhouse in the Cubs' broadcast booth in 1982 even though Caray was two years his senior. Their careers paralleled each other, and they had more than a few postgame beers together. With Brickhouse in retirement, Caray became a local and national phenomenon thanks to WGN's nationally televised games, and he helped turn Wrigley Field into the world's largest neighborhood tavern.

When Caray died shortly before the 1998 season, the Cubs quickly announced a statue would be erected outside Wrigley Field. While getting ready for Caray's funeral, Brickhouse felt numbness in his leg and soon learned he had a brain tumor. He passed away on August 6, 1998.

On the day the Caray statue was unveiled, the Cubs also honored Brickhouse by emblazoning his memorable "Hey, Hey!" home run call atop the left field foul pole. It seemed like Caray got the grand prize and Brickhouse was given a ribbon just for showing up.

Several friends of Brickhouse's started a group called Citizens United for Brickhouse Statue (CUBS) and raised $150,000 to build and erect a statue in his honor. Brickhouse's career was filled with so many achievements—he was the voice of the Bears for 24 years and the voice of the White Sox for 27—they needed all four sides of the statue to catalog them all.

The statue was dedicated on Thursday, September 14, 2000, and rests just south of the Tribune Tower, several miles from Wrigley Field.

14 Slammin' Sammy

He was one of the greatest power hitters in baseball history whose role in the Great Home Run Race of 1998 electrified the nation, carried the Cubs into the playoffs, and turned a poor kid from the Dominican Republic into an international superstar sought out by advertisers, movie stars, and heads of state.

That's slammin' Sammy.

He was a petulant, selfish cheater who cared more about his own glorified statistics than he did winning baseball games, flashed a fake smile only when it suited him, and when the going got rough deserted his teammates then blatantly lied about it.

That's slammin' Sammy.

Who is the real Sammy Sosa? He's certainly somewhere in between these two wildly diverging versions, but in the court of public opinion, the pendulum has swung far in the direction of the latter.

Samuel Peralta Sosa was born on November 12, 1968, in the baseball-crazed town of San Pedro de Macoris and signed with the Texas Rangers when he was just 16. He first arrived in Chicago during the summer of 1989 when the White Sox acquired him in a trade for Harold Baines. Less than four years later, his potential still unrealized, he was dealt on March 30, 1992, to the Cubs along with reliever Ken Patterson for veteran outfielder George Bell.

The trade was viewed as a swap of disappointing hitters, but there was still something untapped and unknown about the 23-year-old the Cubs had just acquired. Hall of Fame sportswriter Jerome Holtzman described him as having a "quiet personality."

In Sosa's first season with the Cubs he had two long stints on the disabled list, first due to a broken finger and then to a broken ankle that ended his year on August 6. The following year Sosa, then a lithe speedster with good power, hit 33 homers and stole 36 bases to signal his arrival as a burgeoning star.

During the next four seasons he became the best player on mostly mediocre Cubs teams and wasn't more than a regional hero, though in 1995 he finished eighth in the MVP voting as he put together his second 30–30 season and drove in more than 100 runs for the first time. Even so, in a postseason wrap-up, Cubs president Andy MacPhail presciently declared Sosa "has not reached his full potential."

In 1996, with Ryne Sandberg returning from early retirement, Sosa was starting to take on a greater leadership role. Years later, Sandberg would use his Hall of Fame speech to lecture players who didn't play the "right" way in what was viewed as a slap at Sosa. Ironically, back then Sosa looked to Sandberg as a role model. "I have to be like Sandberg," he told the *Chicago Tribune*. "Do you want to be a leader? You go outside and do your job. When [a guy] goes outside and gives 100 percent, that's what I call a leader."

Sosa's work ethic was never questioned over the years; he was viewed as someone who would do whatever it took to succeed in baseball. In 1998, all that work paid off in stunning ways. He slugged 13 homers during the first two months of the season, which was typical for him but amazingly he was hitting .343, well beyond his .257 career average at the time.

Then as June got underway, Sosa took the next step. After missing the final three games of May due to a swollen left thumb, he hit two home runs on June 1, including one off Florida rookie Ryan Dempster. The next game he stayed in the park but then homered in five straight. He went on to post a three-homer game and had two more multi-homer games en route to finishing with 20 homers and breaking Rudy York's 61-year-old MLB record of 18 in a single month.

When June ended, Sosa trailed Mark McGwire by four homers and their epic race to No. 62 and surpassing Roger Maris was on. McGwire got there first—on a September night at Busch Stadium against the Cubs—and beat out Sosa for the home run title 70–66. But it was Sosa who was named the National League MVP, and led his team to the playoffs and where McGwire was cautious and cantankerous, Sosa was wide-eyed and lovable. At least in the public eye.

Cubs' All-Time Home Run Leaders

Nobody is likely to crack the Top 10 for several years. With 133 homers at the end of the 2016 season, Anthony Rizzo is 16th overall, but after him there is a long wait to find the next active player still wearing a Cubs uniform. Remarkably, Kris Bryant's 65 homers put him second on the list of current Cubs.

1. Sammy Sosa, 545
2. Ernie Banks, 512
3. Billy Williams, 392
4. Ron Santo, 337
5. Ryne Sandberg, 282
6. Aramis Ramirez, 239
7. Gabby Hartnett, 231
8. Bill Nicholson, 205
9. Hank Sauer, 198
10. Hack Wilson, 190

It was about this time that Sosa's growing entourage and demand for special treatment started to consume the Cubs. When he arrived to training camp in 1999, he began what would become his annual routine of arriving as late as possible and then asking, "Did you miss me?"

The Cubs chose to ignore the clubhouse issues mainly because Sosa was a cash cow who also kept up his incredible pace on the field, hitting 63, 50, and then 64 homers over the next three seasons. He then demanded—and received—a four-year, $72 million extension that ran through 2005. But he started to lose his teammates, in no small measure because of his beloved boom box, which would play his favorite music—and only his music—over and over again.

By 2003, Sosa's numbers started to drop to pre-1998 levels and his act started to get harder to stomach. Whispers of steroid use—which have never been proven—were nonetheless eating at his credibility but not nearly as much as on June 3 when one of his bats cracked open during a game and cork flew out.

His detractors pounced and Sosa's explanation—that he had accidentally grabbed a batting practice bat—was ridiculed. This was the beginning of the end for Sosa, who was no longer even the best player on his own team. In 2003, that honor went to Mark Prior, and in 2004 Moises Alou, Aramis Ramirez, and Derrek Lee were not only better offensively but stayed healthy. The "Gladiator," as Sosa and Sosa alone referred to himself, spent a month on the disabled list after sneezing and tweaking his back. He was 35 and on his way out.

As the 2004 season wound down with the Cubs still vying for a playoff spot, Sosa embarrassed himself by prematurely doing the "bunny hop"—his reaction to a sure-thing home run—and started to jog to first base. Unfortunately, the ball hit off the wall and Sosa was thrown out at second.

Then on the final day of the season, with the Cubs eliminated, Sosa asked manager Dusty Baker for the day off, and his request was granted. After the game had started, Sosa quietly dressed and drove away from Wrigley Field before the first inning was over. Not only was this unacceptable, but Sosa then lied and said he had stayed until the seventh inning. The Cubs, done covering for Sosa after years of enabling him, released a surveillance tape that revealed the truth.

It wasn't easy for the Cubs to deal a fading and insolent player owed $18 million, but as they've done so many other times due to bad contracts, they dumped Sosa on the Baltimore Orioles for Mike Fontenot, Jerry Hairston, and a minor leaguer.

That was the end of an era, but not the end of the story. By every statistical measure, Sosa should have easily gained entry into the Baseball Hall of Fame when he became eligible in 2013. His 609 homers are good for seventh on the all-time list. But based on the reaction to other players linked to illegal performance-enhancing drugs, it's unlikely he'll get in for years, if at all. In 2016, McGwire failed to get in after his 10th and final year of eligibility.

The next question is simpler—can Sosa ever show his face again at Wrigley Field? He has yet to sing the seventh-inning stretch or participate in any team-sponsored event since he left in 2005. Either Sosa isn't welcome in his "house" or he doesn't want to go home.

And love him or hate him, that's sad.

15 Merkle's Boner

Before Steve Bartman, there was Fred Merkle. And before a century of black clouds, bad baseball, and bad luck, the Cubs were the beneficiaries of the most controversial on-field moment in baseball history.

The 1908 National League pennant race was coming down to the wire with the Cubs, New York Giants, and Pittsburgh Pirates all within striking distance of each other. There were still about two weeks left in the season when the Cubs and Giants met on September 23 at the Polo Grounds, and there is no doubt the Cubs should have lost 2–1 on that fateful day.

The play that should have ended the game was exciting but routine. With two outs and the score tied 1–1 in the bottom of the ninth, Merkle was on first and Moose McCormick was on third. Giants shortstop Al Bridwell singled to center to easily score McCormick, who touched home plate with what should have been the game-winning run.

But Merkle, just 19 years old and making his first start of the season in place of the injured Fred Tenney, failed to touch second base before heading to the Giants clubhouse to avoid the happy mob of fans racing onto the field. That was never really in dispute despite later claims from some Giants that Merkle did indeed touch second.

It wasn't that Merkle forgot to touch the bag; he was simply following the accepted protocol of the era. Even though the rule-book stated that a runner must always touch the next base even when a winning run is scored, the little-known rule wasn't always followed or enforced.

In fact, on September 4, 1908, the Cubs were playing in Pittsburgh when the Pirates got a bases-loaded single in the bottom of the ninth to win the game. But the Pirates' Warren Gill, just as Merkle would later do, ran to the clubhouse instead of touching second base.

Johnny Evers, the Cubs cranky but astute second baseman, retrieved the ball and alerted umpire Hank O'Day that Gill should be a force out at second and the run should not count. O'Day, who later managed the Cubs to a 78–76 record in 1914, would not change the call and despite a protest filed with the National League the call was upheld and the Cubs lost the game.

Nineteen days later, the Cubs were playing in New York and as fate would have it, O'Day was one of the two umpires working the game. Of course, Evers was manning second for the Cubs and it was his quick thinking that led to Merkle's being called out.

After Bridwell's hit, Cubs outfielder Solly Hofman threw the ball back to the infield but it rolled to Giants pitcher Joe McGinnity. Just what happened to the baseball at this point is still in dispute, but Evers told his version of the story in John Carmichael's *My Greatest Day in Baseball.*

"We grabbed for his hands to make sure he wouldn't heave the ball away but he broke loose and tossed it into the crowd," Evers said. "I can see the fellow who caught it yet…a tall, stringy, middle-aged gent with a brown bowler hat on. [Harry] Steinfeldt and Floyd Kroh…raced after him. 'Gimme the ball for a minute,' Steinfeldt begged him. 'I'll bring it right back.' The guy wouldn't let go and suddenly Kroh solved the problem.

"He hit the customer right on top of that stiff hat, drove it down over his eyes and as the gent folded up, the ball fell free and Kroh got it. I was yelling and waving my hands out by second base and Tinker relayed it over to me and I stepped on the bag and made sure O'Day saw me…he was waiting for that very play…he remembered the Pittsburgh game…and he said, 'The run does not count.'"

There were thousands of fans on the field, and as word spread that O'Day had called Merkle out, a near-riot ensued. There was no way to continue the game even though the score was still tied 1–1. Protests were filed with the National League office by both clubs with the Giants claiming they won fairly and the Cubs claiming they should be awarded a forfeit victory since the Giants fans had made the game impossible to complete.

The outcome of the game wouldn't matter if one team was able to win the pennant outright, but the Cubs beat the Pirates 5–2 in their final game to eliminate them and the Giants won their final three games to end the season tied with the Cubs. A decision was made to replay the tied game in its entirety on October 8 at the Polo Grounds.

Despite Cubs manager Frank Chance getting bloodied by a beer bottle thrown from the stands and starting pitcher Jack Pfiester not making it out of the first inning, the Cubs won 4–2 to win the pennant as Mordecai "Three Finger" Brown came on in relief to outduel Christy Mathewson. They went on to beat the Detroit Tigers in the World Series in five games.

While the Giants had lost the pennant, Fred Merkle had lost his good name. Newspaper accounts had referred to his "bone-headed" decision, and the expression "Merkle's boner" quickly was adopted as the catch-all for the entire affair. Fair or not, Merkle had to live with his last name becoming a verb that came to represent doing something stupid.

By all accounts, Merkle was a good and intelligent man. His teammates never blamed him for what had happened, and he stayed with the Giants until 1916. A year later, ironically enough, he joined the Cubs and helped them win the 1918 NL pennant. But after Merkle retired, the incident continued to haunt him and his family.

In *More Than Merkle: A History of the Best and Most Exciting Season in Baseball History*, Merkle's daughter told Keith Olbermann about how the family was living in Florida in the 1930s when a visiting minister attended their church.

"I want to begin by admitting to you an ugly secret," the minister said. "I am from Toledo, Ohio, birthplace of the infamous Fred 'Bonehead' Merkle.

The entire family got up and left.

16 Jolly Cholly

The numbers don't tell the Charlie Grimm story, the laughs do.

You can go through the statistical record and discover Grimm played 20 years in the big leagues, including his last 12 with the Cubs after getting traded from Pittsburgh. You can see he was a pretty fair ballplayer, too, knocking out 2,299 hits during a career launched in 1916.

A glance at his managerial record reveals he won 1,287 games and three National League pennants in 19 seasons as a big league manager, including 14 spread over three separate stints with the Cubs. Those are the indisputable, important, impersonal numbers, and they only begin to tell the story of the man called Jolly Cholly by countless friends, teammates, and admirers.

"We'd book Charlie into the old Wisconsin and Riverview theatres during the off-season," Bill Veeck Jr. told the *Chicago Tribune* after Grimm passed away in 1983. "He was a wonderful entertainer. He would sing and play the banjo, and he was a great storyteller. Many of us believed he could have been a professional vaudevillian."

In the foreword to Grimm's 1968 autobiography, *Jolly Cholly's Story: Baseball, I Love You!*, co-author Ed Prell relays the story of the time Grimm was struck by a beanball in an era when players didn't wear helmets. Several men in the stands rushed to Grimm's side and one of them, when asked his qualifications to help, said he was not a doctor but a pharmacist. This perked up Grimm, who managed to blurt out, "What do you charge for a pint of gin, Doc?"

Grimm's good humor and laid-back approach is widely credited for turning around the 1932 season for the Cubs, who were disintegrating under Hall of Famer Rogers Hornsby, a remarkable player but an uninspiring and difficult manager. With his trademark banjo by his side, Grimm took over as player-manager in late July and led the Cubs to a 37–18 record and the NL pennant.

Grimm stayed on as manager until 1938 when it was his turn to get ousted in the middle of the season. But unlike Hornsby, who left in a huff, Grimm switched to the broadcast booth and cheered on the Cubs as they again won the NL pennant.

In 1944, with the Cubs again in need of a change, Grimm returned for his second term as manager and in 1945 took them to their fifth World Series in 17 seasons. Although he wasn't manager during the 1938 Series, Grimm was the only person to be in a Cubs uniform for each of those five pennant-winning seasons.

"Oh, Jesus, Charlie was really funny," former Cubs second baseman Don Johnson told author Peter Golenbock in *Wrigleyville*. "In [the minors with] Indianapolis one ballgame, it started to rain about the seventh inning. It just rained, rained and rained...and the umpire wouldn't stop the game.

"Grimm found a great big beach umbrella someplace. Where in the hell he ever got it, I don't know. He walked out to protest to the umpire, and subconsciously the umpire got under the umbrella with him! When he realized what he had done, he kicked Grimm out of the ballgame with his umbrella."

Cubs owner Phil Wrigley found Grimm to be one of the few people in baseball he could trust, and after the 1959 season he installed him for the third time as Cubs manager. Instead of presaging another pennant, however, it turned into one of the oddest baseball trades of all time. After just 17 games, Grimm and WGN Radio broadcaster Lou Boudreau swapped jobs.

Grimm remained with the Cubs as a vice president for many years, and when Wrigley sold the Cubs in 1981, one of the stipulations was that Grimm would remain on the payroll. When he passed away in 1983, Grimm's last wish was that his ashes would be scattered at Wrigley Field.

"Charlie Grimm was great," Boudreau told author Carrie Muskat in *Banks to Sandberg to Grace*. "He was great for ballplayers, great for the fans, and great for the Cubs."

17 The Comeback

No game was really over for the 1989 Cubs, who made a habit during their march to the National League East crown of finding a way to win when all hope seemed lost. From July 20 to August 27, the Cubs won six games after trailing in the seventh inning or later, including four when they trailed in the ninth.

One of the most miraculous comebacks came on July 20 at Wrigley Field when San Francisco led 3–0 with two outs in the ninth before rookie Dwight Smith and reserve infielder Curtis Wilkerson tied the game on run-scoring singles. An 11th inning double by Les Lancaster, a relief pitcher, won it for the Cubs. It was Lancaster's only RBI of the season.

But there didn't seem to be any room for miracles on August 29 when the Cubs fell behind the Houston Astros 9–0 before 25,829 on a Tuesday afternoon at Wrigley Field. Mike Bielecki, a former first-round pick of Pittsburgh who finally was living up to his promise with a breakout season, had one of his few poor starts and didn't make it out of the fifth.

By the time the Astros worked over reliever Dean Wilkins, who gave up a grand slam to light-hitting shortstop Rafael Ramirez, they had their nine-run cushion. This was a game that was over. This became clear when both club's skippers made moves to indicate they thought the outcome was settled.

Even after finally getting on the scoreboard with a pair of two-out runs in the sixth, Cubs manager Don Zimmer pulled Andre Dawson to start the seventh, replacing him with Smith, an NL rookie-of-the-year contender who was in a dreadful 2-for-30 slump.

Meanwhile, with their lead down to 9–5, Houston manager Art Howe let reliever Brian Meyer labor through the eighth so Howe could save his bullpen for the following day. But Meyer gave up a single to rookie catcher Joe Girardi, and after Vance Law flied out to center, Jerome Walton reached on an error. Ryne Sandberg's RBI single made it 9–6.

"I'm thinking we've got it won," Howe said.

There was at least one person in Wrigley Field who believed in the Cubs, and not surprisingly that person was parked in the bleachers. The legendary Arne Harris, who was WGN's executive producer of Cubs telecasts for many years, located a fan in left field holding a notebook with the numbers 1–9 written on it followed by "More To Go." As the comeback progressed the fan, dutifully putting an "X" through another number, kept track of how many runs the Cubs needed to tie the game.

After Sandberg's single, Howe finally replaced Meyer with Danny Darwin, who promptly gave up an RBI single to Lloyd McClendon, a former Little League World Series hero. Lefty reliever Juan Agosto came in to face Mark Grace, whose base hit made it 9–8.

Smith, a lefty, was up next, and Zimmer wouldn't have shocked anyone by pinch-hitting him for Darrin Jackson, a righty. But Zimmer always managed with his gut, and on a day when faith mattered he put his in Smith, whose sacrifice fly tied the score.

Neither team scored in the ninth, and the Astros went down in order in the 10th, but the Cubs rallied in their half. Walton, who beat out Smith as the NL's top rookie, walked and moved over to second on a Sandberg bunt. The game almost ended on

McClendon's single to center, but Walton had to hold up. After an intentional walk to Grace, Smith came to the plate again.

With the crowd in a frenzy, Smith dropped a single into right field as Walton raced home to complete the Cubs' biggest comeback of the 20th century. The 1930 team also came back from a nine-run deficit to beat Cincinnati 13–11, but that game was on the last day of the season and the result didn't have pennant implications.

"I've been asked so many times lately, 'Is this the biggest game you've won?'" Zimmer said afterward. "This was the biggest."

18 Listen to Lee Elia's Rant

If you want to hear Lee Elia's infamous 1983 postgame news conference ripping Cubs fans, it's not hard to find. All it takes is a quick Google search for "Lee Elia tirade," "Lee Elia rant," or if you want you can just go with a simple "Lee Elia."

Lee Elia will never be able to escape the incident in which his use of the "F" word isn't even as shocking as the way he ripped Cubs fans. The rant will be in the first paragraph of his obituary no matter how the rest of his life turns out, and so a few years ago he finally tried to have some good come out of it.

As the 25th anniversary of the rant approached, Elia partnered with a collectibles company and autographed baseballs with the words, "And Print It!"—one of the most memorable non-expletive portions of the rant—written on the bottom. Part of the proceeds went to Chicago Baseball Cancer Charities.

There may not be a more well-known, not to mention cuss-filled, rant in baseball history, and if it weren't for longtime

Chicago broadcaster Les Grobstein's tape recorder Elia's three-minute speech would have disappeared into thin air.

The April 29 game itself had been a disaster. Cubs closer Lee Smith threw a wild pitch in the eighth inning to let in the game-winning run in a 4–3 loss to the Los Angeles Dodgers, dropping the Cubs to 5–14. Afterward, Elia was meeting with reporters when he let loose. Grobstein was the only reporter to record the event.

Knowing he had gold on his hands, and realizing Elia's job was about to be in danger, Grobstein hustled to get the audio edited and within an hour or so was airing on WLS-AM. Separately, he played the tape for Cubs officials, including General Manager Dallas Green, who summoned Elia to his office.

A press conference was hastily called, and Elia spent the entire time apologizing and desperately trying to take back what he had said. In an interview with the *Tribune*'s Fred Mitchell in 2008,

A Bleepin' Excerpt

"We've got all these so-called fuckin' fans that come out here and say they're Cub fans that are supposed to be behind you rippin' every fuckin' thing you do. I'll tell you one fuckin' thing, I hope we get fuckin' hotter than shit, just to stuff it up them 3,000 fuckin' people that show up every fuckin' day, because if they're the real Chicago fuckin' fans, they can kiss my fuckin' ass right downtown and PRINT IT.

"My fuckin' ass. What the fuck am I supposed to do, go out there and let my fuckin' players get destroyed every day and be quiet about it? For the fuckin' nickel-dime people to show up? The motherfuckers don't even work. That's why they're out at the fuckin' game. They oughta go out and get a fuckin' job and find out what it's like to go out and earn a fuckin' living. Eighty-five percent of the fuckin' world is working.

"The other fifteen come out here. A fuckin' playground for the cocksuckers. Rip them motherfuckers. Rip them fuckin' cocksuckers like the fuckin' players. We got guys bustin' their fuckin' ass, and them fuckin' people boo. And that's the Cubs? My fuckin' ass."

Elia said the sight of fans cursing and throwing beer at right fielder Keith Moreland and shortstop Larry Bowa had set him off.

However, in a *Tribune* story that ran the day after the incident, Elia said he wasn't aware Moreland had almost gone after a group of fans. "My frustrations just peaked," Elia said in the news conference about his tirade. "It's obvious the fans have the same frustrations, and I was out of line."

Elia hung onto his job but only for another 104 games. It was another postgame comment by Elia, this one about how the Cubs had never heard of Atlanta Braves rookie Gerald Perry after Perry had homered against them that Green cited on the day Elia was let go. He didn't mention the rant.

Elia, who was 46 at the time of the rant, briefly managed Philadelphia in the late 1980s and has been a respected coach and adviser for many years since, including his current stint as a Senior Advisor to Player Development for the Atlanta Braves. In an interview with the *Atlanta Journal-Constitution* during spring training in 2011, Elia admitted that after 25 years he had finally listened to the tape.

"Pulled the tape out of a drawer about three, four years ago," he said. "Hadn't heard it since it happened. Me and my wife sat there and listened to it, about 10:00 in the morning over a cup of coffee. We couldn't stop laughing."

19 There Really Was a Harry Caray

There's never going to be another Harry Caray, and sometimes it's hard to imagine there was even one of him. Who would have thought that a short, stout former Cardinals and White Sox

Chicago Cubs announcer Harry Caray sits in the broadcast booth on Tuesday, May 19, 1987, at Wrigely Field during the first inning of the Cubs-Reds baseball game. This was Caray's first day broadcasting that season after recovering from a stroke he suffered during spring training. (AP Photo)

broadcaster with enormous glasses and an inability to pronounce the names of ballplayers—forward or backward—would be the most beloved figure in the history of the Cubs franchise?

Think about any player, and their popularity pales compared to that of Harry Caray. Nobody even comes close. In fact, take any three of the most popular Cubs players of all time, and their combined popularity wouldn't exceed that of Harry, who could never take more than three steps before getting mauled by adoring fans. And he loved every minute of it.

Born and raised in St. Louis, Caray spent the first 25 years of his career broadcasting Cardinals games. He was the enemy of Cubs fans then, for his allegiances and an annoying little refrain that went "*The Cardinals are coming, tra la tra la.*"

It was the Cubs good fortune that St. Louis let Caray go and that after one season in Oakland he came to broadcast White Sox games in 1971. It set him up perfectly to replace Cubs broadcaster Jack Brickhouse, who retired following the 1981 season.

Caray was close to returning to the White Sox for the 1982 season, but new Sox owners Jerry Reinsdorf and Eddie Einhorn had plans to put the South Siders on pay TV, a move that might earn money but would certainly shrink the viewing audience. On the other hand, the Cubs were on WGN-TV, a cable superstation. That troubled Harry, who told Reinsdorf and Einhorn it wouldn't work (it didn't) and his thoughts turned to the Cubs.

There was only one problem: The Cubs hadn't called Harry about their broadcasting job. So Harry called them. A few days later, a deal was struck and a 16-year party began at Wrigley Field.

There was initially some thought that the staid Tribune Co. wouldn't want Harry singing "Take Me Out to the Ballgame" during the seventh-inning stretch, a Harry Caray staple that former White Sox owner Bill Veeck helped launch. But from his perch behind home plate, Harry was soon leading fans as only he could, waving his microphone and belting out the tune before finishing with, "Let's get some runs!"

Along with singing the stretch, Harry brought his trademark "Holy Cow!" with him and a rapturous home run call that went, "It might be! It could be! It is! A home run!" Harry's commercials for Budweiser turned him into a "Cubs fan and a Bud man," and he became so popular longtime broadcast partner Steve Stone titled his autobiography, *Where's Harry?*

A statue to Harry Caray greets fans at the corner of Waveland and Sheffield outside Wrigley Field, and there are successful Harry

Caray's steakhouses in Chicago, all filled with photos, memorabilia, and a smiling bronze bust of the legend himself. And make no mistake, he was a legend even to other legends.

Shortly after Harry's death in 1998, longtime Cubs fan and actor Bill Murray was reminiscing about the day in 1987 that he spent filling in for Harry in the broadcast booth. Murray was just one of many celebrities who filled in for several weeks while Harry recovered from a stroke.

"It was sort of like when you come down on Christmas morning and you look and the milk has been drunk and the cookies have been eaten and there's a bite out of the carrot that you have left for the reindeer," Murray told the *Chicago Tribune*. "It was like that when I went into the booth at Wrigley Field and sat in his chair and noticed there was a small refrigerator under the table and there was beer in it. It was like there really was a Santa Claus.

"And there really was a Harry Caray."

20 Baseball's Sad Lexicon: Tinker to Evers to Chance

These are the saddest of possible words:
"Tinker to Evers to Chance."
Trio of bear cubs, and fleeter than birds,
Tinker and Evers and Chance.
Ruthlessly pricking our gonfalon bubble,
Making a Giant hit into a double—
Words that are heavy with nothing but trouble:
"Tinker to Evers to Chance."

—Franklin P. Adams,
New York Evening Mail, July 12, 1910

For the record, they did have first names. It was Joe Tinker, Johnny Evers, and Frank Chance—the "trio of bear cubs"—who gained baseball immortality together thanks to Chicago native Franklin P. Adams' simple eight-line poem.

Now it would stand to reason that this double play combination, the most famous in baseball history, was exceptional, and surely it was. Each man had a long, distinguished playing career, and at one time each managed the Cubs. But has their prowess as a double-play combo been overstated?

In 1947, Evers published a piece for a college magazine that was reprinted in the *Chicago Tribune*. He wrote, "We set a mark for double plays that has never been equaled. I don't recall the exact number, however."

As is the case in baseball, you could look it up. And in 1954, a National League publicist, Charles Segar, did just that. A review of the box scores revealed that during their heyday—from 1906 to 1909—Tinker, Evers, and Chance only participated in 54 double plays. Even more incredible, the specific combo of Tinker to Evers to Chance—that's a 6–4–3, if you're scoring at home—only turned 29. They never led the National League in double plays in any season.

So who were these men who rode Franklin P. Adams' pen all the way to the Baseball Hall of Fame?

Frank Leroy Chance was undoubtedly the greatest manager in Cubs history and bore a nickname by which newspapers of the day often referred to him: Peerless Leader. It was under their Peerless Leader, who became manager in 1905, that the Cubs won four NL pennants and their only two World Series titles in 1907 and 1908.

He joined the Cubs in 1898 and spent five unspectacular seasons mainly as a backup catcher before his predecessor as manager, Frank Selee, permanently moved him to first base. Through parts of 17 seasons, his final two starting in 1913 as player-manager of the New York Yankees, he hit .296 and stole 403 bases.

John Joseph Evers, known as "The Crab" both for the way he chased after ground balls and for his usually sour disposition, joined the Cubs in 1902 and became player-manager in 1913 after Chance was forced out after a feud with owner Charles W. Murphy.

Though he had good speed and stole 324 bases during his career, Evers only hit better than .300 twice and had a lifetime batting average of .270. He was a heady ballplayer who, if "Baseball's Sad Lexicon" had never been penned, would probably be best known as the player who realized Fred Merkle had failed to touch second base during the famous "Merkle's Boner" game of 1908.

Joseph Bert Tinker, who played more games at shortstop than any other Cub until Don Kessinger broke his mark, was nearly identical to Evers as a ballplayer. Smart and with an overwhelming desire to win, he too joined the Cubs in 1902 and depended on great speed to make up for an average bat, stealing 336 bases while only hitting .262.

While Chance started to sit himself more and more starting in 1909, Tinker and Evers remained regulars until the end of the 1912 season when Tinker was shipped to Cincinnati. The pair also engaged in a feud that, according to legend, began when Tinker took a cab without waiting for Evers. Some accounts say the pair didn't speak for 30 years; others say it was just a few years. What seems certain is the pair, despite playing side by side for 11 seasons (or rather because of it), didn't like each other very much.

On April 12, 1912, Tinker, Evers, and Chance appeared in a game together for the last time. Chance was still the Cubs' player-manager but only played in two games. At the end of the season he wasn't given a new contract, and he went on to manage the New York Yankees the next two seasons.

Chance's health began to fail soon after he left the Yankees and he didn't manage again until 1923 when he took over the Boston Red Sox. The following season, he was hired to manage the

Chicago White Sox when he again fell ill. Stepping in for him was his old pal Johnny Evers. A few months later, Chance was dead at the age of 48.

In 1946, baseball writers failed to elect anyone to the Hall of Fame. Chance had come the closest, followed by Evers, while Tinker only garnered the 15th-most votes. A special committee was impaneled to select some old-timers, and on April 23, 1946, Joe Tinker, Johnny Evers, and Frank Chance were elected to the Hall of Fame. Together.

21 8/8/88

Shortly after the first night game was played at Cincinnati's Crosley Field on May 24, 1935, Bill Veeck Jr. went to owner Phil Wrigley and told him he wanted lights for Wrigley Field.

"Just a fad," Wrigley responded. "A passing fancy."

For the next 53 years many people had a hand in denying night baseball at Wrigley Field, including mayors, aldermen, and residents who lived near the ballpark. But nobody played a bigger role than Wrigley.

There was a brief attempt to install lights in 1941 and the necessary materials were ordered, but when World War II broke out he donated it all to the war effort and by the time the war ended he had evidently changed his mind.

"We believe that baseball is a daytime sport and will continue to play it in the sunshine as long as we can," Wrigley said after the 1945 season. By 1948, after the Detroit Tigers added lights to Briggs Stadium, every other major league ballpark had lights. Still, Wrigley wouldn't budge.

Wrigley Field, the last major league ballpark with day-only games, glows under the lights during the first night game in the 74-year history of the park on August 8, 1988, in Chicago. (AP Photo/John Swart)

During the 1962 winter meetings, the National League owners practically pleaded with Wrigley to add lights. They compared the Cubs woeful attendance of 609,802 to that of the Los Angeles Dodgers, who drew 2,755,184. Wrigley, who wasn't present at the meetings, replied the following day: "We don't need lights in Wrigley Field; we need a contender."

In 1966, a Cubs stockholder, William Shlensky, filed suit to force the Cubs to install lights. The suit was thrown out and Wrigley responded by saying the Cubs indeed planned to put lights in one day—but only so day baseball games could be completed.

It wasn't until after Wrigley's death in 1977 and the subsequent sale of the team to Tribune Co. in 1981 that talk of adding lights grew serious and contentious. Cubs General Manager Dallas

Green became a fierce advocate for lights, while state legislators passed a noise pollution law in 1982, the purpose of which was to ban night baseball.

After legal tussles and threats to move the Cubs out of Wrigley Field, the Chicago City Council voted 29–19 on February 25, 1988, to allow eight night games to be played during the 1988 season and 18 games per year in subsequent seasons.

The race to 8/8/88 was on.

During the next few months the Cubs set about the physical task of installing lights, but that was a piece of cake compared to the battle being played out among Cubs fans and armchair psychologists. The question being asked everywhere: Would lights ruin Wrigley Field? Everyone had an opinion, including Cubs broadcasters Harry Caray and Steve Stone, who didn't agree on what lights would mean.

"The kids who ride the 'L' to come to the park in the daytime are not going to do that at night," Caray said. "And their parents can't drive to the ballpark, because there's no place to park. I think what you lose when you play a lot of night games is that kids develop other interests."

Stone disagreed, arguing Wrigley Field wasn't changing at all and one of its greatest advantages could never be altered by night baseball. "I don't think that will be changed by turning on lights at 7:30," Stone said.

The anticipation for the first night game was all anyone could talk about in Chicago during the summer of '88, and the mad scramble for tickets delved into madness. Cubs manager Don Zimmer even changed his answering machine message to include, "And I ain't got no tickets for the first night game."

Cubs pitcher Rick Sutcliffe said it best. "It's history," he declared. "You know there's going to be a World Series X, World Series XI and so on. There's only going to be one [first night game]. This is it."

6/25/43—The Real First Night Game

When 6:00 PM rolls around, it's night. Even if it's not dark. So wouldn't you agree if the Cubs scheduled a game for 6:00 PM it would qualify as a night game?

Okay, maybe we can quibble about the definition of what a night game is, but it's a matter of historical record that on June 25, 1943—a Friday—the Cubs played a home game at light-free Wrigley Field that started at 6:00 PM.

Most games in those days began at 3:00 PM to accommodate work schedules but in 1943 the Cubs experimented with "off-time contests," as the *Chicago Tribune* called it. They had a couple of 11:00 AM starting times during June, as well.

The summer solstice had passed just a few days earlier so there was plenty of sun left when Hi Bithorn took the mound against the St. Louis Cardinals. The game ended two hours and seventeen minutes later, or at roughly 8:22 PM, with Bithorn still on the mound to finish off his two-hitter, a 6–0 win in the first night game at Wrigley Field.

Or not.

When it was finally time to get the game between the Cubs and Philadelphia Phillies underway, 91-year-old Harry Grossman, a season-ticket holder who went to his first game in 1906, hit the switch that lit up Wrigley Field as the crowd screamed out, "Let there be light!"

After the Chicago Symphony Orchestra played the National Anthem, the mechanics of a baseball game got underway. The fourth pitch of the game from Sutcliffe was hit out of the park by Philadelphia's Phil Bradley, and in the bottom of the inning Ryne Sandberg hit a two-run homer to keep the frenzied crowd on its feet.

The early scoring was exciting but hardly atypical. There was just no way the game could possibly be memorable enough to live up to expectations. But then in a weird way it actually did. Seventy-five minutes after the first pitch, a torrential downpour stopped the

Lights Out

After manager Herman Franks quit the Cubs at the end of the 1979 season, the first choice to replace him was Whitey Herzog, who had just been fired by Kansas City after—the horror—coming in second place after winning three straight American League West titles.

A brilliant motivator loved by his players, Herzog may have brought some stability to the Cubs, who had gone through three managers in less than eight seasons since the firing of Leo Durocher in 1972.

Before the Cubs could approach him, however, he was quoted as saying, "I'd become an alcoholic if I managed in Chicago and had my nights free." The sensitive Cubs' management looked elsewhere and instead hired Preston Gomez—then fired him midway through his first season.

Going without lights may have cost the Cubs one of baseball's best managers, Herzog was instead hired by the hated St. Louis Cardinals and led them to three NL pennants and the 1982 World Series title.

ballgame and after a two-hour rain delay the umpires called it. The first official night game would not be played for another 24 hours.

The rain didn't dampen the spirits of those at Wrigley Field even if it did deprive them of night baseball. Fans in the bleachers basked in the rain while some jumped to the field and successfully outran security guards to dive onto the wet tarp before being arrested. On the other hand, four Cubs—Jody Davis, Les Lancaster, Al Nipper, and Greg Maddux—avoided arrest despite diving on the tarp themselves to the delight of the crowd.

In the end, it was a memorable night—if not a memorable game—as lights finally came to Wrigley Field.

22 Game 163

Some teams have to back into the playoffs. In 1998, the Cubs and the San Francisco Giants were mediocre enough that they each had to back into the *playoff* for the playoffs.

Both the Cubs and the Giants lost what was supposed to have been their final game of the regular season in gut-wrenching yet similar fashion. The Cubs led their finale against Houston 3–1 in the bottom of the eighth before losing in 11 innings.

In a contest between future Cubs managers Dusty Baker and Don Baylor, the Giants led 7–0 in the fifth until Colorado came roaring back and won the game in the bottom of the ninth on a home run by light-hitting Neifi Perez.

Both teams engaged in extensive scoreboard watching as each game progressed at a similar pace and ended within minutes of each other, lending drama to what had been a thrilling National League Wild Card race. The New York Mets were also in contention before dropping their last five and failing to force a three-team playoff.

Thanks to winning a coin flip a couple weeks earlier, the tiebreaker was held at Wrigley Field on a Monday night as the rest of baseball either headed for winter break or enjoyed a day of rest to prepare for the postseason.

Even though the game was considered part of the regular season, it most certainly felt like a playoff game. Michael Jordan threw out the first pitch, Bill Murray sang the seventh-inning stretch, and the famous Wrigley Field scoreboard was nearly barren, save for the only baseball game being played that day. "What a strange sight," Cubs general manager Ed Lynch remarked.

It had been a long, tortuous march to this winner-take-all contest for the Cubs, the first of its kind at Wrigley since Game 7 of the 1945 World Series. All of Cubdom had been dealt a devastating blow in February when beloved broadcaster Harry Caray passed away. The grief then turned to amazement as Sammy Sosa turned in a 66-homer season for the ages.

One of the most memorable regular season games in Cubs history had taken place on September 23 in Milwaukee when Brant Brown dropped a fly ball with the bases loaded and two outs in the ninth inning to cost the Cubs a precious game. Nobody needed a win in the tiebreaker more than Brown, who never made it off the bench.

Cubs manager Jim Riggleman chose human rain delay Steve Trachsel to start while Mark Gardner took the hill for the Giants, whose roster was filled with ex-Cubs Joe Carter, Shawon Dunston, and Rey Sanchez not to mention future Cubs third baseman Bill Mueller.

Trachsel was hardly stellar with six walks, but he didn't allow a hit through 6⅓ innings. By that time the Cubs had gone ahead thanks to two unlikely heroes: Matt Mieske and Gary Gaetti. A little over a month earlier, Gaetti had been released by St. Louis and on August 19—his 40th birthday—signed with the Cubs. In just 37 games, he hit .320 with eight homers and 27 RBIs, including a two-run homer off Gardner in the fifth inning to give the Cubs a 2–0 lead.

Mieske, a right-handed hitting reserve outfielder, had been up and down from the minors and was hitting .130 as a pinch-hitter when he hit for Henry Rodriguez, a lefty, with one out and the bases loaded in the sixth. His two-run single put the Cubs ahead 4–0 and all eyes turned to Trachsel. By the time he departed with one out in the seventh, he had only given up one single. The forever-maligned Matt Karchner and Felix Heredia, a couple of middle relievers Lynch had obtained in July for former No. 1 draft picks, took over and got the Cubs out of the inning.

The Cubs tacked on a run in the eighth when Sosa scored on a wild pitch, and they entered the ninth inning with what any rational observer would have said was a secure 5–0 lead. When it comes to the Cubs, there is no such thing and they proved that in the ninth.

Kevin Tapani, who had pitched a scoreless eighth, gave up back-to-back singles to Brent Mayne and Mueller before giving way to Terry Mulholland. Things were just getting interesting. Mulholland gave up an RBI single to Stan Javier and then walked Ellis Burks, bringing up Barry Bonds. This was in Bonds' days before performance-enhancing drugs but well into what was already an incredible career.

Riggleman stayed with the lefty Mulholland against Bonds, who in the seventh inning had grounded out to first with the bases loaded. This time he ripped a screamer to right that luckily found Sosa's glove but still allowed Mueller to tag up and score from third, making it 5–2.

The Cubs closer in 1998 was Rod "Shooter" Beck, one of the most intimidating-looking yet affable and fun-loving guys you could ever hope to come across in the clubhouse. He saved 51 games in his only full season with the Cubs, none more important than this one. Beck, who passed away in 2007 at the age of 38, got Jeff Kent to hit into a fielder's choice and then jammed Carter, whose meek pop-up along the first-base line landed gently in Mark Grace's glove for the final out.

A wild scene broke out at Wrigley with players dancing on the field, champagne being sprayed into the crowd, and Sosa racing toward his most devoted fans in the right-field bleachers to bask in their glow.

Finally, the Cubs had won a big one. Even if it wasn't the biggest one.

23 Spend a Day in the Bleachers

Take heed of the warnings that you need to be very careful when you sit in the bleachers. You're liable to enjoy yourself too much and may never want to sit anywhere else.

Wrigley Field's gorgeous, sun-drenched bleachers aren't for everybody. If you don't like loud, rowdy people or if you've got a bad back and need a standard seat with a back rest, then go to the grandstand. If you want to keep an opponent's home run ball, head over to U.S. Cellular Field.

Detractors will say the bleachers are just an oversized bar, that fake fans drink too much, the girls show too much skin, and fights get in the way of a good time. Well, sure. On occasion that's all true. Deal with it.

A day in the bleachers is a chance to experience arguably the most famous section of any ballpark ever built. So get yourself a bleacher ticket, sit down, and prepare to chant, "Right field sucks!" Unless you're sitting in the right field bleachers, in which case you probably want to yell that left field sucks.

The bleachers were built in 1937 when Cubs owner Phil Wrigley green lit additions that included the same manually operated scoreboard that is still there today. There was an expansion in 2005 to add several thousand seats, but the bleachers are essentially the same as they were 75 years ago.

Today, the term "Bleacher Bum" is used to describe anybody sitting in the bleachers whether they're one of the regulars or a tourist from Dubuque. But in 1969, when the Bums became a local and then a national phenomenon, they were an actual organization with an actual president. They even had a cheerleader and kindred spirit in Cubs relief pitcher Dick Selma, who directed them with waves of his arms from the left-field bullpen.

Ron Grousl was a 24-year-old who didn't work much but because bleacher tickets were just $1, only went on sale the day of the game, and weren't nearly in as much demand as they are today, he and the rest of the Bums never had any problem getting into games. Grousl was the president of the Bleacher Bums, who wore yellow construction worker helmets, carried membership cards, and heckled the bejeezus out of any player not wearing a Cubs inform.

Many opposing players came to despise the Bums, but there was also a grudging respect and playfulness with the rabid fans. In August 1968, in the ninth inning of an 8–0 St. Louis victory, Cardinals outfielder Lou Brock came out to his spot in left field with a sign reading, "We're Still No. 1," taped to his back.

Bleacher Bums: The Play

The 1977 play *Bleacher Bums* isn't the story of the actual Bleacher Bums. The fictional characters sat in right field while the real Bums were in left, and the eight disparate characters didn't always get along while the real Bums were a close-knit group.

The real Bums also didn't enjoy nearly as much success as the play, which premiered in 1977 at Chicago's Organic Theater and was conceived—where else?—in the Wrigley Field bleachers by actor and longtime Cubs fan Joe Mantegna.

"I had the idea start germinating in my head when I was, like, 18 or 19 years old," he told the *Chicago Sun-Times*' Bill Zwecker in 2004. "I thought, 'Wouldn't it be interesting to do a play about this group of people I sit with every day in the bleachers?'"

Mantegna's idea turned into an improvised play that also starred Dennis Franz and ran in Chicago for two years before going to Broadway for a short run and then to Los Angeles for 13 years.

One of the original stage performances was taped by PBS in 1979 and can still be seen in its entirety with Mantegna and Franz in the roles they originated. A made-for-TV version was made in 2002.

But his teammate Ron Davis, who claimed he was hit in the back by a battery during that Cardinals win, was shellshocked. "You know, I just got back from two weeks of army training and that was safe compared with playing the outfield here if you don't wear a Cub uniform," he told the *Chicago Tribune*. "Come to think of it, I ought to get hazardous duty pay when I play here."

The Bums began their days at Ray's Bleachers, now known as Murphy's Bleachers, and ended them there, as well. Among the 300 Bums were teens and seniors, including a 72-year-old Bum and a Gramma Bum. Grousl limited official membership but the Bums eventually started to become victims of their own fun.

"Now everyone wants to be a Bum and sit in the bleachers," one of the original Bums, Jim Donohoe, told the *Tribune* in June 1969. "We've really got to get up early to get to our seats."

The highlight of the 1969 season for the Bums came when Wrigley bankrolled a trip to Atlanta for 100 of their lot. The trip proved to be a great success as the Cubs swept the Braves. As Rick Talley wrote in *The Cubs of '69*, the Bums also were at the top of their game "...with one Bum trying to lasso the Atlanta mascot, Chief Noc-A-Homa, another trying to burn down his tepee, and another being hospitalized after taking a 22' plunge off the railing of the left-field stands."

The disappointment of 1969 didn't prevent 1970 from starting off with a bang. After the Cubs nearly blew their home opener before a sellout crowd, a riot broke out as fans stormed past Andy Frain ushers and raced onto the field. Cubs second baseman Glenn Beckert was attacked by three fans, according to a *Tribune* story. The same story was careful to point out that "the Bleacher Bums were not involved" in the riot.

However, the bleachers were becoming an increasingly difficult place to police, and the following day a no-standing policy was enforced at the start of the game. With only a few thousand people in Wrigley Field the rule was relaxed by the end of the game but changes were being planned.

A few days later, the Cubs announced beer would only be sold at concession stands in the bleachers and they would stop the practice of selling 750 standing-room-only bleacher tickets. The biggest change, however, was to add a wire-mesh basket to prevent beer cups as well as people from entering the Wrigley Field playing field. The first game with the basket was played on May 7. Three days later, Billy Williams became the first player to have a home run land in the basket.

The conversion of the bleachers from an inexpensive way to catch a game to huge moneymaker began in 1985 when the Cubs ended the practice of only selling tickets on the day of the game. Within a few years the prices started to skyrocket, and by 2016 the top price for a general admission bleacher ticket was $72.80.

Occasionally incidents show the bleachers in a negative light, such as the time in 2009 when one fan threw a beer on Philadelphia outfielder Shane Victorino during a nationally televised game only to have an innocent fan ejected.

But the bleachers are still a tremendous place to watch a baseball game. Even if it doesn't cost a buck anymore.

24 Billy Williams: The Quiet One

There may not have been a more soft-spoken superstar in Cubs history than Billy Williams, except maybe the painfully shy Ryne Sandberg. Williams wasn't shy, however, he was a quiet, confident man who came to play every day and let others do the yapping.

That approach worked for years until late in his career, after destroying pitchers for an entire season and getting bypassed for recognition, Williams, who a *Chicago Tribune* writer called "the quiet man of the club," got fed up.

In 1972, Williams not only had his best season—he had one of the best years any Cub had ever put together, maybe even better than any by former teammate Ernie Banks, who had retired after 1971. Williams came within three homers and three RBIs of capturing the National League's Triple Crown, hitting .333 with 37 homers and 122 RBIs. And for his efforts he felt he got kicked in the teeth.

Cincinnati catcher Johnny Bench beat out Williams for the National League's MVP award even though Bench hit only .270, 63 points less than Williams. Bench was the one who denied Williams the Triple Crown, hitting 40 homers, driving in 125, and playing a demanding position. The real difference was Bench's Reds had made the playoffs and Williams' Cubs, as usual, stayed home.

Williams was immediately and publicly critical of the vote, and he had a right to be. On one ballot he was completely left off. The writer either didn't think Williams had been one of the top 10 most valuable players in the NL that year or he was rigging the vote in Bench's favor. The hurt hadn't worn off by the following spring, and Williams, who came into camp having settled for a one-year $150,000 contract well below market value, made his feelings known.

"I've been a nice guy too long, and it has cost me money and endorsements," he told the *Chicago Tribune*'s Ed Prell. "I'm convinced it helps an athlete to pop off and that the fans don't care if you're right or wrong, as long as it's controversial. You'll get more attention than if you make eight hits in a row."

Players try out all sorts of new things in the spring before going back to their old ways, and it was the same with Williams.

Hall of Famer Billy Williams addresses the crowd outside Wrigley Field after a statue of him was dedicated before a game between the Houston Astros and the Cubs on Tuesday, September 7, 2010, in Chicago. (AP Photo/Charles Rex Arbogast)

He remained the calm, thoughtful player he had always been, and history remembers him for his beautiful left-handed swing that brought him to the major leagues and carried him on to the Baseball Hall of Fame in 1987.

Plain-spoken and with a permanent twinkle in his eye, the kid from Whistler, Alabama, didn't hit as many home runs as Ernie Banks, throw no-hitters like Ken Holtzman, or click his heels like Ron Santo. He just played and played, every single day. And along the way, he hit seemingly almost every day.

From his first full season in 1961 up until 1973, Williams was practically slump-proof despite averaging 159 games and setting a National League record by playing in 1,117 consecutive games. He drove in at least 84 runs for 13 straight seasons and during that span averaged 29 homers and 98 RBIs.

When he retired in 1975 following two final seasons with Oakland, Williams had 426 homers and 1,475 RBIs to go with a .290 batting average. He also had his work cut out for him to get into the Hall of Fame. If it was possible to hit a quiet 426 homers, Williams had done it. Never playing in the postseason for the Cubs didn't help, and neither did going 0-for-7 in his lone postseason appearance with the A's in 1975. In his first year of eligibility, Williams only drew 23 percent of the vote and had to wait six years before his election.

But on the day he was inducted Williams used his bully pulpit to speak out for the rights of African American players, coaches, and managers. He never forgot the virulent racism he encountered in the minor leagues that forced him to stay in different hotels, eat in restaurant kitchens, and put up with repeated chants of "nigger."

If it weren't for legendary Cubs scout and coach Buck O'Neil, who went to Alabama in 1959 to convince the proud, angry 21-year-old Williams to return to his minor league team, Cooperstown would have had one less bust. And so on July 26, 1987, after finally getting elected in his sixth year of eligibility, Williams went to Cooperstown to speak up for himself and others. His induction came just a few months after Los Angeles Dodgers GM Al Campanis was forced to resign after saying on national TV that African Americans might not be suited for managerial and executive positions.

"The next courageous step rests with the owners of 26 major league ballclubs. They can make the difference by not looking at the color of a man's skin but by examining his ability, talent, knowledge, and leadership. If this is the land of opportunity, then let it be true to become the land of opportunity for all.

"Questions have been raised in recent months by the media about the participation of blacks and other minorities in decision-making positions in baseball. The issue wouldn't have come up if every job in baseball was open to every league, creed, race, and nationality. But this is not the case.

"We minorities, for the past four decades, have demonstrated our talents as players. And now we deserve the chance and consideration to demonstrate similar talents as third base coaches, as managers, as general managers, as executives in the front office, and yes, owners of major league ballclubs themselves."

"Baseball has become considered America's favorite pastime. Now let's make this sport that reflects the true spirit of our great country and nation that more than 200 years ago was dedicated to the proposition that all men, all men are created equal. Yes, plans and words can be transformed into actions and deeds.

"We ask for nothing less but we seek what is just. I know the experience I've had over the past years as a coach have helped me to prepare myself for the days when I'd be considered for managerial or executive position with a major league ballclub."

Williams never became a big-league manager, but he paved the way for others. His call for justice was similar to how he played the game, with a quiet dignity and an uncanny ability to know just when to speak up.

25 The 71-Year Pennant Drought Ends

To win the World Series you first have to get there, and while 1908 was a year to dwell on in Cubs lore, to a nearly equal extent so was 1945.

It had been 71 years since their last appearance in the World Series when the Cubs began the 2016 National League Championship Series against the Los Angeles Dodgers, a franchise with a fabled past but no NL pennants since 1988. Theirs was not quite a legendary drought, but long enough that about half the Dodgers weren't alive the last time a World Series had been played at Dodger Stadium.

Thanks to a 103-win regular season, the Cubs had home-field advantage throughout the NL playoffs—and thanks to closing out the San Francisco Giants in four games in the Divisional Series, they were able to set their starting rotation just as they wanted to face the Dodgers, who didn't have the same luxury. The Dodgers needed five games to turn back the Washington Nationals in their NLDS and relied heavily on baseball's best pitcher, Clayton Kershaw, to finish the job.

Kershaw threw 110 pitches in Game 4 and then, on a day of rest, came on in relief to get the last two outs of the Game 5 clincher. This was not insignificant for a pitcher who had missed nearly half the season with a bad back. Overusing him was not part of the game plan, but the Dodgers simply had no choice if they wanted to get back the Nationals.

Once they did, the Cubs had the advantage. Jon Lester was rested and ready for Game 1 against Dodgers rookie Kenta Maeda, who was not sharp in Game 3 against Washington, having given up four runs in three innings. Lester, on the other hand, had a long history of playoff brilliance with the Boston Red Sox and a few days earlier had thrown eight shutout innings in beating the Giants to kick off that series. The Cubs got three early runs again against Maeda, tacked on a 5-spot in the eighth, and easily won 8–4.

A good thing, too, because the Dodgers owned the Cubs for the next two games. Kershaw and Kenley Jansen combined for a two-hit shutout in Game 2. Then, after the series moved to Los Angeles, four different Dodgers, led by former Cub Rich Hill,

Sidebar Head

Prior to Game 4 of the NLCS, Addison Russell and Anthony Rizzo were a combined 3-for-50 with no home runs and no RBIs in the 2016 postseason. They each broke their slumps with Game 4 home runs and that led to remarkable performances during the remainder of the playoffs.

Russell went 12-for-40 (.300) with 3 homers and 13 RBIs over the last 10 games, while Rizzo hit .410 (16-for-39) with 3 homers, 10 RBIs, and 10 runs scored including the deciding run in Game 7 of the World Series.

shut out the Cubs again in Game 3. Trailing two games to one, the Cubs weren't quite on the brink but the disappearance of their offense was troubling.

The Dodgers went with another rookie, Julio Urias, in Game 4, and he began by not allowing a hit through the first three innings. When cleanup hitter Ben Zobrist came to the plate leading off the fourth, the Cubs not only had no hits but hadn't scored for 21 straight innings. So what does a cleanup hitter like Zobrist do? He lays down a bunt single, of course. It's amazing what the tiniest bit of momentum can do.

Javier Baez and Willson Contreras followed with singles to get the Cubs on the board. Then, one out later, Addison Russell homered to put the Cubs up 4–0 and send a signal that they were far from dead. There had been some clamoring to bench Russell, who had started the playoffs in a dreadful 1-for-24 slump, but Cubs manager Joe Maddon never considered taking his defense out of the lineup.

Not quite as troubling but of concern was Anthony Rizzo, whose own 2-for-26 slump was marked more by bad luck than a poor approach at the plate. But just as Russell had obliterated his slump with a home run, Rizzo came to the plate in the fifth inning and launched a homer to increase the Cubs' lead to 5–0 and propel them to a 10–2 victory. Game 5 was a close affair that turned on Russell's tiebreaking two-run home run in the sixth inning, and when their 8–4 victory was over, the Cubs were one win shy of getting to the World Series. But Kershaw was rested and ready for Game 6 back at Wrigley Field.

Over the years you could point to certain moments when, perhaps, you knew the tide was about to turn against the Cubs. There was the black cat in New York in 1969, Leon Durham's error in 1984, and, of course, the comedy of errors in the 8th inning of 2003's NLCS. Finally, the Cubs had a moment that would help them immeasurably. The Cubs had already got to Kershaw in the first inning when Dexter Fowler hit a leadoff double and Kris Bryant followed by dropping a single into right field. 1–0 felt good, but this was Kershaw on the mound; this might be all the Cubs would get. Thanks to Dodgers left fielder Andrew Toles, they'd get more.

Toles somehow dropped an easy fly ball to left field, the kind an outfielder may never drop in an entire career, and instead of having one out with only one on the Cubs had runners on second and third with only one out. Zobrist's sacrifice fly made it 2–0 and it just felt like this was going to be a night to remember, which it turned out to be. Kyle Hendricks threw the game of his life, allowing two measly hits in 7⅓ innings, and Aroldis Chapman got the final five outs to give the Cubs a stunningly easy 5–0 victory that launched an uproarious celebration inside and outside Wrigley Field.

After 71 years, the Cubs were once again champions of the National League.

26 P.K. Wrigley: The Man Who Invented the Cubs

The Cubs were founded in 1876 and experienced their glory years around the turn of the 20th century, but the franchise as it's known today wasn't invented until many years later.

Philip Knight Wrigley was a tinkerer who would purchase expensive automobiles and immediately take them to his busy workshop where he would take them apart just for the pleasure of trying to make them better. Among his inventions was a non-slippable screwdriver, which he created on purpose, and the Cubs as lovable losers, which he created by accident and never came close to perfecting despite many years of tinkering.

"What is the combination? Why are we losing?" he once lamented to the *Chicago Tribune*'s David Condon. "I can't pinpoint it, but you know in flying we have an indefinable explanation when a crash cannot be explained. We call it pilot error. Sometimes I wish I wasn't the Cubs pilot."

Wrigley inherited the Cubs from his father, William Wrigley Jr., in 1932 and for the next 45 years—until Philip's death at the age of 82 in 1977—presided over the franchise in a way that was always futile, often admirable, and occasionally bizarre.

The last four seasons the Cubs made the World Series—in 1932, 1935, 1938, and 1945—all came under P.K. Wrigley's watch, although the first three are credited to his father and team president Bill Veeck Sr. and the last one to the dilution of baseball talent due to World War II.

Blame for the long run of losing that took place after the 1945 season is heaped on the shoulders of Wrigley, whose interest in the sport of baseball was minimal at best. The legendary Bill Veeck Jr., who worked for Wrigley for eight years beginning in 1933, wrote in his autobiography *Veeck—As In Wreck*, "If he has any particular feeling for baseball, any real liking for it, he has disguised it magnificently."

Wrigley's first concern was always the comfort of fans, although he never was able to quite understand the emotional discomfort wrought by losing. He once ripped out hundreds of box seats at Wrigley Field at considerable cost because he felt they weren't wide enough, a move that decreased capacity among the most expensive seats.

Yet over the years he lowballed superstars like Ernie Banks when baseball's reserve clause made it easy to do so, and he bristled when free agency arrived in the 1970s saying "nobody is worth over $100,000."

Despite his stinginess with baseball players, Wrigley didn't define himself by his wealth and was generous with fans. He would answer his own phone at work, surprising more than a few Cubs fans calling to complain who never expected to get the owner himself. In 1969, during the height of that crazy season, he even arranged for dozens of Bleacher Bums to attend a three-game series in Atlanta.

Some of the ideas he brought to the Cubs were ahead of their time, such as having computers track hitting and pitching trends and having the scoreboard flash "hit" or "error" to let the fans know the outcome of a questionable play.

But he was wrong about night baseball, calling it a "fad" when it first became popular in 1935 and after a brief flirtation with lights in the 1940s refused to permit night baseball at Wrigley Field, in part out of devotion to local residents.

Wrigley had many downright goofy ideas, including using psychologists to discover what separates the best ballplayers from the worst. "We didn't find out much about the 1 percent of the boys who could make the major leagues," Veeck Jr. told the *Chicago Tribune*. "But we did find out a lot about the 99 percent who can't."

In 1961, Wrigley decreed the Cubs would not have a manager but instead would have a rotating "college of coaches." This came about in part because of Wrigley's distaste for firing people and also because he had noticed the dictionary defined "manager" as being a "dictator." He disapproved of the definition. The experiment lasted five years, whereupon Wrigley hired Leo Durocher, a dictator if there ever was one.

Probably the strangest thing Wrigley ever did came just a few years after he assumed ownership of the team. He paid $5,000 to an "Evil Eye," whose job was to sit behind home plate and put a "whammy" on opposing teams. Not much else is known about this odd event but one thing is certain—it didn't work.

Wrigley, who was demonstrably shy, stayed away from the ballpark during his final years, an irony because his greatest legacy is the ballpark. He poured millions of dollars into it out of a certainty that Wrigley Field was the greatest sales tool he had.

Decades later, as millions still pour into the Friendly Confines during losing seasons, it's clear Wrigley was ahead of his time about that, as well.

27 Click Your Heels Like Ron Santo

Please be careful when you try this, if you think jumping into the air and clicking your heels is easy, it isn't. Ron Santo's jubilant jump on June 22, 1969, thrilled Cubs fans and spawned a summer of imitators, at least two of whom ended up on the disabled list. Even Santo didn't come away unscathed. On his inaugural leap he cut himself on the leg with one of his cleats.

"I'd see kids come along my car and be clicking their heels," Santo said in *What It Means to be a Cub*. "It was fantastic. I got a card from two elderly people, and each of them had a leg up on a coffee table. They had tried to click their heels and both of them broke their ankles, but they sent me a card."

Oh, Nooooo!!!!!!!!!

The beauty of Ron Santo the radio announcer was that he was a fan first and a broadcaster second, and there really was nothing he or anyone could do about it.

Not that anyone ever wanted Santo to hide his undying love for the Cubs or his desire to see them win a World Series, that would be as foolish as asking a bird not to fly, a fish not to swim, or Ronnie Wickers not to "woo woo."

It's no surprise then that the defining moment of his broadcasting career—which began in 1990—came during one of the worst moments in Cubs history. Some people call it the "Brant Brown" game, but it's really the "Oh, nooooo!" game. The background: In the final days of the 1998 regular season, Brown dropped a fly ball with the bases loaded and two out in the ninth inning that cleared the bases and gave Milwaukee an 8–7 victory.

It was an utterly shocking moment in every aspect that led to an iconic moment. Just as the ball bounced off the heel of Brown's glove and it dawned on Santo what had happened, his instincts took over and he was no longer in the broadcast booth. After the game, Cubs manager Jim Riggleman was in the unusual position of having to console Santo.

"I had to laugh," broadcast partner Pat Hughes said in his eulogy at Santo's funeral. "Here was a manager cheering up a broadcaster. This has never happened in the history of American sports.... Do you think Mike Ditka ever cheered up Wayne Larrivee?"

Santo was a fan aghast at what he had just seen, and the guttural yawp that emerged from his mouth when Brown dropped the ball became the way generations of Cubs fans would affectionately mimic him.

Jack Brickhouse had his signature "Hey, Hey," Harry Caray had his "Holy Cow," and now Santo had his, "Oh, nooooo!"

There isn't much unbridled joy allowed in baseball, not when "unwritten" rules state any such act will result in a beaning. Later in the season, Santo was pulled aside by St. Louis Cardinals catcher Tim McCarver, who explained his pitchers didn't like when he clicked his heels, even if it was only after the game and only at Wrigley Field.

"Timmy," Santo said, "when I go across those white lines, nobody is my friend. You just let them know I don't care."

That one act perfectly reflected a player—and later a broadcaster—whose emotions could never be buried.

Ronald Edward Santo was born in Seattle, Washington, on February 25, 1940, and 20 years later he was in training camp with the Cubs with his sights set on Wrigley Field. Manager Charlie Grimm told him he'd made the team, but just before camp broke the Cubs traded for veteran third baseman Don Zimmer.

The disappointment devastated Santo, who had passed on contracts worth two or three times as much as the Cubs offered because he believed their inferior lineup would allow him to reach the major leagues quicker. After threatening to not report to the minors, Santo cooled off and reluctantly headed off to Triple-A.

Three months later, the Cubs called him up and on June 26, 1960, he went 3-for-7 with 5 RBIs in a doubleheader at Pittsburgh. He played in his first game at Wrigley Field two days later, going 1-for-4 against the Milwaukee Braves. He was home.

"I walked on the field, and there was atmosphere," he said in *Banks to Sandberg to Grace.* "There's nothing like it. The stands were empty. It was so beautiful. It was like playing in my backyard."

He quickly became a fan favorite and perennial All-Star selection all while harboring a secret he'd learned after undergoing his first Cubs physical in 1958—Santo was a diabetic. It took him a few years to understand the needs of his body, but he still rarely missed games. During his first nine full seasons, he sat out a total of 11 games.

In 1971, Santo revealed he had diabetes, and raising money for research became the cause of his life. He raised $60 million through his foundation during his lifetime, and he never turned down a request to talk to any person—young or old—about the ups and downs of living life as a diabetic.

On the field, Santo seethed at all the losing the Cubs did during the first six years of his career when they lost more than 90 games four times, including a pair of 103-loss seasons. So when the core of Ernie Banks, Fergie Jenkins, Billy Williams, Don Kessinger, Randy Hundley, Glenn Beckert, and Santo started to win, it was a revelation.

It was during the fabled 1969 season that Santo reached his high—seeing the Cubs in first place deep into the season—as well as his low, which came when his criticism of center fielder Don Young's misplayed balls led to a torrent of media criticism and boos at Wrigley Field.

The season, of course, ended horribly. And Santo's hatred of the New York Mets, who surged past the Cubs that season, was so complete he wouldn't even take the field against them 15 years later during a 1984 reunion game. After the 1973 season, the Cubs decided they wanted to trade Santo, who was coming off a year in which he hit .267 with 20 homers and 77 RBIs. Not the same numbers as when he averaged 29 homers and 106 RBIs from 1964 to 1970, but he was still only 34 years old heading into the season. He had some baseball left in him.

The Cubs didn't agree. They had just traded for third-base prospect Bill Madlock and put together a deal that would have sent Santo to the California Angels. As a player with 10 years in the major leagues and five with the same team, Santo had veto rights and rejected the trade. He just didn't want to leave Chicago. So the Cubs arranged a trade to the White Sox, and Santo accepted it.

Santo agreed to the trade so he could stay in Chicago and continue his career, but the Sox already had a third baseman in Bill Melton and tried to fit Santo in at second base. He ended up hurting his arm, played only 117 games, and retired at season's end with 342 homers and 1,331 RBIs.

He had a thriving oil business and other investments to fall back on and spent the next 15 years enjoying his retirement. The disappointments of not getting into the Hall of Fame began in 1980 when he only received 4 percent of the vote in his first year on the ballot, below the 5 percent threshold he needed to remain on in subsequent seasons.

The travesty of that vote was addressed in 1985 when Santo and several other deserving players had their eligibility restored, but he never got more than 43 percent of the vote, far short of the 75 percent required for enshrinement. There was so much hope that Santo would get elected by the Veterans Committee in 2003 that television cameras were with him when the call arrived.

"Nobody got in?" was his stunned response.

Toward the end of the 2003 season, the Cubs surprised Santo again. They told him his No. 10 would be retired, joining Banks' No. 14 and Williams' No. 26 as the only Cubs to be given that honor. Ryne Sandberg's No. 23 was retired in 2005.

"Now I really don't care if I get into the Hall of Fame anymore," Santo said in an emotional press conference after the announcement. "This is my Hall of Fame."

Santo's 20 years broadcasting Cubs baseball on WGN Radio introduced him to another generation of Cubs fans, who grew to admire his great courage and relentless good cheer after having part of both legs amputated due to complications from diabetes. He was finally elected to the Hall of Fame on December 5, 2011. But it came a year and two days to late for Santo to enjoy it.

On December 3, 2010, Santo passed away after a long battle with bladder cancer, an illness he kept hidden from the public. He died too young but at the height of his popularity as thousands mourned the loss of this old Cub.

So step back to get a running start, then click your heels for Ron Santo and don't give a damn what anyone thinks.

28 Room 509 of the Sheffield House

There was an old hotel at 3834 N. Sheffield Avenue, roughly four Dave Kingman moon shots north of Wrigley Field, where back in the day a few Cubs resided during the season.

It used to be called the Hotel Carlos and then the Sheffield House, and on July 6, 1932, it's where Violet Valli, a drunk and lovesick 21-year-old chorus girl, went to Room 509 with a loaded pistol and shot Cubs shortstop Billy Jurges.

Not only did Jurges survive taking bullets to his left hand and ribs, but he was back in the Cubs' lineup 16 days later. Jurges hit in seven straight games immediately upon his return and then hit .364 in the 1932 World Series. The shooting was a huge news story in Chicago and really took off as Jurges' relationship with Valli was revealed.

The two had been an item for around a year, and their relationship only came to an end at the urging of veteran Cubs right fielder Kiki Cuyler, a teetotaler, who thought Jurges was being led down the wrong path by Valli.

A note police discovered in Valli's room at the Hotel Carlos following the shooting illustrated how distraught she was over the break-up. "To me life without Billy isn't worth living," she wrote. "But why should I leave this earth alone? I'm going to take Billy with me."

An Earlier Tragedy at the Hotel Carlos

At about 2:00 AM on May 28, 1930, veteran Cubs pitcher Hal Carlson woke up from his bed in the Hotel Carlos with tremendous pain in his stomach. Less than two hours later, with an ambulance on the way, he died in the lobby of the hotel from a stomach hemorrhage.

The 38-year-old Carlson had been gassed during World War I, according to a May 29, 1930, *Chicago Tribune* article, and he had experienced health problems since joining the Cubs in 1927. But he had started on May 23 and was apparently ready to make his next start when he passed away.

Carlson had been a sub-.500 pitcher with Philadelphia and Pittsburgh, but after the Cubs acquired him in a mid-season trade in 1930 he went 30–17 while being used as a starter and a reliever.

On May 30, the *Tribune* wrote, "No official announcement was made but it was learned yesterday that the club will pay to Mrs. Carlson the salary due on the unexpired portion of her husband's contract."

While Jurges was recuperating in a hospital, Valli, who suffered a gunshot wound to the wrist during a struggle for the gun, immediately started talking to the press from her own hospital bed. In a *Chicago Tribune* story published on July 8 she blamed what she had done on "too much gin."

"I had been drinking before I wrote that note," she said. "And when I went to Billy's room I only meant to kill myself. He knows that. I got a note from him today, after I wrote him one. He said he'd do anything he could to help me."

And in fact, he did. Jurges refused to press charges against Valli, and nine days after the shooting the two stood feet apart from each other in a Chicago courtroom as Judge John Sbarbaro set Valli free. "The case is dismissed for want of prosecution," the judge said. "And I hope no more Cubs get shot."

Some believe this incident was the inspiration for Bernard Malamud's *The Natural*, but the 1952 novel was actually based on the shooting of Philadelphia's Eddie Waitkus, an ex-Cub who

in 1949 barely survived being shot by a deranged fan at Chicago's
Edgewater Beach Hotel.

29 Go to Spring Training

The weather is perfect, the setting is slow and intimate, autographs
are plentiful, and chances are pretty good you'll run into old Cubs
like Fergie Jenkins or Billy Williams wandering around the Sloan
Park concourse.

So why is it again you haven't gone to spring training?

At least once in your life you have to make the easy trek to
Mesa, Arizona, the spring home of the Cubs since 1979 and for the
foreseeable future. On November 2, 2010, Mesa voters approved
legislation to let the city spend $99 million on a new facility that
includes an entertainment complex. It's on the site of Riverview
Park, about 3½ miles west of HoHoKam, the Cubs' former spring
training facility, and it opened in 2014.

With the ability to fill stadiums no matter where they play, it
was paramount that Arizona keep the Cubs and the estimated $138
million they bring to the local economy from leaving. That is why
the Cubs owners, the Ricketts family, had the hubris to try to get
the Arizona legislature to pass what became known as the "Cubs
tax." This would have added a surcharge to every Cactus League
ticket sold, all to benefit the Cubs' new complex.

The ill-conceived plan was shot down by Commissioner Bud
Selig and they moved on to the next plan, which became reality
after the Cubs started negotiating to move their spring operation
to Naples, Florida.

As with almost everything they touch, the Cubs are a phenomenon even for spring-training-crazed Arizona, where they've

had eight of the top 10 highest single-season attendance marks in Cactus League history. Tickets to HoHoKam can be difficult to come by, but with road games just a few minutes away, your chances of seeing the Cubs are always doubled.

Even if you can only make it there in February before Cactus League play begins you'll be able to be part of spring training. The Cubs spend the first couple of weeks working out adjacent to Sloan Park, where you can watch their light workouts and then hit them up for autographs as they leave the field.

There's plenty to do in Arizona but one can't-miss place to stop when you're away from the ballpark is Don & Charlie's restaurant in Scottsdale, where on any given day you're likely to find scouts, broadcasters, coaches, and players from every Cactus League club.

30 Ferguson Jenkins: In a Class by Himself

Go ahead and try to pigeonhole Ferguson Jenkins. It's just not possible. If you try to squeeze him into one category of pitcher you'll come up short, which is the way he wanted it.

The 6'5" Canadian wasn't just a power pitcher, though he struck out 3,192 hitters in his 19-year major league career. His fastball, almost always low and away, was better than most but not on par with the great power pitchers of his day like Bob Gibson, Tom Seaver, and Nolan Ryan.

He wasn't just a control pitcher, though he's one of only four pitchers—along with Greg Maddux, Curt Schilling, and Pedro Martinez—to have given up fewer than 1,000 walks while striking out more than 3,000. He was almost always unflappable despite the frustration of pitching in Wrigley Field, where baseballs flew into the bleachers by the case, though during one memorable game in August 1973 he coolly walked off the mound before throwing bat after bat out of the dugout in the general direction of the home-plate umpire.

Hell, Jenkins wasn't even just a baseball player. Hockey was his first love growing up in Chatham, Ontario, and he was a solid prospect before signing with the Philadelphia Phillies in 1962. Following the 1967 season he even toured with the Harlem Globetrotters for a handful of games.

So if any other hockey-playing, globetrotting, power pitchers with unusually good control are out there, let him come forward now. Fergie Jenkins was simply one of a kind, and on September 8, 1972, after he won his 20th game to reach the milestone for the sixth straight season, he announced that to the world. "I think that Ferguson Jenkins belongs in a class all by himself," he told the Cubs' beat writers.

It was an unusual burst of arrogance for Jenkins, whose arrival in Chicago as a 22-year-old rookie in April 1966 was so unheralded that the *Chicago Tribune*'s headline referred to him as one of the "others" brought over in a trade with Philadelphia. The Cubs also got center fielder Adolfo Phillips and John Herrnstein and sent pitchers Larry Jackson and Bob Buhl to the Phillies, both of whom were out of baseball within three years. If this wasn't the greatest trade in Cubs history, it's certainly on par with the best of them.

It took Jenkins five months to break into the rotation, but his first appearance in a Cubs uniform was a strong indication of things to come. On April 23, 1966, he threw 5⅓ innings of shutout relief and also homered in a 2–0 win over Los Angeles. It was the first of 167 games he would win in a Cubs uniform.

During the next six seasons, Jenkins put together a resume nearly unimaginable in the 21st century. He went 127–84 with a 3.00 ERA that was punctuated by—and this is not a typo—140 complete games. It's been three decades since Philadelphia's Steve

Ferguson Jenkins delivers a pitch en route to a victory at Wrigley Field on Friday, April 24, 1983. He beat the San Francisco Giants and recorded his 279th career win and the first of this season. Chicago won the game 7-2.
(AP Photo/John Swart)

Cubs' 20-Game Winner Trivia
Questions
1. Who was the first Cubs pitcher in the 20th century to win 20 games?
2. What's the longest stretch the Cubs have gone without a 20-game winner?
3. Who was the only other Cubs pitcher to win 20 games during Ferguson Jenkins' streak of six straight 20-win seasons?
4. Before Jenkins, who had been the Cubs most recent 20-game winner?
5. Since Jenkins won 20 games in six consecutive seasons, how many Cubs pitchers have won 20 games in a season?

Answers
1. Jack Taylor, who went 23–11 in 1902.
2. 18 years. In 1945, Hank Wyse had a 22–10 mark and Hank Borowy went 21–7, although his record came with the Yankees and the Cubs. It wasn't until 1963 that they had another 20-game winner when Dick Ellsworth went 22–10. Ellsworth also lost 22 games in 1966, the most ever by a Cubs' left-hander.
3. Bill Hands, who went 20–14 in 1969.
4. Larry Jackson, who went 24–11 in 1964 and two years later was traded to Philadelphia for...Ferguson Jenkins.
5. Five pitchers. Rick Reuschel (1977), Rick Sutcliffe (1984), Greg Maddux (1992), and Jon Lieber (2001) each won exactly 20 games, and Jake Arrieta won 22 games in 2015. Sutcliffe won four of his games with the Cleveland Indians.

Carlton became the last major league pitcher to throw 300 innings in a season. Well, Jenkins *averaged* 306 innings during his incredible six-season run as arguably the best pitcher in baseball.

His only Cy Young Award was won in 1971 when he went 24–13 with a 2.77 ERA, but some think his 1968 campaign was his best as a Cub. Jenkins finished 20–15 but on five occasions was on the losing end of 1–0 decisions.

Jenkins came to the Cubs just a few weeks after Leo Durocher—who Jenkins once called "tougher than a night in jail"—managed his first game on the North Side. Their relationship was tested in 1969 when Durocher told Jenkins he was a "quitter" in front of the whole team the day after a late-season loss to Pittsburgh. But

Jenkins, who towered over Durocher, didn't have a problem with him.

"The thing to remember about Leo: the next day the slate was clean," Jenkins told former *Tribune* columnist Rick Talley in his book, *The Cubs of '69.* "He just gave me the ball and didn't take it away from me until I didn't pitch right. I knew that faith was there, and that's one reason I had so many complete games."

The end of Jenkins' first go-round with the Cubs—he returned in 1982 for two seasons and notched his 3,000th strikeout in blue pinstripes—approached as his contract demands and his chagrin over having to pitch in Wrigley continued. Jenkins asked the Cubs to trade him following the 1973 season and they accommodated him, dealing him to Texas for Vic Harris and Bill Madlock, a young third-base prospect. Jenkins won 25 games in 1974 for the Rangers and later played for Boston, winning 110 games from 1974–80.

In 1980, his reputation took a major hit when was arrested in Canada for drug possession, although charges were later dropped. Jenkins went on to win 20 games again for the Cubs, but it was stretched out over his final two seasons. He went 14–15 in 1982 and 6–9 in 1983, and he was cut the following spring just 16 victories shy of his 300th win.

Instead of going after that important milestone, Fergie signed on with a semi-pro team in Ontario and settled into a life away from Major League Baseball that has too often been touched by tragedy. In 1990, Jenkins' wife, Maryanne, was critically injured in a car accident and died four days after word came that he had been elected to the Baseball Hall of Fame. Two years later, Jenkins' girlfriend, Cynthia Takieddine, committed suicide and also took the life of his 3-year-old daughter near their Oklahoma ranch.

Jenkins and Greg Maddux, another legendary Cubs pitcher who had a memorable but abbreviated stay on the North Side only to return years later, had their No. 31 retired together in 2009 in a ceremony at Wrigley Field.

Years earlier, after Jenkins had been released by the Cubs in 1984, he told the *Tribune* how proud he was to be the final player from his era to still be with the organization. And that's how he wanted to be known.

"I want people to remember me as the last Cub," he said. "The last of the real Cubs."

31 Visit the Mordecai "Three Finger" Brown Memorial

It's only about a three-hour drive from Chicago to Nyesville, Indiana, the tiny town where Hall of Fame pitcher Mordecai "Three Finger" Brown grew up and earned his nickname.

Don't expect to find much besides the typical joys of small-town life, but that's not the reason for a Cubs fan to pay a visit. You'll go to see a 3' granite memorial erected in 1994 by devoted relatives and to imagine that day, more than 100 years ago, when what turned out to be a happy accident altered Brown's life forever.

It's within walking distance of the memorial that Brown, at either the age of five or seven depending on who's telling the story, took a dare from one of his brothers and stuck his hand under a corn chopper. The blade tore into his right index finger, causing it to be amputated, and damaged his pinkie.

A few weeks later he fell and injured his hand again, leaving him with no index finger and three disfigured digits. The result was a badly mangled hand that was able to do magical things with a baseball.

Brown started out playing semi-pro ball and didn't make it to the big leagues until he became a 26-year-old rookie with the St. Louis Cardinals in 1903. He was dealt to the Cubs in 1904 after he went 9–13 his rookie season. The Cubs only made the deal, according to Glenn Stout's book *The Cubs*, because ace Jack Taylor, for whom Brown was traded, had been telling people he had been on the take during a postseason exhibition series against the White Sox.

It turned out to be a steal. During the next eight seasons Brown used his devastating curveball to win 186 games and lead the Cubs to World Series titles in 1907 and 1908. He threw a seven-hit shutout in his only start of the 1907 Series and the following year won Game 1 in relief and then threw a four-hit shutout in Game 4. Brown's streak of six consecutive 20-win seasons, accomplished from 1906–11, has only been matched by Ferguson Jenkins in Cubs history.

Brown went to Cincinnati after the 1912 season and spent time in the short-lived Federal League, including a year with the Chicago Whales when brand-new Weeghman Park, later renamed Wrigley Field, was their home field.

Brown, who finished his career with a 239–130 record, returned to the Cubs for one more season in 1916 but only appeared in 12 games. On September 4 he lost to old friend and fierce rival Christy Mathewson, who Brown had once beaten nine straight times in their heyday, in what turned out to be the final game of both their illustrious careers.

There was some concern among Chicago sportswriters as Brown and other players from his era were initially bypassed for induction into the Baseball Hall of Fame, which opened in 1936. But in 1949, a year after his death at the age of 71, Brown was enshrined.

The memorial in Nyesville wouldn't exist if not for the determination of Fred Massey, a great-nephew of Brown who came up with the idea and turned it into a labor of love. Many others contributed, as well, including Three Finger's descendants Scott Brown and Cindy Thomson, who published *Three Finger: The Mordecai Brown Story* in 2006.

In it they share sweet tales of Cubs fans leaving tributes to Mordecai, like the time during the 2003 playoffs when a Cubs coaster, a can of Bud Light and a baseball were found by the memorial. On the baseball, according to the book, the fan had written:

"Thank you, Three Finger Brown! The Cubbies couldn't have done it without you. This Bud's for you. Go Cubs!"

32 The Sandberg Game

The most famous game in the historic Cubs-Cardinals rivalry was played on June 23, 1984, at Wrigley Field. And it belongs to Ryne Sandberg, as you can see from the title of this particular entry.

But Sandberg has always shared it with every Cubs fan in attendance and the millions watching and listening at home. This was a game that became an event, the kind you never forget where you were and what you were doing when it happened.

The Sandberg Game, as it came to be known almost immediately, was NBC's Game of the Week and introduced the nation to the Cubs' 24-year-old second baseman, a smooth fielder who was only just emerging as an offensive force. Going into the game he was hitting .321 with seven homers, above what he'd produced during his first two full seasons with the Cubs but not enough to cause anyone to think a Hall of Famer was waiting to bust out.

The Cardinals jumped out to leads of 7–1 and 9–3, knocking out Cubs' left-hander Steve Trout before the end of the second

The Sandberg Game Trivia
Questions
1. What was the name of the Cardinals' starting pitcher?
2. Who scored the game-winning run?
3. Who were the game's winning and losing pitchers?
4. Who was the only other Cub to have more than one RBI?
5. Which Cub was thrown out at second base in the sixth where he would have been the potential game-tying run?

Answers
1. Ralph Citarella, a right-hander who started only one other game in his career. His last season came in 1987 when he appeared in five games for the White Sox.
2. Leon Durham, who was traded to the Cubs for Bruce Sutter in 1980.
3. The Cubs' Lee Smith and the Cardinals' Dave Rucker. However, Rucker only faced one batter, and it was Jeff Lahti who gave up the game-winning hit to Owen.
4. Bobby Dernier, who had a two-run double in the sixth.
5. Ryne Sandberg, who was thrown out trying out on a double on a two-run single that made the score 9–8.

inning and silencing most of the 38,079 fans, but not the thousands of Cardinals fans who still routinely venture to Wrigley Field. The Cubs scored five runs in the sixth to make it 9–8, but they couldn't complete the comeback and with two outs in the seventh Cardinals manager Whitey Herzog turned to his closer, Bruce Sutter.

Bringing in a closer in the seventh is unheard of today but it was run of the mill for Sutter, who had outings of two innings or more in 41 of his 71 appearances in 1984. Sutter was still a master of the split-finger fastball, which he had learned while in the Cubs' minor league system and perfected during his five years with the Cubs from 1976–80. As usual with the Wrigley-owned Cubs, money became an issue and Sutter was traded to the Cardinals for Leon Durham, Ken Reitz, and Ty Waller. Just as with Lou Brock almost 20 years earlier, the Cardinals rode their recently acquired former Cub to a World Series title in 1982.

So the sting of losing Sutter was still very fresh in 1984, and it didn't help that Sutter was nearly untouchable after a subpar 1983 season. Going into the game, Sutter had a 1.19 ERA and had given up three home runs all season. This wasn't going to be easy, and Sutter retired the first four Cubs he faced on grounders. The split-finger was working splendidly.

Sandberg, who was 1-for-10 lifetime against Sutter, surprised just about everyone by knocking out his eighth home run of the season while leading off the ninth inning to tie the score 9–9. There was tremendous excitement, sure, but little did anyone know this was just the warm-up act.

In the top of the 10th, skinny center-fielder Willie McGee rapped an RBI double off Lee Smith that not only put the Cardinals ahead but allowed McGee to hit for the cycle. They tacked on another run and went to the bottom of the inning secure that Sutter, who was still in the game, wouldn't blow it again.

Sure enough, Sutter got two quick ground outs before narrowly walking Bobby Dernier on a 3–2 pitch that was just a touch low and easily could have gone the other way. But there Dernier stood at first, and there Sandberg once again stood at the plate.

If you watch closely, there's very little different about Sandberg's ninth-inning homer and the one he sent soaring into the left-field bleachers in the tenth that tied the game, leading NBC's Bob Costas to scream, "Do you believe it!" and sending Wrigley Field up for grabs.

What gets lost in the hysteria is that Sandberg, who finished 5-for-6 with seven RBIs, didn't even figure into the final inning of the game, in which the Cubs got three straight walks—two of them intentional—and then won it on Dave Owen's RBI single.

After the game no amount of hyperbole was good enough for Herzog, who declared, "Sandberg is the best player I have ever seen." Sandberg, as shy and reserved a superstar as baseball ever had, was in shock afterward. "I don't even know what day it is," he said.

It was the day that changed Sandberg's life and the memories of Cubs fans forever.

33 The Hawk

In 1987, I thought about giving up the game or maybe going to Japan. But I knew there had to be a place where the game could be fun again. I found that place. It's called Wrigley Field. It reminded me that if you love this game, the game will love you back.

—Andre Dawson, Hall of Fame induction, Cooperstown, New York, 2010

It's remarkable to think about what Andre Dawson had to go through in order to become a Cub, and it's even more remarkable to think about what he did once he became one.

There weren't many options for a free agent in 1987; collusion among major league owners had made player movement very difficult. But Dawson simply had to leave Montreal's Olympic Stadium and its rock-hard artificial turf. His knees wouldn't have it any other way. Dawson knew where he wanted to be, and that was playing day baseball on the Wrigley Field grass. Going into 1987, he had hit about 100 points higher during the day and was a lifetime .346 hitter at Wrigley. It was a perfect fit.

Only the Cubs didn't see it that way, or rather collusion didn't allow them to see it that way. Instead of embracing Dawson, they treated him like a poor relation who kept showing up on their doorstep asking for a handout. In fact, Dawson did show up on the Cubs' doorstep. After trying to secure a two-year, $2 million contract over the winter, negotiations broke down in January. When training camp began, Dawson and his agent, Richard Moss, went to Mesa anyway and held a press conference to announce Dawson had signed a contract and the Cubs could fill it in with whatever dollar figure they wanted.

Cubs president and general manager Dallas Green, whose club had finished 70–90 in 1986, was ticked off by this because he was doing everything he could to not sign Dawson. "In my heart I don't feel that we need Andre Dawson," Green had told the *Tribune*. "We need every one of those guys in that locker room. They are signed, they're Chicago Cubs. And some of them have not performed too well in the past. If they perform up to their past capabilities, and what we feel are their present capabilities, I'm not sure we need Andre Dawson."

It took several days for the Cubs to agree to this radical proposal that was so incredibly tilted in their favor. They eventually gave in to Dawson's "demand" and paid him $500,000 plus incentives. Finally, with three weeks left in camp, the Hawk was a Cub. That's when the fun really began.

Dawson put the negotiations behind him and turned in a season for the ages that initiated a love affair with Cubs fans and in all likelihood elevated him to Hall of Fame status. Secure in his new home, Dawson hit .287 with 49 homers and 137 RBIs and became the first player to ever win the Most Valuable Player Award for a last-place team. The Cubs were actually decent that year and despite a 76–85 record, Dawson and Rick Sutcliffe, who went 18–10, kept the Cubs above .500 through early September.

Wrigley Field was the haven Dawson imagined it would be. In 74 home games, he hit .332 with 27 homers and 71 RBIs compared to .246 with 22 homers and 66 RBIs on the road. Nothing could stop him, not even a beanball from San Diego's Eric Show on July 7 at Wrigley Field that left Dawson's face bruised, bloodied, and with 22 stitches.

The beaning, which came two innings after Dawson's 24th homer, resulted in a bench-clearing brawl led by Sutcliffe, who tore after Show from the dugout while Dawson still lay on the ground writhing in pain. When he finally regained his faculties, Dawson ripped himself away from those attending to him and made his own attempt to get to Show, who was whisked away to the Padres' dugout. Incredibly, Dawson was ejected from the game while Show, though replaced by a reliever, was not.

Dawson missed just two games and after slowing down for a few weeks went on to have a monster August, slamming 15 homers. He then put the final touches on his magical season by homering in his final home at-bat of the season.

Dawson spent five more seasons with the Cubs and averaged 25 homers and 90 RBIs, good numbers but nothing approaching the 1987 season. When the Cubs went to the playoffs in 1989, a

Hall of Famer Andre Dawson thanks the Chicago fans as he is honored by the Chicago Cubs before a game against the Pittsburgh Pirates on Monday, August 30, 2010, at Wrigley Field in Chicago. (AP Photo/Charles Rex Arbogast)

year when Dawson only played 118 games due to knee problems, he went 2-for-19 and didn't hit a home run.

After the 1992 season, when he was 38, Dawson left for Boston and criticized Cubs' management. "I'm just excited that an organization, for once, has shown me the decency and respect that I think I didn't get when I was in Chicago," Dawson told the *Chicago Tribune.*

There would be one more bittersweet moment involving the Cubs, and that was on the day the Baseball Hall of Fame announced Dawson would be immortalized with a Montreal Expos hat on his plaque. That wasn't what he wanted. But he made his true feelings known in a moving speech that singled out Cubs fans who embraced him in 1987 when it appeared nobody else in baseball wanted him.

"And from my heart, from my heart, thank you, Cub fans," Hawk said. "You were a true blessing in my life. I never knew what it felt like to be loved by a city until I arrived in Chicago. And though it wasn't my way to show it, I can't express to you enough how I appreciate what you did.

"You gave me new life in baseball when I arrived in Chicago, and you are the reason I continued playing the game. I can't thank you enough for how good you were to my family and me. You were the wind beneath the Hawk's wings."

34 95 Years Later, the Cubs Win a Playoff Series

Futility can take many forms, and aside from not making the playoffs for decades, the Cubs also didn't know how to handle themselves when they got there.

After beating Detroit in five games to win the 1908 World Series, they lost 10 straight postseason series, including seven Fall Classics. A 39-year playoff drought ended in 1984, but a heartbreaking loss to San Diego that season was followed by rather mundane postseason defeats by San Francisco in 1989 and Atlanta in 1998.

There wasn't much reason to think 2003 would be any different. The Cubs won the National League Central with a mere 88 victories and didn't clinch until the next-to-last day of the regular season.

Meanwhile, the powerful Atlanta Braves won 101 games, tying the New York Yankees for the most wins in the majors, and had six players with 20 home runs and four with 100 RBIs during the regular season. The Cubs did have one distinct advantage. Their top two starters—Kerry Wood and Mark Prior—were the most dominant starters on either team, an invaluable commodity in a short series.

The other thing giving the Cubs hope was they were not the same team they had been 2½ months earlier. On July 23, Cubs general manager Jim Hendry sent Jose Hernandez, minor leaguer Matt Bruback, and a player to be named later (it wound up being Bobby Hill) to Pittsburgh for power-hitting third baseman Aramis Ramirez and aging center fielder Kenny Lofton.

The Cubs were 50–49 when the trade was made and desperately needed help at both positions. They had first tried Mark Bellhorn at third, but he wasn't hitting and on June 20 he was sent to Colorado for Hernandez. Five weeks, 26 strikeouts, and a .188 batting average later, he was sent packing and replaced by Ramirez, who proved to be the answer. He hit 15 homers after joining the Cubs.

Corey Patterson, 23 years old on Opening Day, was fulfilling his promise as the Cubs' center fielder of the future by hitting .298 with 13 homers, 55 RBIs, and 16 stolen bases as the All-Star break approached. But on July 6 he blew out his knee against St. Louis and was lost for the season. Lofton was at a point in his career where he was becoming a wanted man by playoff teams at the trade deadline. The previous year he had helped Cubs manager Dusty Baker lead the San Francisco Giants to the World Series. In 56 regular season games after joining the Cubs, he hit .327 and stole 12 bases. It was a masterful trade, easily Hendry's best, and set up the Cubs perfectly for the playoffs.

In order to win the series the Cubs would have to win at least one road game, which also meant snapping an eight-game road losing streak in the playoffs. Their last win away from Wrigley in the postseason had come in Game 3 of the 1945 World Series when Claude Passeau one-hit the Detroit Tigers. Wood didn't throw a one-hitter in Game 1 at Turner Field, but he came pretty close. In six powerful innings, Wood allowed just two hits and struck out 11 in 7⅓ innings. He also went 2-for-4 with a team-high two RBIs in the Cubs' 4–2 victory.

Baker decided to go with 22-year-old Carlos Zambrano in Game 2, and even though he pitched well, the Braves got a pair of eighth-inning runs to snap a tie and deliver a 5–3 victory. The series went back to Wrigley Field all tied up.

A loss in Game 3 would have probably forced Baker to use Wood on three days' rest, but Prior didn't allow that to happen. In a 133-pitch, two-hit performance, he won a 3–1 decision over the Braves' Greg Maddux to bring the Cubs to the brink of a series win. There was hope that in Game 4 the Cubs could break another streak. The only two postseason series they had ever won had both come on the road in Detroit during the 1907 and 1908 World Series. It wasn't to be as the Cubs' Matt Clement fell behind 4–1 after five innings and the Braves held on for a 6–4 win.

Sammy Sosa, who wound up 3-for-16 in the series without an RBI, nearly produced the most thrilling Cubs playoff moment in several generations when he came to the plate with two outs and

Damian Miller on second base in the bottom of the ninth. His drive on a 3–2 pitch couldn't escape Wrigley Field and the teams headed back to Turner Field to decide the series.

The previous time the Cubs had played a winner-take-all playoff Game 5 was in the 1984 NLCS in which they led San Diego 3–0 in the sixth inning with their best pitcher on the mound before falling apart. There was even a mishap involving a glove just like there was in 1984 when a bucket of Gatorade was spilled on Leon Durham's glove before he committed a fateful error that led to a bucketful of runs. Wood's glove didn't make the trip to Atlanta; he had forgotten it in his North Side apartment while rushing to pack for the flight. He had been so confident the Cubs wouldn't need a Game 5 that he hadn't packed for a road trip.

You can debate whether Wood or Prior was the Cubs' best pitcher in 2003, but as in 1984 this Game 5 followed a similar pattern as the Cubs built a 4–1 lead. Moises Alou, who went 10-for-20 in the series, had an RBI single in the first, and Alex Gonzalez hit a solo homer an inning later.

Ramirez, who had a lone RBI in the first four games, put the Cubs up 4–0 in the top of the sixth inning with a two-run blast off Mike Hampton. A controversial call in the bottom of the inning led to the Braves' only run of the game, but it could have been worse for the Cubs. With nobody out and Marcus Giles on first base and Rafael Furcal on second, Gary Sheffield hit a liner to center that Lofton appeared to have caught. Furcal thought the ball had dropped and kept running while Giles hesitated. If the umpires' call had come right away he could have made it to second, but there was no immediate call on the field.

Finally, right-field umpire Gary Cederstrom signaled that Lofton had trapped the ball, but Giles wasn't able to get to second in time to avoid a force out. Even though Furcal scored on the hit, which replays showed Lofton had actually caught, the damage was mitigated.

The Braves only managed two more hits over the final three innings and never brought the tying run to the plate before closer Joe Borowski pitched a 1–2–3 ninth to win the game and close out the series. The Cubs had at long last won a playoff series, defying tradition and putting their demons to rest.

For a little while anyway.

35 Curse the Cubs at the Billy Goat Tavern

During the 2004 Cubs Convention, a few months after a mysterious force seemed to help end the Cubs' season in stunning fashion, Dusty Baker was asked what the biggest surprise was during his first season as manager.

"The strength and magnitude of the goat," he replied. There was laughter all around, and Baker was clearly trying to play to the crowd, but if you think there wasn't at least some truth in what Baker said, you're kidding yourself.

The curse of the Billy Goat dates to the 1945 World Series against Detroit, when tavern owner Billy Sianis purchased two box seats to Game 4 at Wrigley Field. One was for himself, and the other was for his pet goat, Murphy. That part of the story seems to be undisputed. An account in the October 7, 1945, edition of the *Chicago Tribune* by the legendary "In the Wake of the News" columnist Arch Ward, who created baseball's All-Star Game, read:

"Andy Frain employed 525 ushers and other attendants to handle the capacity throng.... He had trouble with only one fan, Billy Sianis, owner of a tavern near Chicago Stadium, who insisted on bringing a goat into the box seat section.... Sianis had a ticket for the goat, which was paraded thru the American league area

How to Get to the Billy Goat Tavern

The original Lincoln Tavern, bought by Sam Sianis in 1934 and renamed the Billy Goat Tavern soon after, was at 1855 W. Madison Street about a block from where the Bulls and Blackhawks play at the United Center.

The Billy Goat, also made famous in the 1970s by *Saturday Night Live*'s "cheezborger" sketches, has been at its present location at 430 N. Michigan Avenue since 1964.

of front box customers…the critter wore a blanket on which was pinned a sign reading, 'We Got Detroit's Goat.'"

There's no mention of Sianis, or Murphy for that matter, being ejected. But according to the curse, the goat made a nuisance of himself and Sianis was told Murphy would have to leave Wrigley Field. In response, Sianis wired Wrigley a message after the Cubs lost the World Series in seven games: "Who stinks now?"

At some point, Sianis is alleged to have placed a curse on the Cubs that would stop them from ever winning another pennant, and indeed they have not.

But was there ever really a curse? There was little written about any curse before a series of columns in the late 1960s by Ward's "In the Wake of the News" successor, Dave Condon. The first of the columns appeared on December 26, 1967, and explained the hex Sianis had put on the Cubs. However, Condon wrote, Cubs owner P.K. Wrigley had asked that it be removed in 1950, and Sianis had agreed.

In his book, *A Chicago Tavern: A Goat, a Curse and the American Dream*, author Rick Kogan writes that the idea to forgive Wrigley was a publicity stunt hatched from the mind of *Sun-Times* sports editor Gene Kessler and Sianis, as big a showman as Chicago ever had, was eager to play along.

On April 15, 1969, another Condon column raised the issue. He wrote that Wrigley had requested that the hex be lifted in September 1950 with a personal note to Sianis: "Will you please extend to Murphy my most sincere and abject apologies for what-ever it was that happened in the past."

While Murphy accepted Wrigley's apology, Condon wrote, Sianis apparently did not and the curse remained for another 19 years. With the Cubs off to a fast start in 1969, Sianis decided it was time. And so, according to Billy Sianis himself, the curse he placed on the Cubs was lifted more than 40 years ago. When the Cubs completed their 1969 collapse, Sianis and Condon again collaborated on a goat-related column, this time so Sianis could explain why the Cubs failed to beat the Mets. Did he blame the curse? Uh, no.

"The Cubs lost because the New York Mets just played like hell!" Sianis rationally explained.

Ever since, each time the Cubs contended the curse of the Billy Goat was raised and exploited. Publicity stunts, barely disguised as efforts to lift the hex, were executed and the tale lived on.

The story of the curse of the Billy Goat is too much a part of Cubs lore to ever fade away, even now that the Cubs did finally return to and win the World Series. Real or not, the curse was known to every player, coach, and manager who had a hand in whether a World Series would again come to Wrigley Field.

36 Rick Monday... You Made a Great Play

It was an odd sight to see on a Sunday afternoon at the ballpark, though certainly not completely out of the ordinary. Two people—a man and a boy—had left the stands at Dodger Stadium and were running across the outfield.

Happens enough that Rick Monday, who was patrolling center field for the Cubs on April 25, 1976—the 100th anniversary of the

Cubs' first game—thought they were just a couple of punks. Have your fun and get off the field, he thought.

Moments later, Monday realized fun wasn't what was on their mind. He saw the man, later identified as 36-year-old William Thomas, spread an American flag on the outfield grass in left-center not far from him. Thomas' 11-year-old son was kneeling by his side.

If Monday had been a linebacker in a previous life, maybe he would have mauled the man as he was desperately trying to light the flag on fire. But he was a former Marine, so he had his priorities straight.

"I was just going to run them over until I saw them with the can of lighter fluid. I could see they were going to try to burn it," he told reporters after the game. "If you're going to burn the flag, don't do it in front of me. I've been to too many veterans' hospitals and seen too many broken bodies of guys trying to protect it."

Monday arrived in time, scooped up the flag, and carried it to safety before it could be set ablaze. Thomas was so stunned all he could do was rise to his feet and throw the lighter in Monday's direction. Thomas and his son were taken away by security, and the next time Monday came to the plate the grateful Dodgers organization declared, "Rick Monday...You Made a Great Play" on their scoreboard. Later on, the electrified crowd spontaneously belted out "God Bless America."

The event became a national story, and even without any video of the incident—the Dodgers weren't televising the game and it wasn't until 1984 that a Super 8 film was discovered—Monday's life was instantly transformed. He went from being an above-average but not very well-known outfielder on a crummy team to an American hero who saved our national symbol from ruin. Decades later that's still what he's best known for, despite hitting a very respectable 241 home runs in 19 seasons, including 106 during a five-year stint with the Cubs from 1972–76.

Monday, who was traded to the Dodgers nine months after the incident and later became a radio broadcaster for the team, has never stopped insisting the public reaction hasn't been for what he did but for what the American flag represents. Monday kept the flag and more than 35 years later it remains in his possession.

"I feel honored and proud when I am asked about the flag, not because I stopped two people from burning the flag that afternoon in Los Angeles, but because it represents a lot of rights and freedoms," he told WGN-TV's Bob Vorwald. "A lot of years have gone by, but it is still important enough that people still discuss. That flag is still a part of my life, and my wife and I have been blessed to be able to take it around the country and raise a lot of money for charities. It's meant a lot to me."

37 Cubbie Occurrences

Thank you, Lou Piniella. Even if you hadn't helped the Cubs to two division titles and mostly good baseball during your nearly four years managing on the North Side, you would still be remembered for coining a most apt and memorable term: Cubbie occurrence.

It came about during spring training of 2008 when Piniella was telling reporters his starting rotation would soon be set, "unless there's an injury or a Cubbie occurrence."

So what exactly is a "Cubbie occurrence?" Longtime *Chicago Tribune* Cubs beat writer Paul Sullivan asked Piniella to define what he meant by the term, but he wouldn't bite. There was so much attention to it that Piniella actually banned the term being used around him the following season.

There's little doubt Cubbie occurrence will remain part of the Cubs' lexicon for years to come, so it seems important to come up with a proper definition. Maybe it's best to start with what it's not. It's not anything positive. Perhaps after the Cubs win a few World Series titles thanks to the Yankees doing something interminably stupid or suffering from a stroke of impossibly bad luck, a Cubbie occurrence could be a good thing. But we're not quite there yet.

Would a trend, such as the Cubs' inability to find a decent manager over time, be a Cubbie occurrence? No, an occurrence is more specific. It is the "action, fact, or instance of occurring." By definition it has to be an instance and trends will not be allowed. There also has to be an element of oddity or surprise to it. Players get injured in baseball all the time, and there's no documentation that the Cubs have had more than their fair share. But they have had some pretty strange ones that certainly qualify.

The entire 1985 starting rotation going on the disabled list at the same time isn't a Cubbie occurrence. But Steve Trout, who was a member of that rotation, falling off a stationary bicycle and going on the disabled list is. The 2004 collapse isn't a Cubbie occurrence, but Kyle Farnsworth had one late that season when he kicked an electric fan after a bad outing and ended up on the disabled list.

Farnsworth's injury was part Cubbie occurrence and part stupidity, which is also how you'd describe what Mike Harkey did on September 6, 1992. The former No. 1 draft pick was 4–0 with a 1.89 ERA and pitching the best baseball of his career when he did a cartwheel on the Wrigley Field outfield grass and ended up with torn ligaments in his knee.

Seemingly typical injuries can also qualify. On June 4, 1981, Bobby Bonds tripped while running on Pittsburgh's Three Rivers Stadium's astro turf and broke the little finger on his right hand. A routine injury? Sure, but it's a Cubbie occurrence because the injury came in the first inning of his first game since the Cubs acquired him from Texas. Bonds was injured before he even had one at-bat.

There have been other bizarre injuries, from Jose Cardenal's stuck eyelid to Sammy Sosa hurting his back when he sneezed to Ryan Dempster breaking his toe hopping over the dugout fence following a Cubs win. Mike Remlinger once got his pinkie caught between a pair of recliners and had to go on the DL.

But enough with the silly injuries. Let's move on to the hard-core Cubbie occurrences, the ones that have kept Cubs fans awake at night. The earliest one might be Babe Ruth's Called Shot in the 1932 World Series. Whether he actually did it or not, the home run was on a huge stage at Wrigley Field and has brought years of ridicule. That kind of thing just doesn't happen, yet it did to the Cubs.

Fast forward to Shea Stadium in September 1969. The Cubs were already in the throes of their historic collapse and had enough bad luck when a black cat ran onto the field. Sure enough, it headed straight for the Cubs dugout.

A little more than 15 years later the Cubs got past the New York Mets and were in the National League Championship Series against the San Diego Padres when first baseman Leon Durham let a ball get through his legs. It was the only error on a ground ball he had committed all season and also the first time he had to play with a sticky glove that a teammate had accidentally doused with Gatorade.

In 1998, the Cubs were in Milwaukee and Brant Brown was patrolling left field as a late-inning defensive replacement. The Cubs led 7–5, there were two outs, the bases were loaded, and Ron Santo was ready to scream "Yeahhhh!" when a fly ball came Brown's way.

Instead of ending the game, the ball hit the heel of his glove and fell to the ground. Santo screamed "Oh, nooooo!" and the

Cubs lost. Because they made the playoffs that year, this incident pales compared to the biggest Cubbie occurrence of all time.

Hint: It involves a guy named Bartman.

38 Horrible Playoff Collapses, Part 1: 1906

If you think a Cubs–White Sox World Series would be epic today, of course you're right. Bigger than in 1906? Even in the age of ESPN, that's debatable.

What's not up for debate is that the 1906 Cubs, who went 116–36 and still hold the major league record for highest single-season winning percentage, choked badly against their city rivals.

It wasn't a Crosstown Classic right after the turn of the century. The Sox were playing at the 39th Street Grounds, four blocks south of where U.S. Cellular Field stands now, and the Cubs' home was about five miles away at the West Side Grounds, now occupied by the University of Illinois Medical Center.

The ballparks were much tinier then and only 12,693 could crowd into the Cubs' park for Game 1, which was played as the city remembered the Great Chicago Fire that had raged 35 years earlier. Chicago's windy politicians closed City Hall, and thousands packed the Chicago Auditorium and other venues to follow the game on manually operated scoreboards.

The 1906 White Sox were a middling team until a 19-game winning streak propelled them to the top of the American League. Yet even in the dead ball era, they had little by way of offense and were dubbed "The Hitless Wonders," a nickname they'd initially live up to against the Cubs.

The Cubs, on the other hand, were on the verge of a dynasty. The famed infield of shortstop Joe Tinker, second baseman Johnny Evers, and first baseman Frank Chance, in his first year as manager, was still in its youth. Chance was the veteran of the group at 29, Tinker was 25, and Evers just 24.

The pitching staff was led by Mordecai "Three Finger" Brown, who went 26–6 and had a 1.04 ERA, barely above that of Jack Pfiester (20–8, 1.51) and Ed Reulbach (19–4, 1.65). Even though *Chicago Tribune* columnist Hugh Fullerton predicted a White Sox victory, he was thought to be daffy and the paper wouldn't even print such an outlandish prognostication. Few gave the Sox any chance of competing, let alone winning. That is, until the games started.

The Sox were going to have spitballer Ed Walsh start Game 1, but chilly temperatures led player-manager Fielder Jones to give Nick Altrock the ball. They also had to contend with a back injury to shortstop George Davis and reconfigured their infield, moving third baseman Lee Tannehill to short and replacing him with backup George Rohe, a fateful decision.

Brown started Game 1 and was perfect through four innings until Rohe lashed a triple, equal to the number he had during the regular season. He came around to score on a fielder's choice, and to the shock of Chicago's rabid baseball fans, the Sox held on behind Altrock's stellar pitching for a 2–1 victory.

The Series shifted back and forth between each team's park, and Game 2 at the 39th Street Grounds was a cakewalk as expected. The Cubs scored three second-inning runs, and Reulbach allowed only one hit in a 7–1 victory to even the series. But with Walsh's spitball holding the Cubs to just two hits in Game 3, the Sox came back for a 3–0 win.

Brown served up his own two-hitter in Game 4, beating the Sox 1–0. These Cubs were masters of what today might be called "small ball," and they scored their only run on a single, a pair of sacrifice bunts, and finally an RBI single by Evers.

Even though the Sox had only a total of 11 hits so far, Chance was feeling pressure and decided a change was needed. Neither team had been able to win in its home park, so when Game 5 commenced at the West Side Grounds, Chance had the boys wear their road flannels. Just like future efforts to end the Billy Goat curse, this non-baseball measure proved futile.

The previously punchless Sox pummeled Reulbach and then Pfiester in relief as they won 8–6 despite committing six errors. On the verge of a humiliating defeat, the Cubs had no more room for error so Chance turned to Brown, who had pitched so brilliantly two days earlier.

But the move backfired. Brown had little left, giving up eight hits and seven runs in 1⅔ innings. Game 6 did have a controversy on par with other Cubbie occurrences of later years. According to a story in the October 15 edition of the *Chicago Tribune*, a Chicago policeman kicked Cubs outfielder Frank Schulte as he raced to snare a fly ball with two on and two out.

True or not, and accounts of the incident differ, it may not have mattered. White Sox starter Doc White stifled the Cubs en route to an 8–3 win and the South Siders' first World Series title. As the final out was recorded, fans of both clubs raced onto the field and there were reports of distraught Cubs fans attacking supporters of their rivals.

Only after the Series was over did the *Tribune* print Fullerton's prediction, and even then it was still hard to believe.

"I can't understand it," Johnny Evers lamented. "But probably I will in two or three days."

39 Baseball's First Modern Dynasty— and the Cubs' Only One

It's hard to imagine but the Cubs were once synonymous with the World Series. Not for missing it but for making it.

In the first three seasons the World Series was played—1903, 1905, and 1906—six different teams won pennants and there was a new world champion each year. After that, the Cubs took over like no team ever had before and laid the groundwork for future baseball dynasties to come.

With an everyday lineup and starting rotation that was young and set in stone, the Cubs averaged 106 wins between 1906 and 1910, winning the National League pennant four times. They were the first team to ever appear in the World Series in consecutive seasons and in three straight seasons. And with titles in 1907 and 1908, the Cubs were the first team to repeat as World Series champs.

It was no coincidence that the dynasty began with the elevation of Frank Chance to manager during the 1905 season. Dubbed "Peerless Leader" in the press, Chance was a 29-year-old first baseman when he began his first season as player-manager in 1906.

Chance's fabled double-play partners—shortstop Joe Tinker and second baseman Johnny Evers—were hardly the only stars. Catcher Johnny Kling, third baseman Harry Steinfeldt, and outfielders Frank Schulte and Jimmy Sheckard would all be part of the nucleus for the next five seasons.

And the starting rotation? The stuff that dreams are made of. Chance didn't have to think much about who to put out there with Mordecai "Three Finger" Brown, Ed Reulbach, and Jack Pfeister on his staff. If that wasn't enough, on June 2, 1906, the Cubs traded Bob Wicker to Cincinnati for 25-year-old Orval Overall. Wicker was a former 20-game winner who finished out the 1906 season and then never pitched in the big leagues again. Overall, who had lost 23 games in 1905, twice became a 20-game winner during the dynasty years.

Except for the 1908 season that famously came down to the wire, the pennant-winning teams of the Cubs dynasty didn't face any real competition. The 1906 club, which has the highest winning percentage of any team since 1900, went 116–36 and finished 20 games ahead of the New York Giants. The 1907 club won the NL by 17 games, and in 1910 they outpaced the Giants by 13 games.

It was not always smooth sailing. Tinker and Evers were in a constant state of war with each other, Kling left the team in 1909

Ed Reulbach's Back-to-Back Shutouts—On the Same Day

Some records are made to be broken but not this one. It's unthinkable that another pitcher will throw two shutouts in the same day let alone be given the opportunity to try.

On September 26, 1908, just three days after the famous Merkle's Boner game, Cubs pitcher Ed Reulbach took the mound in Game 1 against Brooklyn, then known as the Superbas but later as the Dodgers. Reulbach finished up a 5–0 five-hit shutout in 1 hour, 45 minutes.

Feeling pretty good, Reulbach asked Cubs manager Frank Chance if he could go again. And so in the nightcap, he went out and this time pitched a three-hitter, needing just 75 minutes this time to beat the Superbas 3–0.

That's an impressive feat to be sure, but the Superbas weren't exactly world beaters. They finished with a 53–101 record and in the *Chicago Tribune*'s September 27, 1908, game notes it appears they may not have been taking the final games of the season too seriously:

"[Brooklyn manager Patsy] Donovan is trying out a new first baseman from Wesleyan college, who says his name is Smith. He comes out to practice in a bathing suit, so in case he fails to make good he can swim back home."

to try his hand at billiards before returning the following seasons, and during the 1908 season Sheckard nearly blinded rookie Heinie Zimmerman by hitting him in the head with a bottle of ammonia during a fight.

Sure, they had clubhouse spats but so did players like Ron Santo and Carlos Zambrano from time to time without anywhere near the same success. What the 1906–10 Cubs teams did best was win, more than any other lineups in the history of the franchise.

40 Leo the Lip

There was very little that was lovable about ornery, irascible Leo Durocher, whose disdain for losing was so great he once famously declared, "Nice guys finish last."

But by the time Cubs owner Phil Wrigley signed off on Durocher becoming manager following the 1965 season, lovable had been tried and losing was as ingrained at Clark and Addison as Wrigley Field. A dramatic change was needed for a franchise that had averaged a mere 7,727 fans per game the year before Durocher's arrival.

It's not accurate to say Wrigley let Durocher "manage" the Cubs. Wrigley, whose College of Coaches idea had failed miserably and was finally being set aside, didn't like titles. In a prepared statement, Wrigley said no title had been given. Or so he thought.

"I just gave myself a title: manager, not head coach," Durocher declared during a raucous news conference in the Pink Poodle, the Cubs' press lounge.

There's no tidy way to describe Durocher's wild, tumultuous and ultimately futile 6½-year reign as the Cubs manager. There

Manager Leo Durocher in Scottsdale, Arizona, in 1971. (AP Photo/
Robert H. Houston)

were growing pains, controversy both on and off the field, and
one epic failure. There was also more winning than the Cubs had
seen in a generation. In the 19 seasons before Durocher, the Cubs
finished above .500 exactly once. In the 11 full seasons after he was
fired midway through the 1972 season, they never finished with a
winning record.

Durocher not only led the Cubs to five straight winning
seasons—he gave them the kind of consistent, if not stable, leadership that they haven't enjoyed since. He's one of four men
to manage at least 1,000 games in a Cubs uniform, something

high-profile hires like Don Baylor, Dusty Baker, and Lou Piniella couldn't accomplish.

Durocher is synonymous with the great collapse of 1969, and some lay much of the blame at his feet for refusing to give his regulars a day off during the hot summer months. They also point to a bizarre incident during the heat of the pennant race that illustrated his enigmatic character.

On July 26, Durocher told coach Pete Reiser to take over the club after three innings because he was feeling ill. The following day Durocher called in sick again. But he wasn't sick at all—he had decided to charter a plane and go up to Camp Ojibwa in Eagle River, Wisconsin, to surprise his stepson during parents' weekend.

Chicago Today columnist Jim Enright got wind of the visit, and the story took off. Wrigley wondered out loud in the *Tribune* how it looked for the manager to desert the team in the middle of a pennant race. "My concern is that some of the players, who have been busting their boilers to win the pennant, might wonder if their manager is equally dedicated," Wrigley said.

In his 1975 autobiography, *Nice Guys Finish Last*, Durocher wrote that Wrigley should have fired him, and according to some Durocher was fired for a couple of hours. But after a brief meeting, Wrigley's non-confrontational personality asserted itself and he decided to let Durocher keep his job.

This surely pleased Cubs fans, who adored Durocher and many gave him credit for the team's resurgence. On Opening Day in 1968, the *Tribune* wrote, "Manager Leo Durocher got such a deafening, standing ovation that the public address man, WGN's Roy Leonard, had to delay the introductions of the rest of the Cubs for a few moments."

Durocher's arrival with the Cubs coincided with the tail end of Ernie Banks' career, and several times Durocher tried to trade Banks but couldn't get Wrigley to allow it. Their relationship never improved much, but at least it didn't devolve like Durocher's relationship with Ron Santo.

Santo was entering his prime in 1966 and his hatred of losing rivaled that of Durocher, who praised the Cubs third baseman up and down when he was hired. Slowly, however, it became harder for the two fiery personalities to co-exist, and in 1971 it all blew up.

During a team meeting in late August, Durocher and several players—including Santo, Joe Pepitone, and Milt Pappas—got into a shouting match. At one point, Durocher accused Santo of asking for his own Ron Santo Day that was being held at Wrigley Field the following week.

Santo erupted at the suggestion and had to be restrained from going after Durocher, who was also upset from the exchange with the players and nearly resigned that day. A movement to "Dump Durocher" became a cause in the Cubs' clubhouse and led Wrigley to place a full-page ad in the *Tribune* supporting his manager.

"Leo is the team manager and the 'Dump Durocher Clique' might as well give up," the ad said in part. "He is running the team and if some of the players do not like it and lie down on the job, during the off-season we will see what we can do to find them happier homes."

Durocher survived the end of the season, and Wrigley made another announcement in November that Durocher would return for the 1972 season. But with Banks retired and much of the nucleus aging or traded off, the Cubs fell 10 games behind by the All-Star break. On July 24, 1972, Wrigley finally fired Durocher.

"In those early days, he was a son of a bitch," Cubs broadcaster Jack Brickhouse told author Rick Talley in *The Cubs of '69.* "But he was a sharp son of a bitch. But by the time he was finished in Chicago, he was just an old son of a bitch."

The Durocher era was over, and for the next dozen years so were the Cubs.

41 Visit Cap Anson's Grave

In the immediate days after Adrian Constantine "Cap" Anson passed away in 1922, baseball writers and executives bent over backward to pay homage to the first Mr. Cub.

The *Chicago Tribune*'s E.S. Sheridan, a former sports editor who also covered Anson during his heyday in the 1880s, wrote, "Anson brought to professional baseball four great qualities of personal character that helped to make the profession what it is. He had integrity, sobriety, personal purity, and dignity—the last named quality almost to the point of arrogance."

Anson was so revered in Chicago that a Near Northwest Side street, Anson Place, still bears his name. Off the field, he neither drank nor smoked and on it he was a brilliant hitter and strategist. Anson was the first major leaguer to reach 3,000 hits and still holds Cubs career records for most hits, runs, doubles, and RBIs.

Anson joined the Cubs, then known as the White Stockings, in the off-season before their first National League game was played on April 25, 1876, and was in the lineup that day against Louisville, going 1-for-4. Three years later he was named player-manager, a dual role he held until his contract wasn't renewed following the 1897 season. He was 45.

According to Glenn Stout's *The Cubs*, Anson is credited by some with inventing the hit-and-run and was among the first to use hand signals, platoon players, and pitching rotations, plus he conducted a team-sponsored spring training. In his eulogy, baseball commissioner Kenesaw Mountain Landis said of Anson, "I never knew him to do anything that would not bring respect and admiration."

The Father of the National League

Just down the street from Wrigley Field is Graceland Cemetery, the final resting place of William A. Hulbert, the Cubs' first owner and a towering figure in baseball history who is credited as the Father of the National League. Hulbert also has one of the most interesting gravestones you'll ever see.

In 1876, Hulbert led the charge to bring together baseball clubs from the Midwest and the East coast into one league. According to Glenn Stout's book, *The Cubs*, Hulbert recognized the need to have a member of one of the East coast clubs become league president.

So rather than assume the position himself, he convinced Morgan Bulkeley, owner of the Hartford club, to become the first NL president. The league prospered and after a year Hulbert assumed the presidency until his untimely death in 1882 from a heart attack at the age of 49.

To find Hulbert's gravestone just look for the one shaped like a baseball. Carved on either side are the names of the cities in the NL at the time of his death: Chicago, Cleveland, Buffalo, Detroit, Boston, Providence, Worcester, and Troy.

It wasn't until years later that the unseemly side of Anson was deemed okay to write about and examine. Anson, who played for the Cubs from 1876 to 1897, was also a racist whose actions some believe played a leading role in ushering in baseball's despicable color barrier. The incident most often mentioned took place on July 19, 1887, when the White Stockings went to Newark, New Jersey, to play an exhibition game. Newark's best player was an African American pitcher named George Stovey, who was scheduled to start the exhibition.

Anson reportedly refused to play if Stovey took the field, Stout wrote, and the Newark team subsequently gave in to his demands. The Cubs played the exhibition while Stovey sat out due to an unexplained "sickness." Anson's actions and those of many others resulted in a color barrier being drawn that would continue unabated until 1947, eight years after Anson was elected to baseball's Hall of Fame.

A granite monument with two crossed baseball bats was erected after Anson's death and still presides over his grave at Oak Woods cemetery, located on the city's South Side at 1035 East 67th Street. The cemetery is open for visitation weekdays from 8:30 AM until 4:15 PM.

While there you can also visit the graves of many prominent Chicagoans, including that of Harold Washington and Eugene Sawyer, Chicago's first two African American mayors.

42 The Rise and Fall of Hack Wilson

The homers kept piling up, the runs kept being driven in, and by the time the 1930 season was over, Hack Wilson had put together the greatest year in National League history.

It's not hard to argue the entirety of his .356 average, 56 homers, and 191 RBIs still stands as the best, considering the only comparable campaigns have come from modern players closely linked to steroids. No, Wilson didn't need steroids to bulk up his short but powerful 5'6" frame. The vice that did him in was alcohol, which drove him from the Cubs and from baseball.

"I never played drunk," Wilson once said. "Hung over? Yes, but never drunk."

In 1948, not 20 years after his most memorable season, Wilson was far removed from his day in the sun. He was discovered—alone, forgotten, and destitute—working as a towel boy at a community pool in Baltimore. Shortly afterward, Wilson suffered a fall at his home and died from complications related to the fall, ending the spectacular, colorful, and troubled life of one of the Cubs' greatest sluggers.

Lewis Robert "Hack" Wilson was born on April 26, 1900, and grew up in a small Pennsylvania steel town. A newspaper account during his early playing days said of Wilson that of all the rubes, "He is the rubiest of them all."

Wilson, whose nickname was derived from his physical similarities to Georg Hackenschmidt, a popular pro wrestler of the era, made it to the majors in 1923 with the New York Giants but never cracked the starting lineup for a sustained period. By the time the Cubs snatched him from the Giants in baseball's annual minor league draft of unprotected players, he had hit a respectable but hardly awe-inspiring 16 home runs in 573 career at-bats.

Thus began one of the most remarkable five-year runs by any player in Cubs history. Wilson hit .331 with 177 home runs and 708 RBIs during that span, culminating with his masterful 1930 season. It didn't take long before Wilson's love of the bottle made itself known to the Cubs, as he was arrested at a prohibition-era speakeasy a few weeks after joining the team.

Actually, the Cubs might have known about Wilson's proclivities and tried some tough love with him as a wire service story following the arrest claimed, "The place was raided, it was learned, on complaint of the Cubs' management."

Some of the most memorable moments of Wilson's career had nothing to do with his prodigious power. On June 20, 1928, after grounding out in the bottom of the ninth while the Cubs were trailing St. Louis 6–1, Wilson decided he had heard enough of a rather vociferous fan. Instead of going back to the dugout, he headed after the fan and proceeded to pound him into submission, igniting a melee in the stands.

The following season, he attacked a Reds player in their dugout and later that night, when the two teams ran into each other at the train station while heading out of town, Wilson got into a scrap with Reds pitcher Pete Donohue and decked him, as well.

But those were minor contrivances compared to what happened during the 1929 World Series. The Cubs had lost the first two games to the Philadelphia Athletics but took Game 3 and were primed to tie the series after taking an 8–0 lead in Game 4. However, Wilson lost two fly balls in the sun during a disastrous seventh inning, including one that resulted in a three-run inside-the-park home run, as the A's scored 10 times and went on to win 10–8.

Wilson was devastated but was able to put it behind him and launched into his 1930 season with a fervor, hitting long balls at such a pace that for a time he threatened to break Babe Ruth's newly minted home run record. Despite not breaking Ruth's mark, Wilson's 191 RBIs is still a major league record that few think will ever be broken.

There wasn't much joy for Wilson after that season. His rise to fame led to even more nights out and more drinking, and in early September he and pitcher Pat Malone punched out a pair of sportswriters. That was the end. Wilson was suspended, kicked out of the clubhouse, and never played again for the Cubs. He was traded to the St. Louis Cardinals in the off-season for pitcher Burleigh Grimes.

The Cardinals were forced to dump off Wilson on the Brooklyn Dodgers a month later after they couldn't agree on a contract, and he actually put together a decent season in 1932 as he hit .297 with 23 homers and 123 RBIs. But in 1933 his demise accelerated. Wilson hit only nine homers for the Dodgers that season, and he played his final game on August 25, 1934, for the Philadelphia Phillies. He was 34.

Wilson's death 14 years later came as a shock to the baseball world, which had lost track of him. Informed that Wilson's own son wouldn't claim the body, National League President Ford Frick sent money for a proper burial.

43 Kid K

Here's the thing to know about Kerry Wood: He's as big a Cubs fan, if not bigger, than you are.

The boy from Grand Prairie, Texas, who came to Wrigley Field in 1998 as a 20-year-old with a blazing fastball and just a wisp of facial hair is also now a full-time Chicagoan. Where he and his family spend the rest of their lives seems to be a done deal. It's why he left millions on the table to re-sign with the Cubs in 2011 after a two-year stint with Cleveland and the New York Yankees, and he retired as a Cub in 2012.

"It's about being here at Wrigley, which is home for me," Wood said during a press conference to announce his return. "My wife grew up here. We have family here obviously…we really feel that's where we belong, where I belong."

Players like Wood, who embody the franchise, come around rarely in sports, and Wood's struggle to stay healthy made it even less likely he'd become one of the most beloved Cubs of all-time, on par with Ernie Banks, Ron Santo, Andre Dawson, and Ryne Sandberg.

Think about the way many Chicago fans turned on Mark Prior when his injuries derailed his career or how Bears quarterback Jay Cutler was vilified after leaving the 2010 NFC title game with a knee injury. Wood had to deal with a lot of fans questioning his skill, but nobody ever questioned his heart during any of his 15 stints on the disabled list.

His role as a modern-day Mr. Cub certainly began with the 20-strikeout game on May 6, 1998, in Wood's fifth career start, but it started to cement when he risked his shaky right elbow to start Game 3 of the 1998 National League Divisional Series against

Kerry Wood throws during batting practice at the Cubs' spring training facility on Monday, February 21, 2011, in Mesa, Arizona. (AP Photo/Paul Connors)

Atlanta. Wood gave the Cubs five strong innings that day in what would be his last start for 19 months.

He blew out his elbow the following spring and underwent Tommy John surgery to replace the torn ligament. In his first game back on May 2, 2000, he thrilled the Wrigley Field crowd by not only pitching three-hit ball over six innings in a win over Houston but by homering in his first at-bat.

As expected, he struggled in his first season back and went 8–7 with a 4.80 ERA, his worst as a starter. But in 2001 he began a three-year stretch where he went 38–28 with a 3.41 ERA and made 93 starts while throwing 599 innings, capping it off with the 2003 playoffs and the highs and lows that came with it.

It was Wood who started Game 7 of the 2003 National League Championship Series against Florida, and despite hitting a game-tying two-run homer in the second inning to make up for a three-run first, he couldn't stop the Marlins. He gave up seven runs in 5⅔ innings and when facing the media afterward it was hard for him to even speak.

"You've got to understand," he said. "About 30 minutes ago, I choked."

That wasn't Wood feeling sorry for himself, it was a deep understanding of what the loss and not making it to the World Series would mean to generations of hopeful Cubs fans. In that sense, he was feeling sorry for himself. Because Wood, like you, is a Cubs fan.

The switch from starting to relieving came in 2007 after three injury-plagued seasons in which it became clear his right shoulder couldn't withstand the toll of throwing 100 pitches every outing. Wood embraced the move once it was clear he had no choice, and in 2008 he became the Cubs closer, finishing with 34 saves.

Wood had a very close relationship with former Cubs general manager Jim Hendry, who joined the Cubs in 1995 as an assistant GM a few months before Wood was drafted fourth overall. Hendry encouraged Wood to seek other offers following the 2008 season, knowing he couldn't match other offers or ask Wood to take a hometown discount of around $15 million.

So Wood signed with the Indians for $20 million over two years then was traded to the Yankees for their annual playoff push. When the Hot Stove League got underway before 2011, Wood was a free agent and he was mentioned as a possibility to return to the Cubs. But Hendry's hands were tied by a tight budget, and Wood didn't seem affordable.

That is, until the two had a heart-to-heart talk following Ron Santo's funeral. Whether it was the emotion of Santo's funeral or they just both knew it was right, Hendry and Wood agreed a return to Chicago was the right thing and he was signed to a one-year, $1.5 million deal that was well below market value but came with a priceless result.

Wood was home.

44 The Greatest Rain Delay Ever

It was all going so smoothly. As it turned out, a little too smoothly.

The Cubs only needed four pitches to jump in front of the Cleveland Indians in Game 7 of the 2016 World Series. Dexter Fowler's leadoff homer saw to that. And although the Indians briefly tied it in the third inning, the Cubs added runs in the next three innings to take a 6–3 lead into the bottom of the 8th.

Everything about this Cubs team told you that it was unlike any other, that it wouldn't succumb to collapses as the Cubs did in 1984 and 2003 because they were just too good and too mentally tough and, well, it just couldn't happen again…could it?

Of course it could, and it did. With two outs, a man on, and the Cubs' lead down to 6–4, Cleveland's Rajai Davis, who was 3-for-32 with no home runs in the 2016 playoffs to that point, turned on an Aroldis Chapman pitch and that sickening feeling familiar to generations of Cubs fan returned as quickly as the ball sailed into the bleachers of Progressive Field.

The score was now tied. This was a momentum shift of epic proportions, and though Chapman was able to keep the game knotted up through nine innings, the feeling was that the Cubs had blown their shot. And that's when the deluge started. The rain that was expected to fall began to come down in buckets just before the 10th inning began, and the umpires quickly made the call to get the tarp out and begin a rain delay.

Cubs manager Joe Maddon admittedly hates meetings, so when the team got back to the clubhouse he went off to check a weather map. The players, led by embattled right fielder Jason Heyward, went in another direction. Heyward's first season with the Cubs after signing a $184 million contract was beyond dismal at the plate, but he kept his head up even as Maddon kept him out of the starting lineup for the first three games of the World Series.

"It was starting to rain and I was like, they're going to pull the tarp and we need to get together and have a meeting," Heyward said. "Just needed to let these guys know they're awesome. Don't get down."

The rain delay only lasted 17 minutes, and soon the Cubs were back on the field, seemingly cleansed of any negative feelings that had been creeping in since they blew the lead in the 8th. Kyle Schwarber led off with a sharp single, then pinch-runner Albert Almora made a gutsy decision to tag up and go to second on Kris Bryant's long fly out. The Indians walked Rizzo to bring up Ben Zobrist, who sliced a double down the right-field line for the go-ahead run. Miguel Montero added an RBI single, and the Cubs hung on to capture the World Series with an 8–7 victory.

Collapse averted.

Maybe the Cubs still get to Indians reliever Bryan Shaw in the 10th without their now-legendary clubhouse meeting. But then again, maybe they don't. Fowler had no problem giving credit where credit was due.

"It was the greatest rain delay ever," he said.

45 Horrible Playoff Collapses, Part 2: 2003

If we're going to rank Cubs' playoff collapses—and with a dearth of playoff comebacks it's really our only option—the 2003 version is slightly more vomit-inducing than 1984. After taking a 3–1 series lead, there was simply no way the Cubs would lose three straight games. Consider the following:

They had their best three starters ready in Carlos Zambrano, Mark Prior, and Kerry Wood.

The Cubs hadn't lost three straight since mid-August.

Florida's ace, Josh Beckett, would at best only be available to start one more game.

Game 6 and 7 were scheduled to be played at Wrigley Field.

The Cubs were a team of Dustiny.

Okay, so that last one wasn't quantifiable, but ever since Cubs manager Dusty Baker arrived in Chicago and asked, "Why not us?" at his introductory news conference, it became a far more preferable mantra than the typical Cubs lament of, "Why us?"

Nobody knows why; all we know now are who, what, and where. And given what came later, it's easy to forget the biggest lead the Cubs blew in the 2003 National League Championship Series actually came all the way back in Game 1.

Beckett, who had given up more than four earned runs in a game just twice all season, allowed four runs in the first inning alone on an RBI triple by Mark Grudzielanek, a two-run homer by Moises Alou, and an RBI double by Alex Gonzalez. This was the best the Marlins could offer up?

Well, it wasn't. Beckett settled down and in the top of the third inning Zambrano allowed three home runs in the span of four batters. Marlins catcher Ivan Rodriguez hit a three-run shot, and after Derrek Lee struck out, Miguel Cabrera and Juan Encarnacion hit solo homers to give Florida a 5–4 lead.

By the time the ninth rolled around, the Marlins led 8–6 and things looked bleak. Even with Kenny Lofton's double, the Cubs were down to their last out with Sammy Sosa coming up. This was

The Ex-Marlin Factor

There were at least five and as many as seven past or future ex-Cubs on the 2003 Florida Marlins, depending on your definition of what makes someone an ex-Cub.

The five who actually played in a big-league game for the Cubs were pitcher Chad Fox (2005, 2008–09), utility man Lenny Harris (2003), outfielder Todd Hollandsworth (2004–05), first baseman Derrek Lee (2004–10), and outfielder Juan Pierre (2006).

In Game 6, Fox was the winning pitcher while Pierre, Lee, and Hollandsworth went a combined 3-for-3 with a walk, three RBIs, and three runs scored in the pivotal eight-run eighth inning. Harris started the 2003 season with the Cubs but was released in early August then signed by the Marlins on August 11, making him eligible for the playoff roster.

Two members of the Marlins were in the Cubs organization but never played for the big league club: starting pitcher Dontrelle Willis, an eighth-round draft pick in 2000 who was traded away in 2002 as part of the deal that brought Antonio Alfonseca and Matt Clement to the Cubs; and reliever Braden Looper, who came to training camp with the Cubs in 2011 but retired after being cut a week before Opening Day.

the same Sosa who had a lifetime .161 postseason average (5-for-31) with no homers. Even with first base open, it wasn't a shock that Florida manager Jack McKeon chose to pitch to him.

Big mistake. Sosa turned on a 1–1 pitch from Ugueth Urbina and sent it flying toward Waveland Avenue to tie the game and turn Wrigley Field into a madhouse. The delirium was short-lived, however, as the Marlins' Mike Lowell hit an 11th inning home run off Mark Guthrie and the Cubs went down in order in the bottom of the inning.

Games 2 and 4 were, incredibly, drama-free in the Cubs' favor—both blowouts that an anxious fan base needed after the tense series in Atlanta. Game 3 was similar to the NLCS opener, a see-saw affair that went into extras, but this one was won by the Cubs 5–4 thanks to Doug Glanville's RBI triple in the 11th inning.

Beckett completely shut down the Cubs in Game 5, striking out 11 and tossing a two-hit shutout. That set up Game 6 and, if necessary, Game 7 at Wrigley Field.

Game 6 is not a myth, it actually happened. The Cubs really did lead 3–0 with one out in the eighth and Prior pitching flawlessly. There really is a fan named Steve Bartman who touched a foul ball that could have—*could have*—been the second out of the inning.

And the Marlins really did go on to score eight runs in the inning and walk away with an 8–3 victory, further destroying the fragile psyche of a fan base that knew playing Game 7 was a waste of time. It was over.

Sure, the fans, players, and broadcasters showed up and the game was played, but it was more to see the extent of the car wreck rather than to see if the driver was still alive. Even with Wood, who had pitched so brilliantly in the decisive Game 5 of the National League Divisional Series against Atlanta, the Cubs were overwhelmed by their past.

Wood played like he didn't know whether he should be the hero or the goat. He gave up three runs in the first inning then hit a two-run homer in the bottom of the second to tie it. The Cubs actually went up 5–3 on Moises Alou's two-run blast in the third, but in the fifth the Marlins tallied three runs and went on to win 9–6 and advance to the World Series.

Eleven months earlier, Dusty Baker had asked, "Why not us?"

Finally, he had his answer.

16–1!

More than 30 years later, Rick Sutcliffe still looks remarkably like the youthful man whose near-perfect run following a mid-season trade became the final—and most important—piece to the Cubs' first playoff appearance in 39 years.

The tidy red beard's been trimmed down to a goatee and maybe he's added a few pounds to his 6'7" frame, but he's still the Red Baron, the perfect nickname Harry Caray hung on him during that magical 1984 season.

When Dallas Green pulled the trigger to land Sutcliffe on June 13, 1984, he was getting a former National League Rookie of the Year and American League ERA title winner, who was still largely unknown to the Wrigley Field faithful. He had been exiled to Cleveland by the Los Angeles Dodgers in 1982 and despite a league-leading 2.96 ERA that year and 17 wins the following season had gotten off to a mediocre start in 1984, going 4–5 with a 5.15 ERA in 15 starts.

The Indians didn't think they could sign soon-to-be free agent Sutcliffe in the off-season, so on June 13 they dealt him along with

Rick Sutcliffe gets set to deliver another pitch during the first inning against the San Diego Padres in National League playoff action on October 2, 1984, in Chicago. Versatile Sutcliffe later smacked a home run off his opposing pitcher Eric Show. (AP Photo/Mark Elias)

middle reliever George Frazier and backup catcher Ron Hassey for Mel Hall, top prospect Joe Carter, and a couple other minor-leaguers. The brutally honest Sutcliffe, who had once destroyed Dodgers manager Tommy Lasorda's office after a disagreement, told the *Cleveland Plain-Dealer*, "It's a really bad trade for Cleveland."

And almost immediately it was, but not because of anything that happened on the field. Dallas Green had neglected to clear waivers on any of the four players the Cubs had traded to the Indians, and even though Sutcliffe and the other were definitely Cubs, it took several days before Hall and Carter could play for the Indians. It was a huge embarrassment for Green, who had to wait until June 19 to see his new starting pitcher.

It was worth the wait. Sutcliffe's impact was huge, and it was immediate. He allowed one earned run in eight innings to stop the Cubs' four-game losing streak by beating Pittsburgh in his debut, and in his second start—which came a day after the Sandberg Game—struck out 14 in a five-hitter over St. Louis.

There was something different about Sutcliffe with the Cubs, besides the fact he had jumped 20 games in the standings and had found his breaking ball. He was finally at full strength for the first time all season. A painful root canal earlier in the season that required four days of dental work had left him weak, and although he never missed a start he had lost several miles off his fastball.

Sutcliffe followed up his only loss on June 29 in Los Angeles by winning five straight starts, including two against the San Diego Padres, and finished 16–1 with a 2.69 ERA to win the NL Cy Young Award. He was on the mound in Pittsburgh nailing down another complete-game win when the Cubs clinched the NL East title, their first in 39 years.

The Cubs ended up going 18–2 in Sutcliffe's 20 starts, and on seven occasions he got a win following a Cubs' loss. He was the quintessential stopper, something they simply didn't have in Steve Trout, Dennis Eckersley, or Scott Sanderson.

Traded Between Games of a Doubleheader

On May 30, 1922, Cubs right fielder Max Flack went 0 for 4 against St. Louis at Wrigley Field. On May 30, 1922, St. Louis right fielder Max Flack went 1 for 4 against the Cubs at Wrigley Field.

How did this happen? The Cubs dealt Flack to the Cardinals for outfielder Cliff Heathcote between games of a doubleheader, the only time that's happened in major league history. Heathcote went 0 for 3 in the first game while playing center field for the Cardinals, then after the trade went 2 for 4 in the nightcap while playing right field for the Cubs.

Flack lived a few blocks from Wrigley Field and had gone home for lunch. When he returned, unaware he had been traded, he went to the Cubs' clubhouse and was told he was in the wrong place.

"There wasn't much radio in those days, and of course there hadn't been time to have it published in a newspaper," Flack said years later. "So fans were astonished when they saw us in different uniforms."

The unique trade worked out better for the Cubs. Flack, 32 at the time of the trade, played 3½ seasons mostly as a part-time player with the Cardinals before his career ended. Heathcote was only 24 when he joined the Cubs and in nine seasons appeared in 856 games, twice hitting better than .300.

Unfortunately, it ended too soon. Sutcliffe's Game 1 win over the Padres in the National League Championship Series, in which he also hit a monster home run onto Sheffield Avenue, was followed by a heartbreaking loss in Game 5 that ended the season shy of a World Series.

In Sutcliffe's final start with the Indians at Cleveland Stadium, he had pitched before 3,699 fans. Eighteen days later, he pitched before a crowd of 39,494 in his first start at Wrigley Field, and Sutcliffe got swept up in the hysteria that was the 1984 season.

"Being part of that family, being with people like Harry Caray...those people created me," he told Peter Golenbock in *Wrigleyville*. "I had done some things in L.A. and Cleveland, but there weren't many people who even heard my name, could even spell it. Harry Caray called me the Red Baron. The next thing I knew, it was unbelievable. I get goosebumps just talking about it."

47 May 17, 1979: Phillies 23, Cubs 22

Just look at that score. Even after all these years, it still takes your breath away.

On a Thursday afternoon in front of 14,952 fans at Wrigley Field, with 25-mph winds whipping out of the southwest, the Philadelphia Phillies and the Cubs combined for 50 hits, 45 runs, 11 home runs, and not one lead change.

The first sign of something unusual wasn't when the Phillies went ahead 6–0 in the first inning on three-run homers by Mike "The Cub Killer" Schmidt and Bob Boone. It was when Randy Lerch—the Phillies' starting pitcher—homered to make it 7–0 before the top of the inning was over.

By the time the Cubs came up, their starter Dennis Lamp was out of the game and Lerch, who hadn't given up more than four runs in any of his first eight starts that season, had a seemingly comfortable lead not knowing that on this day such a thing didn't exist.

The Cubs rapped out three straight singles off Lerch, including an RBI single by Bill Buckner before Dave Kingman launched the first of his three home runs on the day, a three-run shot that made it 7–4. Your totals at this point: 11 runs scored, four home runs hit, and three outs recorded.

Two batters later, Lerch got yanked and the Cubs wound up with a couple more runs to end the inning trailing just 7–6. They were almost right back where they had started.

The Phillies went ahead 17–6 and 21–9 before the Cubs launched another comeback. They scored seven times in the fifth on Buckner's grand slam and Jerry Martin's three-run homer, both of which came off Phillies closer Tug McGraw. Yes, Phillies manager Danny Ozark brought his closer on in the fifth inning.

The Cubs scored three more in the sixth to make it 21–19 and, after the Phillies added one more, tied the game in the eighth with five hits, including a pair of two-out RBI singles by Martin and Barry Foote. It was now 22–22.

Probably the two most memorable regular-season games in Wrigley Field history are this one and the Sandberg Game in 1984. St. Louis Cardinals closer Bruce Sutter was twice victimized by future Hall of Famer Ryne Sandberg in that one, but in 1979 he was still with the Cubs and on his way to winning that season's Cy Young Award.

In the top of the 10th, up stepped future Hall of Famer Schmidt, who clubbed Sutter's 3–2 pitch deep over the left-center bleachers for his second home run of the game. Cubs broadcaster

Cubs 26, Philadelphia 23

The highest-scoring game in major league history was also one of the sloppiest. On August 25, 1922, at Wrigley Field, the Cubs and the Philadelphia Phillies combined for eight errors and an incredible 19 unearned runs. There were 51 hits but only three home runs, all by the Cubs.

The Phillies were one of the worst teams in baseball and proved it early on, giving up 10 runs in the second inning and 14 runs in the fourth to trail 25–6 after just four innings. The Cubs actually led 26–9 going into the eighth inning before giving up eight runs in the eighth and six more in the ninth. Incredibly, the Phillies used two pitchers the entire game.

Perhaps even more incredibly, the following day neither team scored a run through 10 innings until the Phillies plated three in the 11th to beat the Cubs 3–0.

Jack Brickhouse could only watch in dismay as the Phillies went ahead once again 23–22.

"Scot Thompson took about four steps out there in center field," Brickhouse told WGN-TV viewers, "and then realized that was a gone goose."

Phillies reliever Rawly Eastwick set down the Cubs in order in the ninth and 10ᵗʰ for the win. Kingman had a shot to tie the game and hit his fourth homer of the day, but he struck out for the second out of the 10ᵗʰ inning. Steve Ontiveros hit a check-swing grounder to Schmidt, who fired to first baseman Pete Rose to end the game.

The four-hour, three-minute game may have really taken a toll on the Phillies. They only scored 31 runs over their next 13 games, which included a mere eight runs during a four-game series in Philadelphia against the Cubs. The Phillies were also shut out three straight times during one stretch.

"It was no fun," Schmidt told the *Chicago Tribune*. "It was a struggle more than anything, and I'm dead tired."

But to the winner goes the spoils, and also the jokes.

"We all knew it was going to be one of those days," Phillies shortstop Larry Bowa said after the game. "I mean, what the heck, the Cubs had a field-goal kicker warming up on the sidelines for three innings."

48 Billy Buck

Bill Buckner hobbled and hit his way into the hearts of Cubs fans during his nearly 1,000 games in blue pinstripes, becoming one of the few players who have defined the franchise for an extended period of time.

It was not love at first sight.

When Buckner and his Marlboro Man moustache arrived from the Los Angeles Dodgers on January 11, 1977, in a trade that also netted the Cubs Ivan DeJesus and a minor leaguer for Rick Monday and Mike Garman, he had to deal with culture shock. The Dodgers were a perennial contender whose Dodger Way of doing things focused on fundamentals, coaching, and pride in the organization from the minors on up. The Cubs were the opposite in just about every way.

In an interview days after being traded, Buckner told the *Chicago Tribune*, "I'm going from a contender to a non-contender...from a city I love to a city I dislike. It's a real drag. I'm very upset about it."

First baseman Bill Buckner on March 1, 1979. (AP Photo)

More than seven years later, having been dealt to Boston in the midst of the Cubs memorable 1984 season, Buckner couldn't hold back the tears during an emotional press conference at Wrigley Field saying, "This is a very tough moment for me."

Buckner, who went by the easy nickname of Billy Buck, was drafted by the Dodgers in 1968 and spent most of his years in Los Angeles as an outfielder. By the time he joined the Cubs, a series of ankle surgeries had forced him to first base and made limping a way of life.

As Buckner's first spring training got underway, there was grave concern the Dodgers had dumped a useless ballplayer on the Cubs, and sure enough Buckner barely played in any Cactus League games and started the season on the disabled list.

He made his debut as a pinch-hitter on April 19 and started a handful of games during the first two months, but it wasn't until early June that he was able to start on a regular basis despite the pain emanating from his ravaged left ankle, which he was forced to ice every day.

Cubs fans discovered they had received a player who approached every game as if it was his last and wasn't content until his uniform had enough dirt on it to make him look like a chimney sweep. A lingering bitterness toward the Dodgers came out during a three-game series at Wrigley Field in August when he went 8-for-12 with three homers and eight RBIs against his former team.

There was only so much Buckner could do, and while the Dodgers wound up in the World Series, the Cubs went from being tied for first place in the National League East on August 6 to finishing an astonishing 20 games back, losers of 37 of their final 55 games.

"The determination of William Joseph Buckner will be remembered as one of the major stories of the Cubs' current season—however it ends," wrote the *Chicago Tribune*'s Richard Dozer on August 14, 1977. "Some will say he personifies the spirit of the Cubs. Unfortunately, not enough of it has rubbed off."

And that's the way it went in his seven-plus seasons with the Cubs. Finally healthy in 1979, Buckner played like a champion on teams that weren't capable of winning championships. His stats weren't gaudy; he averaged just more than 11 homers during his seven full seasons and only drove in more than 75 runs once. But his slap-style left-handed swing produced a .300 average four times, including the 1980 National League batting title when he hit .324, and it made him nearly impossible to fan. In 4,042 plate appearances, he struck out just 159 times.

Buckner had at least two memorable dust-ups with Cubs managers, one an on-field incident and the other basically a bad break-up. When Buckner joined the Cubs in 1977, the manager was Herman Franks, a gruff self-made millionaire who would later serve as interim Cubs GM in 1981.

From the outset, Franks loved Buckner's style of play. After Buckner's bat beat the Dodgers in his first game against his former team after the trade, Dodgers manager Tommy Lasorda said, "Tell my son, even though he beat us, I still love him." Franks shot back: "He's my son now."

Two years later, Franks threw his "son" under the bus after he quit as manager with a week left in the regular season, telling the *Tribune*'s Dave Nightingale, "I thought he was the All-American boy. I thought he was the kind of guy who'd dive in the dirt to save ballgames for you. What I found out, after being around him awhile, is that he's nuts.... He goes berserk if he goes through a game without getting a hit. He doesn't care about the team. All he cares about is Bill Buckner."

Buckner was troubled enough by Franks' comments, which he said were "really making me look like an idiot," that he asked to be interviewed on WGN-TV between games of a doubleheader to get out his side of the story. Franks faded away, and Buckner remained a fan favorite.

Buckner, who played for six different Cubs managers, also got into a fistfight with Lee Elia on May 24, 1982, in San Diego. According to the *Tribune* it was a 15-second bout, and the pair had to be broken up by teammates and coaches. The incident began when Buckner felt a Padres pitcher had thrown at him, and he screamed in the Cubs dugout that he expected retaliation. Cubs reliever Dan Larson's response? His next pitch hit the Padres' Tim Flannery on the hip.

This incensed Elia, who charged to the mound and not so calmly explained to Larson, "I manage this ballclub, no one else." When Elia got back to the dugout, the fight ensued. Afterward, Buckner said Elia "acted like a child" and demanded to be traded. But he later took back the demand and apologized to Elia.

Almost two years later to the day, Buckner was traded to Boston. He had spent most of the 1984 season on the bench relegated to a pinch-hitting role after Leon Durham had taken over at first base.

Buckner never deserved the ignominy that came to him with the Red Sox, where his infamous error contributed to an epic World Series collapse in 1986. On the North Side of Chicago he'll be remembered in a different way—for that painful-looking hobble, his unrelenting play, and as one of the players beloved by a generation of Cubs fans.

49 The College of Coaches

Let's get this out of the way first. The College of Coaches was possibly the worst idea in baseball history, right up there with Charlie Finley's orange ball and outfitting the White Sox in short pants.

The decision to abandon the traditional manager in favor of a rotating group of coaches who would each take a turn being a "head coach" came from the non-fertile baseball mind of Cubs owner Phil Wrigley, who didn't like firing people and was appalled the word "dictator" was in the dictionary's definition of "manager."

Even the press conference announcing the new system was bizarre. Wrigley brought along an odd sign that read, "Anyone who remains calm in the midst of all this confusion simply does not understand the situation." The situation here was that the Cubs were trying something that had never been done before in baseball history. So why now? After using a strange analogy stating that if a bulldozer driver gets sick you just get a new driver, Wrigley seemed

The Athletic Director

Almost as ridiculous but not as well-known to history was Wrigley's hiring of an athletic director prior to the 1963 season. The only man to hold the title before the position was abandoned two years later was Robert Whitlow, a former Air Force colonel who was also the first athletic director of the United States Air Force Academy.

The athletic director was not the same as a general manager; the Cubs still had one of those in longtime GM John Holland. The job, as Wrigley described when the 43-year-old Whitlow was introduced, was to "basically be responsible for the conduct of the club on the field."

Aside from making the decision to keep Bob Kennedy as the full-time head coach before the 1963 season, it was never quite clear what Whitlow did. His attempt to describe his role in a June 9, 1963, article didn't exactly clear things up. "As I see it," he said. "My job is to achieve harmony among the coaches and the players."

Despite a generally cheery disposition, during Whitlow's first season he nearly got into a fight with a member of the Cubs' coaching staff. He quit in January 1965.

"Baseball simply was not ready for an athletic director," Wrigley said. "Maybe in the years ahead baseball will accept one. Whitlow was ahead of his time."

That time still hasn't come.

to stumble on the truth. "We certainly cannot do much worse trying a new system than we have done for many years under the old."

The initial plan was to have each coach take a turn as the head coach, then perhaps do a stint as a minor league manager before returning to the big-league club to coach again. For a franchise longing for any sense of stability, it was lunacy. Officially, the original College of Coaches were: Bobby Adams, Rip Collins, Harry Craft, Charlie Grimm, Vedie Himsl, Goldie Holt, Elvin Tappe, and Verlon Walker. A ninth—Fred Martin—was added before spring training, and Lou Klein, Charlie Metro, and Bob Kennedy joined along the way.

With the coaches changing all the time, players were getting pulled in all directions. The biggest casualty was Lou Brock, who first joined the Cubs in 1961 and spent three frustrating seasons listening to different coaches tell him to focus on speed, then average, then power. It was no surprise he blossomed upon leaving the Cubs for the Cardinals, who stopped tinkering with him.

Wrigley's utopian expectation was that all the coaches would buy into a new system of doing things, but what really happened was far more human. While there weren't specific acts of sabotage, there wasn't always a spirit of cooperation. According to Don Elston, who pitched for the Cubs from 1961 until 1964, the system was at its worst in 1962. Instead of helping the current head coach, Elston said, Metro would spend his time before games hitting pop flies to his son. The other coaches weren't any more magnanimous when the roles were reversed.

At one point, Metro instituted a ridiculous policy in which players were not permitted to shave in the clubhouse before or after games. Klein led a revolt by the other coaches and, after a vote, Metro's policy was reversed. "That was such a biased threesome toward themselves that it affected our ballclub a lot," Elston said in Peter Golenbock's book *Wrigleyville*.

The experiment lasted from 1961 until 1965, but not everybody ended up getting a turn. The first head coach in 1961 was Himsl, who went 10–21 and was followed by Craft (7–9), Tappe (42–54), and Klein (5–6). In 1962, Tappe went 4–16 to start the season and then gave way to Klein (12–18) and Metro (43–69).

There was such ridicule that the experiment was virtually abandoned after 1962, a season in which the Cubs finished 59–103, six games behind the Houston Colt 45's—an expansion team. Kennedy essentially became a permanent head coach in 1963 before Klein took over in June 1965. The College of Coaches officially came to an end in 1966 when Leo Durocher was hired as manager.

"I don't think you will talk to one ballplayer who played under that system that's going to say anything different than it was very hurtful, and it was a very bad situation," Elston said. "In 1961, it all went to hell, no question about it."

50 Attention, Attention Please! Have Your Pencils and Scorecards Ready!

The first legendary voice of the Cubs wasn't Pat Flanagan, Bob Elson, or Jack Brickhouse. It was Pat Pieper, a gravelly voiced boy from Denver who started out as a peanut vendor and talked his way into a job as the Wrigley Field public address announcer—a job he would hold uninterrupted until his death 58 years later.

It was the spring of 1916, and Pieper had been selling peanuts and popcorn at the old West Side Grounds for ten years when a groundskeeper gave him a tip—the Cubs were in need of a new public address announcer for their new home, Weeghman Park.

Pieper, not the shy type, marched over to Cubs owner Charles Weeghman and offered his services, according to his 1974 *Chicago Tribune* obituary. Weeghman wasn't sure the young man could handle it, until Pieper belted out, "You'd better believe I can!" right in Weeghman's ear.

Weeghman believed.

Pieper went on to become an institution at Wrigley Field with Cubs fans just as likely to copy his signature calls as they were Charlie Root's windup or Ernie Banks' batting stance.

"Attention, attention please!" Pieper would bellow in his halting manner. "Have your pencils…and scorecards ready…for the correct lineups…for today's game."

For the first few years of his career, Pieper used a megaphone to scream out announcements and could be seen running up and down the foul lines to keep the fans informed. In 1922, at Cubs President Bill Veeck Sr.'s suggestion, he upgraded to a 14-pound model that led to a tradition. Each day before the game he would go outside and pick a different boy to help him hold it upright.

It's doubtful anybody ever watched more Cubs games at Wrigley Field than Pieper, and it's a virtual certainty nobody was on the field for more historic events. For decades, before getting bumped up to the press box, Pieper did his job positioned on the playing field near the Cubs dugout.

He was there the day the Cubs' Hippo Vaughn and Cincinnati's Fred Toney threw a double no-hitter in 1917, Ernie Banks' debut in 1953, and every game of the tortuous 1969 season. He also witnessed every home World Series game the Cubs ever played, including Babe Ruth's alleged "called shot" in 1932, which he claimed was absolutely true.

Pieper's job wasn't only to serve as field announcer but also to handle baseballs for the umpires, tossing them new balls and pocketing the used ones. He wasn't a member of the media and he was an unabashed Cubs fan, but not during the game. That changed on few occasions, none more memorably than in 1938 when Gabby Hartnett's Homer in the Gloamin' helped spur the Cubs to the National League pennant.

"I have always attempted to handle my job as an announcer with dignity," Pieper told the *Tribune* in a 1953 profile. "But when I saw Gabby's hit soaring on its way over the left-field fence, I picked up the bag of baseballs I keep for umpires and ran to third base to meet him. Then I jogged beside him until he reached home plate. I kept shouting, 'Be sure and touch the plate.'

"Gabby just smiled. I never saw a man so happy. I was 52 years old then. That was no way for me to behave."

Pieper, who was a waiter at Chicago's famed Ivanhoe restaurant during the off-season and when the Cubs were on the road, was so popular and enduring that the Cubs held two Pat Pieper Days for him—one in 1940 and another in 1953 when he was 67 and nearing a retirement that never came.

"I don't give a damn what they say about retiring," he told the *Tribune* in 1971. "If you have all your marbles and can move your arms and legs, don't ever quit. That retirement is for the birds. I'll stay at Wrigley Field until they chase me out."

Pieper died on October 22, 1974, 20 days after completing his 68th year with the Cubs. The following season, Pieper's microphone was still being used—but not at Wrigley Field.

It went on display at the Baseball Hall of Fame.

51 Attend the Crosstown Classic

You have to go to the Crosstown Classic at least once if only to see if any fights will break out. Off the field or on.

Sure, the fans can get rowdy and there may be a love tap or two, but that's to be expected. At least they have alcohol and decades of pent-up frustration as an excuse. Cubs catcher Michael Barrett didn't have the same excuse when he sucker-punched the White Sox's A.J. Pierzynski in 2006.

When the hotheaded Barrett was bowled over by the pesky Pierzynski in a close play at the plate, it was a combustible combination that ended with four ejections and a 10-game suspension for Barrett. Pierzynski got away with a $2,000 fine. Oh, and the White Sox won 7–0. Of all the crazy moments in the relatively brief history of the Cubs and White Sox interleague games, that's the most memorable.

There have been no shortage of others, such as the time Carlos Zambrano got into a shouting match with Derrek Lee in the dugout at U.S. Cellular Field or when Jose Valentin homered for the White Sox then mimicked the way Sammy Sosa blew kisses after going deep.

In most years the Bulls and Blackhawks have already concluded their seasons by the time the first three-game series is played, and with nothing else to cover, every media creature in town is focused on these games, regardless of the team's records. The games are covered as if the team's season is riding on the outcome, and in a sense it is.

Since the series began in 1997, the Cubs have gone to the playoffs six times and the White Sox have made it three times but only once—in 2008—have they played each other when both teams were leading their division. It's one thing to have a bad season, but to suffer the indignity of losing to the White Sox? That's too much to bear. The hard truth for Cubs fans is the Sox have had more success so far. Through the 2016 season, the Cubs have a 51–57 record and have gone 4-10-6 in the 20 seasons. That'll make any Cubs fans sick to their stomach but particularly the older ones who may be experiencing déjà vu.

From 1903 until 1942, the Cubs and White Sox played what was then called the City Series. It took place every October when at least one team did not participate in the World Series. This wasn't just a few exhibition games played with minor-leaguers, all the best players competed, and for many years each team's fans took these games as seriously as if it were the real World Series.

The final game in 1942 only drew 7,599 fans to Comiskey Park, however, and with salaries rising many players didn't need the extra income anymore. The City Series wasn't played in 1943 and concluded with the Sox having won 19 of 25, including the last

Tough Losses

The 20-year-old Crosstown Classic is old enough now that every player who participated in the first series back in 1997 has retired, and in a ghastly twist the first two pitchers of record for the Cubs have already passed away.

Kevin Foster, a hometown kid who grew up in Evanston, won the first-ever interleague game between the Cubs and White Sox on June 16, 1997. With support from Brian McRae and Rey Sanchez, who each had a pair of RBIs, Foster gave up three runs in six innings to beat the South Siders 8–3 at Comiskey Park. After a six-month battle, Foster died of cancer on October 11, 2008, at the age of 39.

The Sox got their first win in the series on June 17 with a 5–3 victory over the Cubs and starter Jeremi Gonalez, who allowed five runs in six innings, including home runs to Chris Snopek and former Cub Dave Martinez. On May 25, 2008, Gonzalez, who had changed his name to Geremi several years earlier, was struck by lightning and killed in his native Venezuela. He was 33.

eight in a row. There were many exhibition games played over the years, including the Windy City Classic from 1986 to 1995 that also didn't fare well for the Cubs, who didn't win a single game and managed just two ties. One of the tie games came in 1994 when a White Sox farmhand by the name of Michael Jordan had two RBIs, including a game-tying double, before 37,825 at Wrigley Field.

"He might have been playing for the Sox," Cubs shortstop Shawon Dunston told the *Chicago Tribune* afterward. "But he is Chicago. Let's not fool ourselves."

And let's not fool ourselves now. No White Sox player will ever get cheered at Wrigley Field ever again.

52 Amazing Grace

Like several decades before it, the 1990s was a bit of a lost decade for the Cubs.

Greg Maddux and Ryne Sandberg were prematurely ripped away, they didn't win a single game in their only postseason appearance, and aside from Sammy Sosa's home runs there was precious little to cheer about at Wrigley Field.

Through it all, Mark Grace persevered. The Cubs' 1985 24th round pick out of San Diego State never hit enough homers to satisfy his critics, but he finished with the most hits of any big leaguer in the 1990s. The most doubles, too. Both accomplishments were great sources of pride for Grace, who never slugged more than 17 home runs in a season. Instead, he made his living as a four-time Gold Glove first baseman who hit .308 in a Cubs uniform and was always among the toughest players in baseball to strike out.

Grace was the blue-eyed, blond-haired face of the franchise during some awfully lean times, and through it all he kept the media stocked with great quotes and kept his fawning fans—not just the women, mind you—wondering what time he might show up at Yak-Zies for a nightcap. Okay, a few nightcaps.

He was never a wallflower, not even as a rookie, and that didn't always set well with veterans who expect rookies to live by a pecking order. On June 4, 1989, Grace stepped into the batter's box to face St. Louis lefthander Frank DiPino, a teammate of Grace's during his 1988 rookie season. His first pitch was inside and tight. Grace

Mark Grace blasts a bases-loaded double to drive in three runs during the sixth inning of an NL playoff game with the San Francisco Giants at Wrigley Field on Thursday, October 6, 1989. Grace helped the Cubs to a 9–5 victory over the San Francisco Giants to tie the series at one game each. Giants catcher Kurt Manwaring is at left. (AP Photo)

stepped toward DiPino and like a couple of hockey tough guys the pair decided to engage. The ensuing brawl left Grace with an injured shoulder that cost him several weeks.

"He was talking all the time like he was a 10-year veteran," DiPino said about his year as Grace's teammate. "That started getting me hacked off. I guess all that stuff went to his head about 'Amazing Grace.' I have nothing against his talent, he is talented. But I just don't like guys who are cocky."

Grace certainly was cocky, but he could back it up. In the 1989 National League Championship Series, which the Cubs lost in five games to San Francisco, he had a team-leading eight RBIs while hitting a remarkable .647 (11-for-17) during the series. Incredibly, that wasn't the top average in the series or the top average by a first baseman. His counterpart, Giants star Will Clark, went 13-for-20, a .650 average.

Grace not only liked to hang out with Cubs fans, it was clear he was one of them and it would have been a challenge to find any player more loyal to the franchise. As he entered his arbitration years and then free agency, Grace knew exactly where he wanted to be even if the Cubs weren't always sure they wanted him.

Over his 13-year career with the Cubs, Grace signed 11 one-year contracts. And even as they kept bringing him back, Cubs management always made sure he had one foot out the door. Until finally one year, he had both feet out. He signed with the Arizona Diamondbacks before the 2001 season.

A breakdown in Grace's relationship with Cubs President Andy MacPhail didn't help matters, but the Cubs' company line was that they didn't want to block prospect Hee-Seop Choi, a reasonable proposition at the time. But Choi failed miserably and over the next three years the Cubs went with aging veterans Matt Stairs, Ron Coomer, Fred McGriff, and Eric Karros at first base. They had more power but couldn't touch Grace defensively, and in the end only Grace ended up with a World Series ring.

When he played his first game in Wrigley Field after signing with Arizona, Grace received a long standing ovation. Clearly, the fans weren't ready to let go, at least not until after the 2001 World Series. It was that Grace made a comment that was directed toward management but Cubs fans didn't remember fondly.

"I wasn't good enough to play first base for the Chicago Cubs, but I was good enough to play first base for the World Champions," Grace said. "And that feels really good."

That helped cement the separation a bit. After a cooling-off period that lasted a few years—and helped out by MacPhail's resignation a few months earlier—Grace was invited to the 2007 Cubs Convention and began his life as an ex-Cub in good graces. Where it will eventually lead nobody knows, but don't be surprised to one day see Mark Grace again drawing a Cubs' paycheck. This time for his work in the broadcast booth.

53 The Gamer

It was rarely pretty and Lord, there were mistakes along the way, but Dallas Green came to Wrigley Field determined to dismantle a culture of losing he abhorred. And that's exactly what he did.

Where the Cubs had been meek for the better part of 50 years, Green was ferocious and unwilling to let the past dictate his moves. He fired dozens of people when he arrived, made risky trades, and took on residents and politicians in an effort to get lights installed at Wrigley Field.

Right or wrong, Dallas put a giddy-up into the Cubs.

Green had been a lifer in the Philadelphia Phillies organization and managed them to the 1980 World Series title, so it was a tough

Dallas Green's Five Best Trades:

1. January 27, 1982: Ivan DeJesus to Philadelphia for Larry Bowa and Ryne Sandberg.
2. March 26, 1984: Bill Campbell and Mike Diaz to Philadelphia for Porfi Altamirano, Bobby Dernier, and Gary Matthews.
3. June 13, 1984: Darryl Banks, Joe Carter, Mel Hall, and Don Schulze to Cleveland for Rick Sutcliffe, George Frazier, and Ron Hassey.
4. January 19,1983: Dan Cataline and Vance Lovelace to the Los Angeles Dodgers for Ron Cey.
5. March 26, 1984: Minor leaguers Stan Kyles and Stan Boderick to Oakland for Tim Stoddard.

decision to leave, and at first he turned down Tribune Co., which had bought the club a few months earlier. But Tribune chairman Andrew McKenna wouldn't take no for an answer, and eventually he got a yes.

Green's initial move was to hire Lee Elia as manager, a coach from his days with the Phillies. It was the first of many involving his old organization, and most of them proved fruitful for the Cubs. He brought in so many ex-Phillies, including Larry Bowa, Gary Matthews, Bobby Dernier, Ryne Sandberg, Dick Ruthven, and Dickie Noles, that the Cubs came to be known as Phillies West. More accurately, they were gamers, a type of player Green sought over all others.

"They're the guys who can put all the frustrations, all the personal problems, all the garbage aside when they hit the white lines," Green told the *Chicago Tribune* in early 1982, a few months after he was hired. "A gamer plays over the problems of life and baseball and gives you everything he's got. He wants nothing more than to play baseball with gusto."

The other major change Green made was to revamp an unproductive minor-league system by hiring Gordon Goldsberry, whose first pick was Shawon Dunston. Subsequent drafts reeled in prospects like Greg Maddux, Rafael Palmeiro, Mark Grace, Jamie Moyer, Jerome Walton, Dwight Smith, and Joe Girardi.

The 1984 season was a testament to Green's ability to recognize talent as well as his impatience. Less than three years after Green took over, the Cubs had six new everyday players in the lineup and an entirely new starting rotation in Dennis Eckersley, Steve Trout, Rick Sutcliffe, and Scott Sanderson, each one acquired through trades.

Green tried to win again with pretty much the same crew the following season, but injuries decimated the rotation. A 13-game losing streak in June after a 35–19 start was the beginning of the end not just for the Cubs but for Green. He had been promoted to club president after 1984 and was spending more time on off-field activities.

The issue of lights at Wrigley Field started to consume more of Green's time, and on June 19, 1985, he sent out a letter to Cubs' season-ticket-holders, letting them know if the Cubs made it to the World Series that season it would be played in another city.

By 1987, most of the holdovers from 1984 were gone and the Cubs were rebuilding again. Green had already fired Elia in 1983 and then Jim Frey in June 1986. In 1987, Gene Michael was hired to manage the Cubs, but on September 8, 1987, he announced he was quitting through a radio interview with Bruce Levine, then a freelance correspondent. Green didn't even know.

It was an embarrassment to Green, who was faced with hiring his fourth manager in six seasons. His first choice for the job? Dallas Green. That option was rejected by his Tribune bosses, and a few weeks later it was clear he'd have to start sharing decision-making, so Green resigned.

Just like Leo Durocher 15 years earlier, a dominating figure had rolled into Wrigley Field and tried to shake things up. But unlike Durocher, Green had actually won something.

54 Jake Arrieta: Surprise Superstar

The trade shipping one of his favorite teammates to Baltimore was done, and Cubs pitcher Jeff Samardzija was not happy. So he spoke up.

"I don't think this team improves by trading Scott Feldman," Samardzija told the *Chicago Tribune* on July 2, 2013.

It was an understandable quote born of frustration over yet another losing season, but it lives on for how comically wrong Samardzija turned out to be. Jake Arrieta, who arrived from the Orioles along with Pedro Strop in exchange for Feldman and catcher Steve Clevenger, has been nothing short of a miracle worker since becoming a Cub.

There were certainly those who believed Arrieta could turn into a solid Major League starter, but nobody could possibly have known what was coming.

The Texas native had developed into a top prospect not long after the Orioles drafted him in the 5th round of the 2007 draft, reaching the Majors in 2010 and even earning an Opening Day start for Baltimore in 2012. But struggles commanding his pitches that led to bloated earned-run averages made him expendable when the Cubs came calling.

Upon his arrival in Chicago, Arrieta was immediately sent to the minors before making nine promising late-season starts for the Cubs. The 2014 season began with Arrieta on the disabled list due to shoulder stiffness, so he only made 25 starts that year but he made them count. On three occasions, Arrieta took a no-hitter into the 7th inning, including on September 16 when he gave up only a one-out single in the 8th inning against Cincinnati.

It was hard to imagine 2015 could be much better, but it was, and it wasn't even close. The first half of the season was much like 2014; Arrieta's 2.66 ERA nearly matched his 2.53 ERA from 2014 as he confirmed his status as an elite pitcher. The second half? It's still hard to believe how good he was because nobody has ever been better. Nobody.

Arrieta allowed a mere nine earned runs while going 14–1 in 15 second-half starts, his only loss coming on July 25 when Philadelphia's Cole Hamels needed a no-hitter to beat him. The 0.75 ERA Arrieta posted was the lowest after the All Star game in MLB history. Overall, Arrieta's 1.77 ERA set a mondern-day Cubs team record as he won 22 games to become the first 20-game winner on the North Side since Jon Lieber went 20–6 in 2001, and the first Cub to win the Cy Young Award since Greg Maddux in 1992.

The dominance of Arrieta's entire second half was such that it actually overshadowed Arrieta's dominance on August 30 when he no-hit the Los Angeles Dodgers at Chavez Ravine. And such is Arrieta's personality that his postgame news conference was nearly as memorable as the game itself when he took a seat wearing pajamas. Before the game Cubs manager Joe Maddon had decreed the team would fly home from their road trip in pajamas, and Arrieta didn't let a little thing like a no-hitter get in the way.

Arrieta's unbelievable confidence was never more present than in the days leading up to the National League Wild Card game against the Pirates in Pittsburgh. In response to a radio host and Pirates fan who proposed the hashtag #WeMatter to excite Pirates fans, Arrieta tweeted the perfect response.

"Whatever helps keep your hope alive, just know, it doesn't matter. @Cubs"

And it didn't. Arrieta threw a four-hit shutout to bury the Pirates.

King Kong
(aka Dave Ding Dong)

When the Cubs signed Dave Kingman prior to the 1978 season, he brought along with him a mammoth bat capable of sending baseballs flying into windows of rooftop buildings across Waveland Avenue.

But he also brought his crusty personality, which was capable of striking out just as often as he did.

"Dave has the personality of a tree trunk," former teammate John Stearns once told *Sports Illustrated*. "He's not a bad guy, but if you try to talk to him, about all he does is grunt."

Kingman both loved and hated the idea of playing at gusty Wrigley Field, knowing the temptation to hit solely for home runs could be too great to resist. Not that he hadn't been striking out a lot already, having fanned 853 times in his first 798 big-league games.

Before joining the Cubs, Kingman played for five franchises in seven seasons, and in 1977 he was either the most wanted or unwanted player in baseball, going from the New York Mets to the San Diego Padres to the California Angels before heading back to New York—this time with the Yankees—for the final three weeks of the season.

So when he arrived on the North Side there was little mystery about what the Cubs were getting—an all-or-nothing slugger who wouldn't win any popularity contests. And that's exactly what they got. Kingman's first season with the Cubs was free of controversy, although it wasn't free of injury. He missed 43 games yet still finished with a team-high 28 home runs on a Cubs team that saw no other players reach double figures.

The 1979 season was Kingman's tour de force but it got off to a bad start, at least with the press. The *Chicago Sun-Times* ran a list of best and worst on the club and Kingman, who usually came to Wrigley Field straight from his boat on Lake Michigan, was named worst-dressed by his teammates.

Naturally, he took out his anger on the print reporters and refused to speak with them the entire season. This posed a problem because he made news all year long, pounding a career-high 48 home runs and hitting .288, a remarkable accomplishment for a .236 career hitter. Twice, he homered three times in a game and incidentally, both times the Cubs lost.

By 1980, Kingman was growling about his contract, which still had three years left at $225,000 annually. His demands to get an extension were met with deaf ears by Cubs' management, who may have also been put off when Kingman dumped a bucket of water on the head of *Daily Herald* sportswriter Don Friske during spring training. Aside from a stiff reprimand, Kingman went unpunished.

That season he also started writing—or at least putting his name at the top of—a column that appeared in the Sunday editions of the *Chicago Tribune*. This made him a competitor of legendary Cubs fans Mike Royko, then a *Chicago Sun-Times* columnist. He preferred to call Kingman "Ding Dong" rather than King Kong so he began a series of parody columns with the byline, "Dave Ding Dong."

In 1980, Kingman missed 81 games due to an injured shoulder. During his second stint on the disabled list, he chose to attend a boat show instead of Wrigley Field on the same day the Cubs gave away 15,000 Dave Kingman T-shirts. He had all but checked out and as the following spring training grew near, his complaints about his contract grew angrier and he threatened to hold out. On February 28, 1980, he was traded to the Mets for Steve Henderson.

Dave Kingman and Bill Buckner (22) at home plate in the sixth inning after Kingman hit his first of three home runs against the Los Angeles Dodgers in Los Angeles on May 14, 1978. (AP Photo/ Wally Fong)

And with that King Kong was gone. All that remained was a new ice cream parlor called Kingman's Landing he had just opened at the corner of Irving Park Road and Western Avenue. Less than a year later, that closed, too.

What a Relief!

So many amazing things took place during a Pirates-Cubs game on July 6, 1980, at Three Rivers Stadium that it's hard to know where to start. So let's start with the outcome, which remained in doubt for 20 innings.

The 5-hour, 31-minute affair—to that point the longest in Cubs history—ended in the bottom of the 20th when Cubs left fielder Dave Kingman couldn't handle Omar Moreno's one-out single off Dennis Lamp and Ed Ott raced home with the winning run.

Now, to the fun stuff.

- The Cubs struck out 18 times, including 12 against Hall of Famer Bert Blyleven, who finished his career with 3,701 strikeouts.
- Kingman, one of the easiest men to whiff in the history of baseball, went 0-for-9 yet didn't strike out once despite facing Blyleven five times.
- The Cubs trailed 4–3 with two outs in the top of the ninth until Cliff Johnson's homer off Blyleven sent the game to extra innings.
- In the top of the 16th, the Cubs had Mike Vail on third with one out but chose to let pitcher Bill Caudill, who finished his career with a grand total of five hits, attempt a suicide squeeze. He missed, and Vail was a dead duck at home.
- Last, but in no way least, after John Milner's two-out single off Cubs starter Rick Reuschel in the bottom of the sixth, the Pirates didn't get another hit until Lee Lacy's one-out single off starter-turned-emergency-reliever Lamp in the 19th inning.

That's right. Cubs pitchers threw 12²/₃ innings of consecutive no-hit ball in a single game—and lost.

56 The Life and Death of Ken Hubbs

Given the measure of time the Cubs have been around it's no surprise tragedy has struck on a number of occasions, just as it has many other clubs, but nothing has proved to be as profoundly tragic as the death of second baseman Ken Hubbs.

Two years after being named the National League Rookie of the Year, Hubbs and a childhood friend, Dennis Doyle, lost their lives when the single-engine Cessna Hubbs was piloting during a snowstorm crashed into a lake near Provo, Utah.

The February 13, 1964, accident took the breath out of a Cubs franchise that seemed ready to turn its back on years of futility. The previous season they had finished above .500 for the first time in 17 seasons, with Hubbs as much a part of the nucleus as guys named Banks, Santo, and Williams. There was actual hope on the North Side of Chicago. As the *Chicago Tribune*'s Ed Prell wrote in his preview of the 1964 club, "The main thing is they have made a move after all these bleak years."

Hubbs was a big part of why fans were encouraged. He was only 20 when he made the jump from the Class B Northwest League to become the Cubs' starting second baseman. In 1962, his rookie season, Hubbs hit a steady .260 with five homers and 49 RBIs, but it was his fielding that won him vast acclaim. Similar to the streaks fellow golden boy second baseman Ryne Sandberg would later put together, Hubbs thrilled Cubs fans by going 78 games and 418 consecutive chances without an error. Both were major league records for second baseman.

As the conservative 1950s waned and Vietnam beckoned, the crew-cut-wearing Hubbs was everything an owner could hope for in a ballplayer. A quiet and unassuming Mormon who didn't

Rookie second baseman Ken Hubbs was surrounded by young fans after he tied the National League record of 57 consecutive games without an error in Chicago on August 14, 1962. The record was set in 1950 by Red Schoendienst of the St. Louis Cardinals. (AP Photo)

drink or smoke, Hubbs was also a doting son whose wheelchair-ridden father was a constant presence in spring training as well as at Wrigley Field.

After finishing up with the Cubs in 1963, Hubbs decided to pursue his interest in flying, something that he had put off during the season. When he took off from Provo on the morning of February 13 after a visit with Doyle's father in-law, he had been a licensed pilot for barely more than a month.

It was a day before anybody realized Hubbs and Doyle hadn't turned up at their intended destination, and vigils were held as word spread in Chicago that the plane carrying the Cubs' starting second baseman was missing. On February 15, the plane and their bodies were discovered.

The ensuing funeral drew 2,000 people to Hubbs' hometown of Colton, California, including dozens of members from the Cubs organization. Teammates Ernie Banks, Ron Santo, Don Elston, and Glen Hobbie were among the pallbearers.

When spring training began days later, the Cubs were still in mourning. There was a season to prepare for, however, and head coach Bob Kennedy, the current prevailing member of the College of Coaches, didn't mention Hubbs' name during his first speech to the club.

"He wouldn't want us brooding about him," Kennedy told the *Tribune*.

The Cubs would bleed through five different second baseman during the 1964 season, including future manager Joey Amalfitano, but none found any success. That paved the way for slick-fielding Glenn Beckert to win the second-base job the following year.

A few weeks after Hubbs' death, the Cubs broke camp and were on their flight back to Chicago when the team found itself over the site where Hubbs' plane had crashed a few weeks earlier.

"What a waste," Kennedy remarked.

57 Mt. Lou Finally Erupts

Lou Piniella watched quietly, almost serenely, for more than two months in 2007, his first season as Cubs manager. He thoughtfully answered questions and appeared almost befuddled when asked about the troubles his hapless Cubs team was experiencing.

This wasn't the same Lou who Cubs fans had hoped for and expected. They wanted the Lou whose hat-kicking, umpire-dusting, base-throwing outbursts would have generations of baseball fans googling "Lou Piniella ejection" for decades to come.

Instead of Crazy Lou they thought they got Placid Lou. What they really got was lulled to sleep.

In addition to expensive on-field acquisitions, GM Jim Hendry spent big to get Piniella, who twice won World Series rings with the New York Yankees as a player and in 1990 managed the Cincinnati Reds to a victory in the Fall Classic. He also was at the helm when the 2001 Seattle Mariners won 116 games then failed to get past the Yankees in the American League Championship Series.

But the Cubs got off to such a slow start in 2007 that by late May Hendry was already fending off questions about whether the Cubs would be sellers at the late July trade deadline. By early June they hadn't improved and internally appeared to be coming apart at the seams.

During a three-game weekend series against Atlanta at Wrigley Field, pitcher Carlos Zambrano and Cubs catcher Michael Barrett memorably brawled in the dugout as the series got underway on a Friday afternoon. Afterward, there were shades of Piniella reaching his breaking point.

"You don't like to see that...you really don't," Piniella said about Zambrano and Barrett fighting. "As the same time, you don't like to see the silliness on the field. I only have so many guys I can play. It's about time some of them start playing like major leaguers or we get somebody else who can catch a damn ball or run the bases!"

That set the tone for the following day, when Piniella had an even more memorable outburst. With the Cubs trailing 4–3 in the eighth inning, outfielder Angel Pagan was called out at third by umpire Mark Wegner in a close play that replays showed was the correct call. Then, almost as if it were planned, Piniella raced out, threw his Cubs cap to the ground, kicked it across the infield and was, of course, immediately ejected.

Piniella didn't stop there. He started kicking dirt onto Wegner's shoes and drew enough contact that he would later serve a four-game suspension. The Wrigley faithful couldn't have asked for a better show and roared their approval as Piniella finally, and calmly, walked off the field.

"The umpire was correct; the guy was out," Piniella admitted after the game. "I was going to argue whether he was out, safe, or whatever. It didn't make a damn bit of difference."

Oh, but it did make a difference The Cubs still lost that day, but something had changed. They beat the Braves 10–1 the following afternoon, and the season seemed to pivot on Mt. Lou's eruption. The suddenly vibrant Cubs went 63–46 the rest of the way and won a weak NL Central with an 85–77 record.

58 Watch a Game from a Rooftop

It's pretty special to watch a Cubs game on any one of the 16 Wrigleyville rooftops even if it can feel more like you're at Club Med than at Wrigley Field.

There's an aura of exclusivity when you're on a spacious rooftop that you don't get when you're in a cramped Wrigley Field skybox, which is why tickets start just shy of $100 and head close to $300. Murphy's Rooftop Company, which sits atop Murphy's Bleachers at 3649 N. Sheffield Avenue, charged $15,000 for a pair of Yankees games in 2011, according to its website.

If you have that kind of cash to spend go right ahead, but chances are if you wait long enough you can snag an invite since many of the rooftops are booked exclusively for corporate outings. There's no question the rooftops have become big business, but what's more remarkable is that it took decades for anyone to figure out they had value.

Watching a game from a rooftop is nearly as old as baseball itself in Chicago. When the Cubs played at the old West Side Grounds from 1893 to 1915, fans would gather on buildings much like they do now.

The Chicago Whales of the Federal League were Wrigley Field's first tenants when it opened in 1914 with some of the buildings you see now already standing, and the Cubs moved in two years later. For decades, the rooftops were little more than a curious place for WGN to focus its cameras and a place for the lucky few who lived there to see Cubs games for free.

Scott Bieber was one of the lucky ones. From 1980 to 1982, Bieber, then a chemical salesman, rented a three-bedroom apartment at 1032 W. Waveland with a couple of his buddies who were

Many empty seats are seen on the bleachers on the rooftops of the buildings across from Wrigley Field outfield during a baseball game between New York Mets and Chicago Cubs on Friday, September 3, 2010, in Chicago.
(AP Photo/Kiichiro Sato)

in medical school. He remembers the day he got a call to come by and see their new apartment and was told, "You will not be disappointed."

"Oh my God," Bieber said when he saw the yellow three-story building right beyond the left-field bleachers. "Don't tell me it's this building."

The owner of the building was a guy named Phil Pappas who was a friend of a friend's sister, Bieber said years later. He charged them $695 in rent. Total. Pappas had put in a deck the previous summer but was paranoid that something bad might happen. The tenants in the building could go to the roof whenever they wanted, but the limit was 20 people, Bieber recalls.

"It's funny to see these enormous bleachers that might hold 100 people," he said.

Elevators have now been installed in many of the buildings to comfortably zip patrons up to the top floors, but in Bieber's day all his building had was a back stairway that led toward the roof. The final part of the journey was on a steep wooden ladder that took you to a hatch that opened onto the roof. It was such a tight fit to get up there that Bieber doesn't recall ever bringing a keg up except on Opening Day. There were some days, incredibly, when he would have the rooftop all to himself.

"It was just a really, really nice thing," said Bieber, who now lives in Houston where he works as a marketing manager for a chemical company. "We had great parties but it never got way out of control. It was just very relaxed, very pleasant, and it wasn't that big a deal. The Cubs just weren't that big a deal.

"But we knew what we had. We knew how cool it was."

Eventually, so did the rooftop owners.

59 The Shawon-O-Meter

The goal was simply to get on TV. Instead, three young Cubs fans made it all the way to the Baseball Hall of Fame. Or at least their creation did.

The Shawon-O-Meter, a measure of Cubs shortstop Shawon Dunston's batting average, was the brainchild of Dave Cihla, Jim

Cybul, and Melinda Lehman, and it came to life during the joyful summer of 1989. With WGN-TV tracking its every move, the Shawon-O-Meter vied for television time, posed for photos with giddy fans and, in the surest sign of its celebrity status, once even got into a drunken brawl hundreds of miles from home, ending up face down in a ditch.

It all began in late May when Cihla attended a Cubs game in Atlanta and, after crafting a sign out of a sheet, was able to draw the attention of WGN-TV director Arne Harris, who gave the sign a few precious moments on television. Cihla was hooked. He returned to Chicago and summoned his roommates, Cybul and Lehman, and as they tried to come up with a way to lure the TV cameras toward them, Cybul hit on an idea. He called it the "Shawon-O-Meter."

The 1989 season was shaping up to be a miserable one for the No. 1 overall pick of the 1982 draft who enthralled fans with his blistering throws to first base but also tortured them with horrible impatience at the plate. After hitting below .200 the entire season, he finally went over the Mendoza Line with three hits on June 4 while the Cubs closed out a road trip in St. Louis.

On June 5, Cihla, Cybul, and Lehman took their usual spots in the left-field bleachers as the Cubs began an important four-game series against the New York Mets. With them was the Shawon-O-Meter.

That week, WGN found time for the Shawon-O-Meter each game, and almost as if on cue Dunston's average kept rising. He knocked out five hits in the series to move to .213, which the Shawon-O-Meter dutifully tracked. Sadly, the original flimsy version was ruined by a lethal combination of mustard, beer, and rain, and at the end of the series the trio left it behind in the bleachers.

But a star had been born. Another Shawon-O-Meter was quickly produced, this time out of a durable foam board and with the words, "We're all behind you Shawon," written on the back.

"When we came back for the next series, people would recognize us," Cihla said. "It sort of caught on pretty quickly. We were kind of blown away at the airtime they were giving it."

As the season went on the trio, who were then all in their mid-20s, brought the Shawon-O-Meter to as many games as they could. When they couldn't make it, they would give it to friends to take. Cihla even brought it to a series in Philadelphia, which is where it got into a tussle with four drunk Phillies fans. They snatched the Shawon-O-Meter and threw it out of the upper deck. With the help of an usher, Cihla was able to safely retrieve it after the game.

If there was a low point for Cihla, that episode in Philadelphia was it. The high point came when he went to San Francisco for Games 3–5 of the National League Championship Series and got a rousing ovation from everyone on the plane, which was full of Cubs fans. Then when he got off the plane, a tall, portly man approached him.

"[Giants pitcher and ex-Cub] Rick Reuschel had just gotten shelled [in Game 2] and he stops me and says, 'Is that the Shawon-O-Meter?'" Cihla said. "He was a fan. That to me was really surreal."

It's hard to say who had a better season, the Shawon-O-Meter or Shawon Dunston, but at the end of the year they were both hitting .278. Cihla was so captivated by its success that he wondered if others might be, too. So in 1990 he wrote the Smithsonian Institution to see if they'd be interested in it. They were.

Another version was produced for the 1990 season, this time with an All-Star Game motif and the words, "The All-American Boy," written on the back. Cihla later wondered if the Baseball Hall of Fame might be interested in it. They were. A third version was made and, well, you get the idea. The Chicago History Museum was interested. Cihla proudly hand-delivered each version to its final destination.

Cihla had a brief encounter with Dunston at the 1990 Cubs Convention, but it wasn't until years later that they had a chance to talk. Dunston was at Wrigley Field to sing the seventh-inning stretch when a friend of Cihla's hustled over to talk to him. The friend got Cihla on the phone and handed it to Dunston.

"I want to thank you," Dunston told him. "You really made my career."

60 Fill Your iPod with Cubs Songs

Dozens of songs have been written about the Cubs over the years, some of which aren't awful.

Some are so bad you'd sooner go on a six-month submarine voyage with Ronnie "Woo Woo" Wickers than listen to even one of them.

And then there are the ones that make your heart soar, your eyes water, and help you realize spending your days and nights brooding over and loving the Cubs might actually be worth it.

The current standard played at Wrigley Field after a Cubs victory is "Go, Cubs, Go," an uplifting celebratory song if there ever was one written by the late, great folk singer Steve Goodman, who grew up a huge Cubs fan in Rogers Park in the 1950s and 1960s and earned fame as the author of "City of New Orleans."

The origins of "Go, Cubs, Go" are tied to another Goodman song, one that is far less celebratory but one every Cubs fans should know. "A Dying Cubs Fan's Last Request" was written in 1981, about a dozen years into Goodman's battle with leukemia. Here's a sampling:

Do they still play the blues in Chicago
When baseball season rolls around
When the snow melts away,
Do the Cubbies still play
In their ivy-covered burial ground
When I was a boy they were my pride and joy
But now they only bring fatigue
To the home of the brave
The land of the free
And the doormat of the National League

The lyrics are bleak and the folksy tune is slow, so it's no surprise the song is best known for its title, which became all the more poignant when Goodman lost his fight with leukemia days before the Cubs clinched the 1984 National League East title.

But earlier that year, shortly before the 1984 season began, Goodman had been commissioned to write a song about the Cubs by former WGN Radio program direct Dan Fabian. He returned with "Go, Cubs, Go," clearly designed to be as optimistic as "Dying Cubs Fan" was pessimistic, though that's certainly open to interpretation. However you view them, they're both classics.

The Cubs song you love the most probably has more to do with the era you grew up in than anything, and for those old enough to remember the 1969 Cubs it's likely that Johnny Frigo's "Hey, Hey Holy Mackerel" is your old standby. The upbeat tune used the home-run calls of Jack Brickhouse and Vince Lloyd to drive its lyrics and became a sensation, and ultimately a sad remembrance of the '69 season.

Even though it seems like "It's a Beautiful Day for a Ballgame" with its focus on day baseball and "taking the afternoon" off was specifically written for the Cubs, it actually wasn't. The song was recorded in 1960 by the Harry Simeone Chorale and for many years introduced WGN telecasts. Some might even say one of the

An Oldie, But Is It a Goodie?

Good luck finding this one for your iPod.

In 1937, a tune called "Come on You Cubs, Play Ball" was written by Whitey Berquist, and on July 16, 1950, it was introduced as the Cubs new theme song, according to the June 30, 1950, edition of the *Chicago Tribune.*

The main verse, "Come on, get hot and drive across a run or two .... Oh! We want a home on Waveland Av-en-oo!

"We're loyal, one and all, so come on you Cubs, play ball! O! We want a homer, we want a homer, in Sheffield Av-en-oo!

Berquist told the *Tribune* it was written while he was in the bleachers during a Cubs rally. He quipped, "I think they got a man as far as third."

most memorable lyrics—"It's a beautiful day for a home run, but even a triple's okay"—is more concerned with being at the ballpark than winning, a stereotype Cubs fans still have to live with.

You can't go wrong adding most renditions of "Take Me Out to the Ballgame" sung during the 7th-inning stretch even the 22-second version butchered by Mike Ditka in 2008 is good for comic relief. But if you need just one version for your iPod, anything by Harry Caray will do just fine. The Cubs put out a CD in 2008 titled, "Take Me Out to a Cubs Game: Music For the Cubs Fan" that contains the September 21, 1997, version, which was sung during Harry's last game at Wrigley Field. He died the following winter.

One of the biggest celebrity Cubs fans is Pearl Jam's Eddie Vedder, who grew up in Evanston and can still be found taking in games in the bleachers every now and then. In 2007, he was asked by Ernie Banks to record his own Cubs song and came up with the haunting "Go All the Way."

"Go, Cubs, Go" might make you clap your hands, and "It's a Beautiful Day for a Ballgame" might take you back to your childhood, but Vedder's song is special. This is the one that brought many to tears the night the Cubs won the World Series.

Don't let anyone say that it's just a game
For I've seen other teams and it's never the same
When you're born in Chicago you're blessed and you're healed
The first time you walk into Wrigley Field
Our heroes wear pinstripes
Heroes in blue
Give us the chance to feel like heroes too
Forever we'll win and if we should lose

We know someday we'll go all the way
Yeah, someday we'll go all the way

We are one with the Cubs
With the Cubs we're in love
Yeah, hold our head high as the underdogs
We are not fair-weather but foul-weather fans
We're like brothers in arms in the streets and the stands
There's magic in the ivy and the old scoreboard
The same one I stared at as a kid keeping score
In a world full of greed, I could never want more

Then someday we'll go all the way
Yeah, someday we'll go all the way
Someday we'll go all the way
Yeah, someday we'll go all the way
Someday we'll go all the way

And here's to the men and the legends we've known
Teaching us faith and giving us hope
United we stand and united we'll fall
Down to our knees the day we win it all

Ernie Banks said "Oh, let's play two"
Or did he mean 200 years
In the same ball park
Our diamond, our jewel
The home of our joy and our tears
Keeping traditions and wishes made new
A place where our grandfathers, fathers they grew
A spiritual feeling if I ever knew
And if you ain't been I am sorry for you
And when the day comes with that last winning run
And I'm crying and covered in beer
I'll look to the sky and know I was right

To think someday we'll go all the way
Yeah, someday we'll go all the way

61 Theo

Theo Epstein is not a Cubs fan, thank goodness. Of course, he wants his employer, the Cubs, to succeed and if and when they do win the World Series there will be nobody more responsible. But a fan? No; and again, that's a wonderful thing.

The last thing the Cubs needed as they set out to rebuild an organization in tatters was somebody with any emotional attachment to the franchise. They needed somebody who was willing to do whatever it took to turn things around, even if it meant tanking a few season to get there.

"There's no glory in 78 wins instead of 73," Epstein famously told the Chicago Tribune's David Haugh before the 2013 season.

That quote, more than any other, epitomizes the difference in Theo Epstein's approach from past attempts to turn things around on the North Side of Chicago. There would be no quick fix, no appeasing season ticketholders, no desperately trying to attain a worthless .500 record.

When the Cubs chairman Tom Ricketts hired Epstein after the 2011 season he was coming off a remarkable run with the Boston Red Sox that had ended on a sour note. The Red Sox, Epstein's favorite childhood team, won the World Series in 2004 to end an 86-year drought then came back again and won it again three years later.

But by 2011, the relationship between Epstein and Red Sox chairman Larry Lucchino had soured

The rebuild centered around two main strategies: Building through the draft and selling off pieces near the trade deadline to acquire younger, cheaper assets.

Who won the Theo Epstein trade?

When Theo Epstein resigned from the Boston Red Sox to become the Cubs' President of Baseball Operations it came with significant controversy. The teams initially couldn't agree on compensation so Major League Baseball stepped in to force the issue, but the teams finally struck a deal.

The Cubs sent the Red Sox minor-league pitchers Chris Carpenter and Aaron Kurcz, with the Cubs receiving 19-year-old infielder Jair Bogaerts, the twin brother of Red Sox shortstop Xander Bogaerts.

So how did it work out? Carpenter pitched six innings for the Red Sox in 2012, walking 10 in six innings, and hasn't been back to the big leagues since. He briefly played in the Japan League in 2014 before signing with Cincinnati in 2015 and being sent to Triple-A. Kurcz was dealt to Atlanta in 2014 and then to Oakland in July 2015.

And what happened to Bogaerts? He was released by the Cubs before the 2012 season even began and retired to become a pro sports agent.

While the jury is still out on Albert Almora, the high school outfielder taken by the Cubs with the sixth overall pick in 2012, they struck gold the next two seasons with a pair of college players. Kris Bryant was the second overall pick in 2013 and Kyle Schwarber the fourth overall pick in 2013. Both are budding superstars who needed just over 500 minor league at-bats before it was clear they were ready.

Starting in 2012, the Cubs began their annual mid-season purge. In 2012, Ryan Dempster was dealt to Texas for third baseman Christian Villanueva and starting pitcher Kyle Hendricks. In 2013, two major deals were made: Steve Clevenger and Scott Feldman went to Baltimore for pitchers Jake Arrieta and Pedro Strop; Matt Garza was sent to Texas for pitchers C.J. Edwards, Justin Grimm, Neil Ramirez and third baseman Mike Olt.

While Arrieta and Hendricks are ensconced in the Cubs' rotation, the coup de grace may have come in 2014 when the Cubs sent Jason Hammel and Jeff Samardzija to Oakland for outfielder Billy McKinney, pitcher Dan Straily, and shortstop Addison Russell, a player previously thought to be untouchable.

Think about all the names you just read: Bryant, Schwarber, Arrieta, Russell, Strop, and Hendricks. All are important pieces who could contribute to the Cubs for years to come, and none of them would have been available if Theo—backed by an extremely capable staff—wasn't committed to a full and unequivocal rebuild.

There was an aura around Theo Epstein based on his success in Boston that suggested just by his coming to the Cubs a World Series title would follow. Incredibly, it did. The Cubs won the 2016 World Series in Epstein's fifth season with the Cubs, and after signing a lucrative five-year contract extension during the season it looks like he'll be around to try and do it again and again and again.

62 Phil Cavarretta: From Lane Tech to Wrigley Field

Growing up in the shadow of Wrigley Field, Phil Cavarretta didn't have money for an elevated train ride let alone a ticket to see the Cubs. So he and his pals would sneak aboard and, after arriving at Wrigley Field, seek out a kindly policeman.

"We'd be there," Cavarretta said in Glenn Stout's *The Cubs*. "And he'd boost us over the fence and into the ballpark."

A few years later, still a teenager, Cavarretta no longer needed any help getting into Wrigley Field. He'd just walk right in with the rest of his Cubs teammates. Cavarretta was just 17 when the Cubs signed him out of Lane Tech High School in the summer of 1934, and in September they called him up to join the Cubs for a few late-season games.

In his first game at Wrigley Field, by now the ripe old age of 18, Cavarretta hit a solo homer on the first pitch he saw in his first at-bat in a 1–0 victory over Cincinnati. It was quite a debut for a hometown boy who would spend the next 20 seasons starring for the Cubs, the longest tenure in team history. Cavarretta's arrival was perfectly timed, as longtime first baseman Charlie Grimm was retiring and a spot was available.

Cavarretta stepped right in as a rookie in 1935 and played like a veteran, hitting .275 with eight homers and 82 RBIs to help the Cubs win the National League pennant. There was little Cavarretta didn't accomplish during his many years with the Cubs. In addition to 1935, the Cubs made it to the World Series in 1938 and 1945, a year in which he hit .355 and was named the NL's Most Valuable Player despite only hitting six home runs. He didn't have much speed or power, but he had a wonderful batting eye. Over

In this September 12, 1945, photo, Phil Cavarretta takes batting practice at Wrigley Field in Chicago. (AP Photo/File)

the course of his career he hit .293 and only struck out 598 times while drawing 820 walks.

You don't play 20 years in one town without earning the respect of the fans, but he also won over the opposition, specifically a first baseman from the New York Yankees by the name of Lou Gehrig. Playing in opposite leagues, Cavarretta and Gehrig hadn't come across each other until they met in the 1938 World Series. In *Wrigleyville*, Peter Golenbock's oral history of the Cubs, Cavarretta explains what happened when he spoke with Gehrig at first base.

"So I was on first base," he said. "Lou was holding me on. Lou was very quiet. Looking back, I could tell from his voice he was starting to get sick then, as young as he was. His voice was very weak. It wasn't a good strong voice.

"He said, 'Young man, you've been in a couple games, but I've watched you play. From what I've seen of you, the way you hustle and the way you give it your best'—this I'll always remember— 'don't change.'"

It's no wonder Gehrig took notice. Cavarretta hit .462 against the Yankees in that Series, despite the Cubs losing in four straight. Seven years later, the Cubs reached the 1945 Series against Detroit and Cavarretta again was a standout, hitting .423 with a homer and five RBIs.

Cavarretta took great pride in the way he played, and later on when he became the player-manager of the Cubs in 1951, he remained honest to a fault. Right before the 1954 season started, Cubs owner P.K. Wrigley asked him to assess the club.

"I told him that our catching staff was shaky, that [Clyde] McCullough isn't getting any younger, and that a year ago [Joe] Garagiola had talked about quitting baseball," Cavarretta told the *Chicago Tribune*. "I reminded him that only a couple of our young ballplayers looked like prospects and that some of our regulars were getting along in baseball age."

For Cavarretta's honesty, after 20 seasons with the Cubs, Wrigley fired him.

Philibuck, a nickname given to Cavarretta by Cubs great Charlie Grimm, moved over to the White Sox for his last two seasons before retiring and becoming a coach and scout for many years. The humble, hard-working kid from Lane Tech passed away on December 18, 2010, at the age of 94 with obituaries stating he was the last surviving player to compete against Babe Ruth.

63 Be Kind to Cardinals Fans

Why be kind to Cardinals fans? Well, when you've dominated another franchise like the Cubs have over the years it's the right thing to do.

It wouldn't be proper for Cubs fans to point out to Cardinals fans that since the two teams first played each other in 1892 it's the Cubs that lead the all-time series, 1,197-1,147. No, that would be wrong to constantly mention. And it certainly wouldn't be nice to gently remind the so-called "Best Fans in Baseball" that the Cubs have never lost a playoff series to the Cardinals.

But just in case you do want to amicably discuss that time the Cubs dismissed the Cardinals from the 2015 playoffs, winning three games to one in the National League Divisional Series, there are some things you need to know.

For example, it's important to know that after the Cardinals easily beat the Cubs in Game 1 and took a 1–0 lead in Game 2 they began to fall apart at the seams. They committed a pair of errors in a 5-run second inning that put the Cubs on top for good.

Make no mistake, this was an historic win. Never before in the history of the MLB playoffs had a team successfully executed two squeeze bunts in the same game and the Cubs did it on consecutive hitters in their 6–3 victory.

It's also good to know that in Game 3 at Wrigley Field, with the wind blowing out and Jake Arrieta on the mound, the Cardinals didn't just lie down and die. They fought to the end, drawing close in the final inning before Cubs closer Hector Rondon nailed down an 8–6 win.

Make no mistake, this was an historic win. The Cubs became the first team in MLB history to hit six home runs in a single playoff game. The first six men in the batting order—Dexter Fowler, Jorge Soler, Kris Bryant, Anthony Rizzo, Starlin Castro, and Kyle Schwarber—each homered before crazed Cubs fans seeing their first home playoff win in 12 years.

That's not all you need to know, of course, because the series didn't end until after the Cubs took care of business in Game 4 thanks to Javier Baez game-turning 3-run homer off Cardinals starter John Lackey and dingers from Rizzo and Schwarber. The home run by Schwarber seemed to get lost in the night as it flew towards Sheffield Avenue before it was finally discovered resting on top of the newly-installed video board.

Make no mistake, this was an historic win. This was the first time the Cubs had ever clinched a playoff series at Wrigley Field. The ensuing celebration after Rondon struck out Stephen Piscotty to cap off a 6–4 win and clinch the series was 99 years in the making.

But don't feel sorry for the Cardinals. Their day will come. Maybe.

64 Horrible Playoff Collapses, Part 3: 1984

Wrigley Field may never have been more beautiful than it was on October 2, 1984. The sky was clear, the sun was shining, and it felt like the center of the universe. If there was a comparable feel to that day it would have been Opening Day, what with the bunting hanging all around and Ernie Banks—Mr. Cub himself—throwing out the first pitch.

But Opening Day is routine; ready or not it comes ever year. To the thousands of Cubs fans there to see Game 1 of the National League Championship Series, it felt magical if not surreal. After 39 years, their Cubs were in the postseason.

Five days later, Wrigley Field was empty. The magic, if there actually had been any, was nowhere to be found and if you weren't numb, then you were sick to your stomach. After 39 years, the Cubs had collapsed in the postseason. The focus will always be on Game 5 and the horrors that befell the Cubs that day in San Diego, but the 1984 National League Championship Series had gotten off to an auspicious start.

Speedy Cubs center fielder Bobby Dernier's home run on the second pitch of Game 1 from Padres starter Eric Show began an onslaught that seemed to exorcise demons that were badly in need of some exorcising. After Ryne Sandberg struck out, Gary Matthews—Dernier's companion in the outfield and the man he was traded to the Cubs with six months earlier—also homered.

Matthews added another home run as did Ron Cey and Cubs starting pitcher Rick Sutcliffe, whose bomb to right field was even more impressive than the two hits he allowed in seven innings. The final score: 13–0.

Dernier got back to basics in Game 2, singling off Padres starter Mark Thurmond and then going from first to third on a routine ground out to third base. It was an incredible show of speed, and when Matthews hit a grounder to short, Dernier came home to again give the Cubs an early advantage.

Steve Trout, whose father, Dizzy, pitched against the Cubs in the 1945 World Series and was the Game 4 winner, took a 4–2 lead into the ninth inning before exiting after a one-out walk that brought the tying run to the plate. Lee Smith came on to strike out former Cub Carmelo Martinez and then terrified the crowd as Padres catcher Terry Kennedy lifted a pitch high into the sky.

Henry Cotto settled under it on the warning track in left field to secure a 4–2 victory and give the Cubs a 2–0 lead in the best-of-five series. The World Series was now one win away. Never before had a National League team won the first two games of a series then lost the final three. This one was in the bag. So when the Padres routed the Cubs 7–1 in Game 3, there wasn't that much worry. Can't win 'em all, right?

Even when Game 4 ended on Steve Garvey's two-run homer off Lee Smith in the bottom of the ninth to set up the series finale a few hours later, there was concern and angst but belief that Sutcliffe, winner of 15 straight games, could not be beaten. And for five innings he looked unbeatable.

While the Cubs were building a 3–0 lead on Leon Durham's two-run homer and Jody Davis' solo shot, Sutcliffe just did his thing. He gave up two hits and a walk before a pair of sacrifice flies in the sixth got the Padres on the board.

Then came the seventh inning, and the series and season crumbled away. It began with a walk to Carmelo Martinez, who the Cubs had dealt for starting pitcher Scott Sanderson. After a sacrifice, Tim Flannery hit a grounder right at Durham. The ball went right under his glove, which had accidentally been soaked with Gatorade during the previous inning. Maybe you don't believe in curses, but if you do, remember that you can't spell Gatorade without G-O-A-T.

Even after the run-scoring error, the game was still tied at 3, but just as Mark Prior remained in too long 19 years later, so did Sutcliffe. He gave up three straight hits, including a two-run double

True or False: Did No Lights Cost the Cubs Home-Field Advantage in the 1984 NLCS?

In Carrie Muskat's terrific book *Banks to Sandberg to Grace*, former Cubs president and general manager Dallas Green pins the blame for the Game 5 loss in the National League Championship Series to the San Diego Padres on the absence of lights in Wrigley Field.

"That's the reason we lost in 1984, in my mind, because we lost the home-field advantage because the television people wouldn't let us have that extra game."

Well, that's false.

In 1984, home-field advantage for the playoffs and the World Series was not based on a team's record or some asinine system of awarding home-field advantage to the winner of the All-Star Game. It was based on a rotating system set up years earlier in which the NL East would get home-field advantage one season, then the NL West the next season. It worked the same way for the World Series. The Padres—winners of the NL West—were entitled to home-field advantage in the 1984 playoffs, just the way it played out.

The confusion has likely come out of what would have happened had the Cubs made it to the World Series that year. In 1984, the NL was due for home-field advantage. But faced with angry NBC-TV executives, baseball commissioner Bowie Kuhn decreed instead that the AL would get home-field advantage.

Cubs manager Jim Frey called it "a stinkin' shame," and shortstop Larry Bowa said, "That's hard to believe." Dallas Green blamed Wrigleyville residents, saying, "I guess the neighborhood got what they wanted then, didn't they?"

So a terrible decision was made to deny the Cubs home-field advantage in 1984. But it was for the World Series, which never came to pass.

by Tony Gwynn that nearly decapitated Ryne Sandberg, before Cubs manager Jim Frey finally yanked him.

The Cubs brought the tying run to the plate in the eighth off Goose Gossage, but Gary Matthews struck out to end the threat. And an inning later when Jody Davis hit into a force, it was all over. One impossibility—the Cubs making the playoffs—had given way to another impossibility. The Cubs really could blow a 2–0 lead.

"It was my loss," Durham said afterward. "My loss. And I don't know quite how to describe the hurt."

More than 30 years later, it still hurts just as much.

65 Visit the Site of the West Side Grounds

There's almost nothing reminiscent of baseball where the old West Side Grounds once stood, just an informational plaque belatedly erected in 2008, so you're going to have to use your imagination a bit.

It isn't too hard if armed with a few facts about the park, such as the names of the old-timers who played there and the history behind some of the games that took place while the Cubs called it home from 1893 until 1915. So just blot out the sterile medical buildings that make up the University of Illinois Medical Center, which now inhabits the block of Wolcott Avenue and Polk, Wood, and Taylor Streets, and let your mind wander.

The double-decked steel and wood structure first opened its doors on May 14, 1893, and it's mandatory to note in any reflection on the Cubs that they, of course, lost their inaugural effort, a 13–12 decision to Cincinnati in which future White Sox owner Charles Comiskey scored the game-winning run.

It cost $30,000 to build, had a capacity of 16,000, and at the time it opened the club was known by any number of nicknames, including the White Stockings, Orphans, and Colts but certainly not the Cubs, a name that didn't come into common use until at least 1903.

This is the place where the legendary Cap Anson became the first major leaguer to collect his 3,000[th] hit, where Tinker, Evers, and Chance inspired a memorable poem and where the Cubs called home while winning four National League pennants and their only World Series titles in 1907 and 1908. If you had stood at this corner on August 5, 1894, you would have seen a fire break out in the stands that destroyed half the stadium and sent thousands clamoring to escape through a barbed-wire fence.

Players had to be called on to tear apart the fence using their bats. There were hundreds of injuries but no fatalities, and the following day the *Tribune* wrote, "That a few dozen people were not killed is exceedingly wonderful."

The group responsible for finally getting a marker erected on the site dubbed itself the The Way Out in Left Field Society, a name based on the slang term "way out in left field," which was possibly derived from the ballpark's proximity to a psychiatric ward. As the story goes, players patrolling left field could overhear patients in the ward. And so the term "way out in left field" came to mean someone was questioning your sanity. The plaque commemorating the ballpark, located next to UIC's Neuropsychiatric Institute at 912 S. Wood, originally referenced this connection, but the sentence was removed after some complaints that it was insensitive.

The final game was played on October 3, 1915, with the Cubs defeating the St. Louis Cardinals 7–2. The following season the Cubs left the West Side Grounds for the North Side's Weeghman Park, later to be renamed Wrigley Field. The ballpark had found a sentimental writer in the *Tribune*'s Ring Lardner, who penned

a poem that was published in the *Tribune* on April 20, 1916, the same day the Cubs played their first game at Weeghman Park. It read:

Now fades the glimmering landscape on the sight.
Save for the chatter of the laboring folk
Returning to their hovels for the night,
All is still at Taylor, Lincoln, Wood, and Polk.
Beneath this aged roof, this grandstand's shade,
Where peanut shucks lie in a mold'ring heap,
Where show the stains of pop and lemonade,
The Cub bugs used to cheer and groan and weep.

66 The Greatest Playoff Comeback Ever

You never want to look beyond the game you're currently playing, and while the Cubs themselves never gave up on Game 4 of the National League Division Series against San Francisco despite trailing 5–2 in the ninth inning, there were no doubt plenty of fans who did. Even worse, what they saw in the future frightened them.

The Giants, winners of 11 straight postseason series and 10 consecutive elimination games, would have stud pitcher Johnny Cueto going in the deciding Game 5 at Wrigley Field, but that wasn't the scariest part. There was little doubt playoff maestro Madison Bumgarner would be called upon to pitch in relief on two days' rest, just as he'd done when he closed out Game 7 of the 2014 World Series with 5 scoreless innings. The duo of Cueto and Bumgarner was by no means a sure thing against Cubs ace Jon Lester and whoever else manager Joe Maddon would have called on. But it was daunting.

The Cubs found the perfect way to foil the Giants' plans: never let Game 5 come to be.

There didn't seem to be any way to avoid it, however, when the Giants easily took control of Game 4 behind the brilliant pitching of left-hander Matt Moore. The Cubs were lucky to only be three runs down, their only runs coming on a David Ross homer in the third and an unearned run in the fifth. When Moore struck out Dexter Fowler looking to end the 8th inning, he'd reached 120 pitches, sure, but he hadn't given up a hit since Anthony Rizzo's leadoff single in the 4th inning.

The Giants bullpen had been one of the worst in baseball all season, and just the night before, in Game 3, they'd blown a 9th-inning lead to the Cubs before prevailing in 13 innings. So it was slightly surprising when Giants manager Bruce Bochy told Moore to call it a night and sent Derek Law out to face Kris Bryant to start the top of the 9th. Bryant found a hole through the infield for a single to start a rally and a merry-go-round of Giants pitchers.

Bochy replaced Law with Javier Lopez to face Rizzo, who promptly walked. Sergio Romo then came on to pitch to Ben Zobrist, who drilled a double down the right-field line to make it 5–3 and put the tying runs in scoring position. Will Smith was called upon to face rookie Willson Contreras, who stunned the crowd with a single up the middle to score Rizzo and Bryant and tie the game.

Jason Heyward tried to bunt Contreras over to second, but his contact was too hard and he hit into a force. Fortunately, Gold Glove shortstop Brandon Crawford threw wildly to first base and Heyward was able to get into scoring position anyway.

That left things up to Javier Baez, who quickly fell behind 0–2 against San Francisco's fifth pitcher of the inning, Hunter Strickland. Inexplicably, Strickland threw a fastball right down the middle on 0–2 that Baez drilled up the middle to miraculously put the Cubs ahead 6–5. The miracle wasn't complete, though. Just as the Cubs had mounted a comeback, the Giants were facing Cubs closer Aroldis

Chapman, who had blown the save in Game 3 the night before and was pitching in his fourth game in five nights. But Chapman easily struck out the side to close out the game and the series.

The Cubs incredible rally was only the fourth time in post-season history that a team trailing by three runs in the 9th inning or later came back to win, and it was the only time in postseason history that any team did it without needing extra innings.

By winning the series in four games, the Cubs were able to set up their rotation for the National League Championship Series just as they wanted. But just as importantly, they avoided playing a Game 5 that nobody in Chicago really wanted to see happen.

67 Remembering Mark Prior

What do you want to remember most about Mark Prior? Because there are options.

You can focus on the way the No. 2 overall pick of the 2001 draft skyrocketed through the Cubs' minor league system in just nine starts, then struck out 10 to beat Pittsburgh in his major league debut at Wrigley Field on May 22, 2002.

Or you can think about how a little more than three months later, he strained his left hamstring running the bases and went on the disabled list for the remainder of the season, finishing 6–6.

You can focus on his glorious 2003 regular season, in which he returned from a four-week stint on the disabled list to go 10–1 with a 1.52 ERA in his final 11 starts to will the Cubs into the postseason.

Or you can think about that postseason when Prior won his first two starts before joining the rest of the Cubs in self-destructing

The Marcus Giles Collision

On July 11, 2003, in the second inning of a game against the Atlanta Braves at Wrigley Field, Mark Prior drew a two-out walk and then took off for second base when the next batter, Mark Grudzielanek, hit a high chopper toward Braves second baseman Marcus Giles.

The resulting collision knocked Giles out cold and left Prior clutching his right shoulder and writhing in pain. Time stood still as Cubs trainer Dave Tumbas came out to examine their prized possession. While Giles left with a mild concussion, Tumbas and the coaching staff allowed Prior to remain in the game. He struck out three of the next four batters he faced but left after $4^2/_3$ innings, having thrown 95 pitches.

Should Prior, who went on the DL with a sore shoulder a few days after the game, have been pulled? And did staying in have an impact on his future? The Cubs may have thought it was a mistake; they didn't retain Tumbas after the season. But Prior's greatest stretch as a Cub came immediately after returning from the injury.

In his first five starts after coming off the disabled list, Prior went 5–0 with an 0.39 ERA, striking out 35 and walking just four in 39 innings. The shoulder was healthy then, and the following spring Prior was sidelined—and missed the first two months of the 2004 season—not by his shoulder but by an inflamed Achilles' tendon.

during that fateful eighth inning of Game 6 in the National League Championship Series.

After that, the memories are pretty much all the same. Prior was healthy at times and on the disabled list at times, but he never again pitched in an important game for the Cubs, other than the ones where fans would watch with hands clasped, praying the old Mark Prior would return to form.

There were a few times he did, like the 16-strikeout game to end the 2004 regular season and the six times he struck out 10-plus in 2005, but there was never any consistency in his performance or in his health.

And so on August 10, 2006, three years to the day after striking out nine in a complete-game win over Los Angeles, Prior allowed six runs on three innings in a start against Milwaukee as questions about his right shoulder, which had undergone arthroscopic surgery, still swirled.

Pitcher Mark Prior throws against the Cincinnati Reds in the first inning on Tuesday, July 19, 2005, in Cincinnati. (AP Photo/Al Behrman)

"We'll see what happens," Prior told the media that day. "Obviously, I haven't pitched well. I didn't pitch well today. We'll see where we're at."

It would be his last appearance as a Cub, and despite years of trying to make a comeback with three different organizations, Prior never returned to the big leagues as a player. He spent 2011 in the Yankees organization but missed three months to a groin injury. In February 2015, Prior became the San Diego Padres' roving minor-league pitching coordinator.

Watching Prior pitch was appointment television for the first two years of his career, not just because he almost always had no-hitter stuff and you wanted to see how many he would whiff, but because it was mesmerizing to see a player with impossible expectations live up to them.

Cubs fans were told he was the perfect pitcher, that his mechanics were so smooth, so sound, that it was impossible for him to break down. He even had a biomechanics guru, former big-league hurler Tom House, who called Prior the "poster child" for the art of using computers, exercise, and coaching in creating pitchers.

Prior was always linked to Kerry Wood, another power pitcher who soared to early success with the Cubs only to be beset by injuries, but Prior never enjoyed the forgiveness Wood received from fans. Where Wood was considered tough, Prior was repeatedly knocked for not pitching through pain.

There was never any validity to the argument, and if anything Prior risked injury and his standing in the court of public opinion by not being more open when he felt pain. Even after his last game with the Cubs, he insisted he felt fine and manager Dusty Baker believed him.

"You take a man at his word when he says he's feeling great," Baker said. "If that's what you think, that's what you say. We just have to see."

68 2007 and 2008: Back-to-Back Titles—and Sweeps

It's amazing what a pile of money spent the right way will do, isn't it?

Okay, not every dollar the Cubs doled out following a 66–96 last-place finish in 2006 went into the most deserving pocket, and some contracts certainly became albatrosses later on, but there can be no doubt that the National League Central titles in 2007 and 2008 were bought and paid for.

After the miserable 2006 season, general manager Jim Hendry handed out contracts worth a total of $209 million to Mark DeRosa (four years, $13 million), Alfonso Soriano (eight years, $136 million), Ted Lilly (four years, $40 million), and Jason Marquis (three years, $20 million).

Add in Aramis Ramirez re-signing for $75 million over five years and a five-year, $90 million deal that Carlos Zambrano inked during the season, and over the course of a few months the Cubs committed more than $360 million to six players.

Hang on, it wasn't over. Hendry also gave Japanese outfielder Kosuke Fukudome a four-year, $48 million contract in December 2007.

That's a lot of Old Style. And it would have been worth it if the Cubs hadn't crapped out in the playoffs both seasons. In their first playoff appearance since 2003, the Cubs opened the 2007 National League Division Series on the road at NL West champion Arizona, a decent but not dominant team. Yet the Cubs were dominated.

In a three-game sweep the Cubs were outscored 16–6 by a Diamondbacks team that finished 14th in the NL in runs scored and dead last in batting average. Aside from the Cubs bats failing to show up, there were two keys to the series.

The first came with the score tied at one in Game 1 when Cubs manager Lou Piniella pulled Zambrano after six innings and only 85 pitches. His reason? He wanted to pitch Zambrano on three day's rest for a potential Game 4. So in the 7th inning, with Big Z on the bench waiting for a Game 4 that would never come, Carlos Marmol gave up a pair of runs and Arizona held on for a 3–1 win.

The most memorable, and somewhat inexplicable moment, came in the bottom of the second inning of Game 2 shortly after the Cubs had gone ahead on Geovany Soto's two-run homer. Lilly served up a gopher ball on a 3–2 two-out pitch to Chris Young that turned a 2–0 lead into a 3–2 deficit.

The Curse of Crane Kenney

The 2008 Cubs were so good and Lou Piniella had done such a good job of ignoring talk about the Billy Goat curse that it wasn't hard to be dumbfounded when Cubs Chairman Crane Kenney inexplicably went and brought in a Greek Orthodox priest to bless their dugout before the start of the playoffs.

Rev. James Greanias was certainly dumbfounded, first when he got a voicemail from Kenney explaining he wanted him to spread holy water in the Cubs' dugout and then a few months later at the 2009 Cubs Convention when Kenney said it was Greanias who had the idea in the first place.

"An e-mail comes in," Kenney told fans, "And this was a huge Cubs fan who wants to get tickets to the game and has a cell phone with a Cubs ring tone on it, and I said, 'Let him go.'"

Greanias responded by telling the *Chicago Tribune* that Kenney was "throwing him under the bus." The idea to bless the dugout with a Greek Orthodox priest because Billy Goat Tavern owner William Sianis was Greek, Greanias said, had come entirely from the Cubs.

"The last thing on my mind was calling the Cubs to ask them to bless the field," Greanias said. "In fact, I thought it was a joke at first."

With the baseball barely departed from Young's bat, Lilly, who once got into a fistfight with his own manager while in Toronto, whirled and with a ferocious turn whipped his glove straight into the ground. It was certainly a huge home run, but Lilly's reaction was way out of proportion to the moment. This was the second inning of Game 2, not the final innings of a potential clincher.

Then again, maybe Lilly knew something. The Cubs never led again in the series, losing 8–4 in Game 2 and then playing like a defeated team in Game 3 at Wrigley Field for a 5–1 loss.

When the 2008 season started, the Cubs were a favorite to again win the NL Central, and they lived up to those expectations despite constant reminders that this was the 100th anniversary of their last World Series title.

Aside from the addition of Fukudome, they had Soto on board for an entire season and his 23 homers and 86 RBIs earned him NL Rookie of the Year honors. Veteran center fielder Jim Edmonds was signed in mid-May after getting cut by San Diego and quickly won over Cubs fans still mindful of his many years in St. Louis.

Not content to wait for the trade deadline, Hendry sent Matt Murton and three prospects to Oakland on July 8 for starting pitcher Rich Harden, whose talent was matched by his inability to stay healthy.

Though he was kept on a tight pitch count and skipped one start in August, Harden pitched brilliantly for the Cubs. He went 5–1 with a 1.77 ERA and allowed three hits or fewer in eight of his 12 starts.

The Cubs led the division most of the season before Milwaukee pulled into a tie on July 26. Two days later, with the lead back up to one, they marched into Miller Park and swept the Brewers in four straight. They never led by fewer than 3½ games the rest of the season and clinched on September 20 at Wrigley Field against the Cardinals.

Pitcher Ted Lilly throws in the second inning against the Florida Marlins during a game at Dolphin Stadium in Miami on Tuesday, September 25, 2007. (AP Photo/Lynne Sladky)

Nothing is ever a foregone conclusion when it comes to the Cubs, but there was an extraordinary amount of confidence heading into the NLDS against the Los Angeles Dodgers, a team that won a weak NL West with 84 wins.

The Dodgers had the best ERA in the National League, but the Cubs outscored them by 155 runs and their starting pitching was so deep that Ted Lilly wasn't going to be needed until Game 4, if it came to that. Well, it didn't.

In an eerie repeat of the previous year's playoff failure, the Cubs again scored a mere six runs in another three-game sweep. Game 1 before 42,099 fans at Wrigley Field was marked by the unraveling of Ryan Dempster, who walked seven and gave up a grand slam to James Loney in the fifth inning to erase a 2–0 Cubs edge, the only time they would lead the entire series.

Game 2 was a disaster. Each member of the Cubs' infield—Derrek Lee, Mark DeRosa, Ryan Theriot, and Aramis Ramirez—committed an error as they fell behind 7–0 en route to a 10–3 loss. Zambrano didn't pitch too poorly, giving up six hits and just three earned runs, but Dodgers starter Chad Billingsley was never in trouble.

There wasn't much need to head to Los Angeles for Game 3. The Cubs were a dead team by this point and quickly fell behind 2–0 in the first inning before losing 3–1. It was their ninth straight playoff defeat, a streak that began with the final three games of the 2003 NLCS.

69 Milt Pappas vs. Bruce Froemming

All that stood between Milt Pappas and a perfect game was one strike. And the way he sees it now, one umpire.

One of the most controversial calls in Cubs history has turned into a bitter 40-year feud between Pappas and Bruce Froemming, the umpire who was calling balls and strikes on September 2, 1972. It was on that day, before a sparse crowd of 12,979 at Wrigley Field, that Pappas retired the first 26 San Diego Padres he faced.

The 27th, a pinch-hitter named Larry Stahl, fell behind in the count 1–2. The next three pitches, according to every eyewitness account, were close. According to Froemming, they were all balls.

TV replays, which haven't helped settle the dispute, show an enraged Pappas immediately move toward home plate and scream a few choice words toward Froemming, who had just turned Pappas into the only pitcher in major league history to lose a perfect game by walking the 27th man he faced.

Pappas, a 33-year-old right-hander in his third season with the Cubs, wrapped up the no-hitter one batter later and showed no ill-will toward Froemming afterward, telling the *Chicago Tribune*, "The pitches were balls. They were borderline but balls. Froemming called a real good game.

"I was just hoping Froemming might sympathize since it was a perfect game. But he couldn't be expected to do that."

Oh, couldn't he be? Since that magnanimous postgame interview, Pappas has changed his tune and will gladly tell anyone within earshot that Froemming should have given him the benefit of the doubt. One of his biggest arguments is that in 1956 when Don Larsen threw a perfect game in the World Series, the home

Pitcher Milt Pappas in a 1971 photo. (AP Photo)

plate umpire appeared to give Larsen a favorable call on the final
pitch.

"It's a home game in Wrigley Field," Pappas told ESPN in
2007. "I'm pitching for the Chicago Cubs. The score is 8–0 in
favor of the Cubs. What does he have to lose by not calling the last
pitch a strike to call a perfect game?"

In 2010, when Detroit Tigers pitcher Armando Galarraga lost
a perfect game on a blown call by first-base umpire Jim Joyce,
the similarities between the two games led to media contacting
Froemming and Pappas to rehash the memory of a game played

nearly 40 years earlier. The biggest difference is that Joyce acknowledged the blown call as soon as he saw a replay, while Froemming made it clear he felt he had nothing to apologize for.

"The pitch was outside. I didn't miss the pitch; Pappas missed the pitch," Froemming told *The New York Times.* "You can look at the tape. Pappas, the next day, said, 'I know the pitch was outside, but you could have given it to me.' That pitch has gotten better over the years. That pitch is right down the middle now."

Pappas retired after getting cut by the Cubs at the end of spring training in 1974 while Froemming, who was in his second season as a big-league umpire in 1972, worked as an umpire for another 35 seasons before retiring in 2007.

The two have run into each other a couple of times over the years, and although they were cordial to each other, Pappas will never forgive and never forget.

"Of course he's never going to change his mind, and I'm never going to change my mind," said Pappas, who passed away on April 19, 2016. "'Til the day I die, it's always going to be the fact that he blew it."

Fiasco: The Milton Bradley Signing

In theory, it all kind of made sense.

See, the Cubs needed a left-handed bat for their lineup, and there was this really good hitter with a whole lot of fire in his belly—a fellow by the name of Milton Bradley—who could not only hit lefty but could draw a whole bunch of walks and pound some homers and boy, if the Cubs could just get him to take their $30 million then they'd be all set.

That was the theory, anyway. In practice, it turned out horribly. The signing of Milton Bradley—coupled with the trade of uber-popular Mark DeRosa to Cleveland—became arguably the worst personnel decision by the Cubs since they thought they needed Broglio more than Brock.

The mystery about the Bradley signing is that he wasn't a mystery when Cubs General Manager Jim Hendry signed him to a three-year, $30 million deal after the 2008 season. Before coming to the Cubs, Bradley had been with six different franchises in nine seasons and often burned bridges.

Cleveland traded him to the Los Angeles Dodgers after he had feuded with Indians manager Eric Wedge, and the Dodgers dealt him two seasons later after he said teammate Jeff Kent, also a prickly sort, "doesn't know how to deal with African American people."

Bradley was with the Padres in 2007 when he got into a run-in with an umpire late in the season and during the argument blew out his knee when one of his own coaches tackled him. A year later he was with Texas and during one game had to be stopped from going into the broadcast booth after hearing a perceived slight.

Still, he hit .321 with 22 homers and drew 80 walks for the Rangers, and he did it as a switch-hitter, which trumped any warning signs that trouble was lurking. On January 9, 2009, Milton Bradley officially became a Cub.

And it might have all worked out if Bradley hadn't forgotten how to hit the ball. Cubs fans have turned on quite a few high-salaried busts over the years—Todd Hundley and Jacque Jones are among the most notorious—but it wasn't because of money, it was because they played poorly.

Bradley started out 3-for-31 and that was pretty much it, he'd lost most of the fans. It didn't help that he was ejected during his Wrigley Field debut for arguing a third-strike call and received a two-game suspension—eventually cut to one game—for making contact with an umpire.

"He's going to swing the bat well, his teammates love him, and we're glad to have him," general manager Jim Hendry said after Bradley's inauspicious Wrigley debut, his head firmly buried in the sand. "He has the respect of the people he has played with in the past and the respect of his opponents, so I would think that says it all."

It was near the end of August when Bradley started to turn on Cubs fans and his meltdown began. On August 25, he told reporters he faced "hatred" on a daily basis in the right-field bleachers, the implication being he was the victim of racist remarks. "All I'm saying is I just pray the game is nine innings, so I can be out there the least amount of time as possible and go home," he said.

Bradley never provided specific examples, and the incident was fading away when on September 17 he told the *Daily Herald*, "You understand why they haven't won in 100 years here.... It's just not a positive environment. I need a stable, healthy, enjoyable environment.... It's just negativity."

In other words, his troubles were everyone else's fault but his own. At this point, Hendry threw up his hands and realized Bradley was a lost cause. He suspended him for the remainder of the season. "The last few days became too much for me to tolerate," Hendry said.

Bradley's teammates, who had defended him during the season, were also fed up. "Sometimes you've just got to look in the mirror and realize that maybe the biggest part of the problem is yourself," Ryan Dempster said.

"In a way, I feel sorry for him," Reed Johnson said. "He can't enjoy the same things the rest of us enjoy."

Even Andre Dawson chimed in, telling the *Tribune*, "You want to give the uniform back, hopefully, on your terms, and not find yourself in the position where you are out of the game or unemployed because of selfish behavior or behavior that is not conducive to what you are trying to accomplish out there on the playing field."

Bradley, who finished the season hitting .257 with 12 homers and 40 RBIs, was pawned off to Seattle in the off-season for Carlos Silva, ending his troubled tenure in Chicago. Meanwhile, the calm, collected, right-handed DeRosa, who hit .250 but clubbed 23 homers, was traded to St. Louis in June where he helped the Cardinals win the National League Central.

The Cubs wanted fire, and that's exactly what they got. They just didn't expect to get burned.

71 The Legend of Kyle Schwarber

As the ball sailed toward the gap between left and center, Kyle Schwarber and Dexter Fowler raced toward it with no sign of slowing down. It wasn't until the last instant that Fowler dipped toward the ground and served as a sort of fulcrum for Schwarber, who flipped over his teammate and rolled onto the warning track before coming to a rest, facedown.

It was evident to anyone who witnessed the violent collision that this had the potential to be a very serious injury, and a day later the news became official: Schwarber had torn ligaments in his left knee and would be out for the remainder of the 2016 season.

A few days later on Opening Day at Wrigley Field, Schwarber, supported by crutches, received a standing ovation from Cubs fans still in shock that they wouldn't get to see him play again until 2017. Cubs management reiterated over the following weeks and months that there was no chance Schwarber would return in 2016. CBSSports.com's Matt Snyder asked a knee surgeon to assess Schwarber's chances of returning, and it wasn't encouraging. "While it is not completely out of the question that he could return for the end of the regular season and postseason," the doctor said, "everything would have to go absolutely perfectly."

The weeks and months of the 2016 season passed, and Schwarber could be seen during home games on a stool in the Cubs dugout cheering on his teammates. Behind the scenes, Schwarber began the grueling and often lonely work of repairing his wrecked knee. In late August, Schwarber hinted a return wasn't out of the question, but Cubs president of baseball operations Theo Epstein shot it down. "No, he can't play this year," Epstein told reporters.

The talk of Schwarber returning had been shot down so swiftly that it was a shock when news trickled out that, as the Cubs were facing the Los Angeles Dodgers in Game 6 of the National League Championship Series, Schwarber would simultaneously be playing in the Arizona Fall League and that the goal was to get him ready to join the Cubs in Cleveland if they made it to the World Series. The Cubs clinched the NL pennant that night and Schwarber went 0-for-3 with a walk for the Mesa Solar Sox as the designated hitter. Two days later, the day before the World Series was scheduled to start, Schwarber appeared in another game and slugged a double in four plate appearances.

The Cubs had seen enough. Schwarber was officially added to the World Series roster and was in the starting lineup as the designated hitter for Game 1 in Cleveland. It had been six and a half months since he'd last faced a major league pitcher, and he was still looking for his first hit of the season. Never before had a non-pitcher had his first hit of the season in the World Series.

Hitting fifth, Schwarber struck out in his first at-bat. But in the fourth inning he drove a pitch to deep right-center that just missed leaving the park. He would end up with a double, his repaired left leg apparently none the worse for wear. This was really happening. Those who doubted Schwarber were stunned as he didn't miss a beat, hitting .412 against Cleveland and becoming a huge factor. When the Cubs took the field in the 10th inning of Game 7, Schwarber was at the plate. He crushed a single to right to start the memorable rally that propelled the Cubs to their first title in 108 years.

A season that began with so much pain and disappointment six and a half months earlier had somehow ended in pure joy, with Kyle Schwarber leading the charge.

There was only one word to describe it: legendary.

72 A Starlin Is Born

If it weren't for hope, Cubs fans wouldn't be Cubs fans and a turnstile of failed phenoms over the years wouldn't have devastated them.

The list of prospects who came to Wrigley Field making hearts flutter but who were eventually run off by a chasing mob includes the likes of Kevin Orie, Felix Pie, Corey Patterson, and the immortal Gary Scott. It was Scott who joined the Cubs in 1991 at the age of 22 saying he'd "like to be the next Ron Santo" and left at 23 with his tail—and a .160 lifetime batting average—between his legs.

So if you weren't expecting a whole lot from Starlin Castro when he joined the Cubs on May 7, 2010, in Cincinnati for his major league debut, who could blame you? A heart can only get broken so many times.

Born and raised in the Dominican Republic, Castro signed with the Cubs at 17 and distinguished himself in two seasons of

Shortstop Starlin Castro throws the ball to first base for the out on the Houston Astros Chris Johnson in the ninth inning on Saturday, October 2, 2010, in Houston. The Cubs won 8–3. (AP Photo/Pat Sullivan)

rookie ball with averages of .299 and .311 before moving on to Single-A Daytona to start the 2009 season.

He headed to Double-A Tennessee after hitting .302 at Daytona and kept it up with a .288 average and the knowledge that he was not only competing but dominating. By then, Castro was considered an untouchable by the Cubs brass, and there was talk of joining the Cubs in 2010, even though he would only turn 20 on March 24.

The Cubs gave him a shot in training camp, but by the end of March Castro had been cut despite a robust .423 batting average in the Cactus League. The only question left was when, not if, Castro would join the Cubs in 2010.

With a .376 average in his first month at Tennessee, Castro was summoned to become the youngest shortstop in Cubs history, bumping Ryan Theriot over to second base in the process.

On the mound for the Reds was right-hander Homer Bailey, himself a one-time phenom. Cubs manager Lou Piniella hit Castro eighth to take a little pressure off him, so his first at-bat didn't come until the second inning with two runners on base.

Of the first four pitches he saw, two were called strikes and on the fifth pitch, Bailey tried to send the bushy-haired rookie back to the bench with a curveball. Castro did head back to the bench after that pitch but not before rocketing it—on the first swing of his major league career—over the right-field fence for an opposite-field three-run homer. Castro had hit only nine home runs in 995 minor-league at-bats, so this was not a matter of a slugger doing what comes naturally.

Three innings later, after lining out, Castro came up with the bases loaded and cleared them with a triple to the gap in left-center, giving him six RBIs in his first three at-bats in the big leagues.

The six RBIs were the most ever by a player in his major league debut, breaking the mark of five held by four other players. Castro also became the sixth Cubs player to homer in his first big-league at-bat.

"I don't believe it," Castro marveled after the game.

The next few weeks indicated Castro was no longer a phenom but a bona fide big leaguer. He hit .310 during the month of May and ended the season at an even .300, finishing with three homers and 41 RBIs. Castro made three All-Star teams and led the NL in hits in 2011 before getting traded to the New York Yankees following the 2015 season.

And a child shall lead them? On a magical Friday night in May, 2010, Cubs fans could only hope.

73 Root for Charlie

It's about time Charlie Root is remembered for what he did than for what Babe Ruth might have done.

What Root did was make more appearances, pitch in more innings, and win more games than anyone else ever has in a Cubs uniform. He also held the Cubs' strikeout record for four decades until Ferguson Jenkins passed him in 1971, a few months after Root's death at the age of 71.

As for Ruth and the supposed Called Shot he hit off Root in Game 3 of the 1932 World Series, there's far more evidence that Ruth was merely gesturing toward Root in anger than pointing toward the seats in center field where his blast ended up.

That part of the story actually makes perfect sense. Root was a tough-as-nails right-hander who backed down to nobody. During the famous at-bat, Root and his teammates were jawing at Ruth. The called shot? It never happened according to Woody English, a Cubs shortstop and third baseman from 1927 until 1936.

"I was right close to it," English says in *Wrigleyville,* Peter Golenbock's oral history of the Cubs. "He's got two strikes on him. The guys are yelling at him from our dugout. He's looking right in our dugout, and he holds up two fingers. He said, 'That's only two strikes.'

Top 10 All-Time Winningest Pitchers Since 1900

If you include the seasons prior to 1900, a couple of 19th-century pitchers would be on this list. Bill Hutchison won 180 games from 1889 to 1895, and Clark Griffith won 152 from 1893 to 1900. However, those were very different times. In 1892, for example, Hutchison went 36–36 and threw 622 innings, completing 67 complete games.

1. Charlie Root, 201
2. Mordecai "Three Finger" Brown, 188
3. Ferguson Jenkins, 167
4. Guy Bush, 152
5. Hippo Vaughn, 151
6. Bill Lee, 139
7. Ed Reulbach, 136
8. Rick Reuschel, 135
9. Greg Maddux, 133
10. Grover Alexander, 128

"But the press box was way back on top of Wrigley Field, and to the people in the press, it looked like he pointed to center field. But he was looking right into our dugout and holding two fingers up. That *is* the true story."

Many others who were at the game give similar accounts, but one who differed was longtime Cubs' public address announcer Pat Pieper who was in his customary spot down the third base line at the time. In 1966, Pieper told the *Chicago Tribune*'s David Condon that Ruth was talking to Cubs pitcher Guy Bush, who was on the bench, when he said, "'That's strike two, all right. But watch this.' Then Ruth pointed to center field and hit his homer. You bet your life Babe Ruth called it."

The legend of the Called Shot had grown to mythical proportions by 1938 when Ed Froelich, a longtime baseball trainer, asked Ruth if he had, indeed, predicted his homer by pointing to the stands. According to Froelich, Ruth's answer was no.

"I may be dumb, but I'm not that dumb," Ruth said. "I'm going to point to the center field bleachers with a barracuda like Root out there?"

Root never stopped telling people the Called Shot never happened and even refused to play himself in the 1948 film, *The Babe Ruth Story*. A couple of grainy films of the historic at-bat were discovered decades later, which made for fun television but resolved little else.

Author Roger Snell, who wrote the richly detailed *Root for the Cubs: Charlie Root & the 1929 Chicago Cubs*, was sympathetic to Root in his portrayal but after viewing film shot by Matt Kandle Sr., he wasn't able to say with certainty what happened.

"The film refutes the exaggeration of Ruth standing defiantly at the plate, pointing toward the fence, obviously calling his shot," Snell writes. "Instead, it is more obvious that Ruth was yelling back to the heckling Cubs that he was going to get even. His bat did the rest."

Root pitched in four World Series for the Cubs, going 0–3 with a 6.75 ERA, and started one of the Cubs most painful losses ever, a 10–8 defeat to the Philadelphia Athletics in the 1929 World Series in which the Cubs led 8–0 in the seventh inning.

When he finally hung up his cleats after the 1941 season, he was 42 years old and had 201 career wins. Given that kind of longevity, it's not surprising his 156 losses are the most by a Cub since 1900. Was he the greatest Cubs right-hander ever? Mordecai "Three Finger" Brown, Ferguson Jenkins, and Greg Maddux might have something to say about that.

But Root was certainly one of the best, even if he won't be remembered that way. He knew this, too, which he told his daughter, Della, on the day he died.

"Isn't it funny?" he said. "I gave my whole life to baseball, and I'll be remembered for something that never happened."

74 The Legend of Tuffy Rhodes

"Tuffy Rhodes" is the answer to one of the great Cubs trivia questions: Which Cubs player once hit three home runs on Opening Day off Dwight Gooden?

"No" is the answer to a related Cubs trivia question: Did the Cubs win the game?

It's unbelievable but sadly also true. In 1994, the Cubs got three homers from their new center-fielder in one of the most electrifying Opening Day performances in baseball history yet still managed to come out on the wrong end of a 12–8 contest.

That is so Cubs.

Karl "Tuffy" Rhodes was a classic "4-A" player. He tore up Triple-A in 1993, hitting .318 with 30 homers and 89 RBIs in just 123 games but never proved he could hit major league pitching. In parts of four seasons with Houston, he hit .219 with a pair of homers and 15 RBIs.

Rhodes was in the Royals farm system when the Cubs picked him up in a 1993 trade deadline deal that sent lefty reliever Paul Assenmacher to the New York Yankees then impressed the Cubs in a late-season call-up by hitting .288 with three home runs.

He came to spring training with the leadoff job his to lose and easily kept it, finishing at .318 with a pair of homers and 11 walks. New Cubs manager Tom Trebelhorn had his Opening Day center fielder.

Dwight Gooden's career had entered its downward trajectory when he got the start to face the Cubs on Opening Day, but the year before he'd won 12 games and had a 3.45 earned-run average.

Rhodes didn't waste any time. He homered in each of his first three at-bats with a 22-mph wind at his back. All three homers went into the left-field bleachers, and after the third an onslaught of hats—a hat trick, get it?—rained down from the stands.

Said Mets manager Dallas Green, "We made him a legend."

"After the first home run, I was geeked. You know, geeked. That's slang for excited," he said after the game. "After the second one, I was a little more calm. I never thought I could hit two homers in a game. Then when I hit the third one, I was frightened."

Imagine how he would have felt if he hadn't walked and singled in his final two plate appearances. All in all, it was a productive day for the 25-year-old. Unfortunately, there weren't many more to follow.

Rhodes finished April with six homers, including a pair he hit against the Astros on April 28, but then he hit just .194 in May and was out of the Cubs' starting lineup by the end of June. He only hit two more before a player's strike ended the season in early August, and in 1995 he didn't break camp with the team and was claimed on waivers by Boston on May 26, less than 14 months after his historic three-homer game.

In 1996, Rhodes went to Japan to play and became a legend once again. His 474 home runs in the Nippon Baseball League are the most ever by a foreign-born player.

75 The Joe Maddon Way

In order for Joe Maddon to become the manager of the Cubs, many things had to happen in fairly quick succession.

The Los Angeles Dodgers had to relieve General Manager Ned Colletti of his duties, Tampa Bay's Vice President of Baseball Operations Andrew Friedman had to get hired away by the

Dodgers, and Maddon had to have a clause in his contract that allowed him to leave Tampa Bay if Friedman ever left his job.

Oh, and one more thing: The Cubs had to fire Rick Renteria, a manager they were perfectly content with. And therein lied the problem with Renteria: he was not special. A good baseball man, certainly. Better than previous Cubs manager Dale Sveum, definitely. But special? No, Renteria was not special.

Joe Maddon? He's special.

So when he became available the Cubs had little choice but to pursue him even though Renteria had just been given a public pat on the back by the organization two weeks earlier. Within days, Renteria was fired, Maddon was hired, and the rebuilding of the Cubs continued with a new man at the helm.

The press conference to introduce Maddon left no doubt the right man had been hired. He held court at the Cubby Bear in Wrigleyville, with quote after quote that indicated he wasn't just any other manager.

On winning a World Series: "I'm going to be talking World Series this year. I promise you, I am. And I'm gonna believe it. And I'm gonna see how this is all gonna play out and it's within our future there's no question about that."

On the pressure to win: "Don't ever permit the pressure to exceed the pleasure."

On his age: "60's the new 40."

And just as it ended, Maddon announced he was buying everyone a round. "A shot and a beer," he said. "The Hazleton way."

The kid from Hazleton, Pennsylvania didn't hide away waiting for spring training to start. He engaged the Cubs community and sent out this tweet via @CubsJoeMadd in early December: "Respect 90...going to make daily push for our players to respect that distance..run hard for 90 feet, and the respect will come back to you."

That demand to respect the game, run out every ball, and play to the last out resonated with Cubs fans, especially when they saw "Respect 90" stenciled into the grass at the Cubs spring training complex in Mesa, Arizona.

Maddon's unconventional ways weren't just theoretical; they carried over into the regular season as well. Most notably in early August when he benched starting shortstop Starlin Castro and gave his job to Addison Russell, a rookie who was only hitting around .235 at the time. There was no attempt to sugarcoat such a move, as previous managers had done. He told Castro upfront this was not temporary.

"You do not paint any kind of obscure picture that he has to read between the lines, and (you're) very upfront about it," Maddon said. "He's a man. He can deal with it. We'll be better for it. He's going to be better for it too. Yes, you're always concerned about the emotional component. But at the end of the day, it's about the Cubs winning."

That's the Joe Maddon way.

76 Tom Trebelhorn's Town Meeting

There is exactly one lasting memory from Tom Trebelhorn's 113-game tenure as Cubs manager, and it didn't take place at Wrigley Field or any other major league ballpark.

It took place at a Wrigleyville fire station with Cubs security guards genuinely concerned for Trebelhorn's safety.

In 1994, the Cubs were not expected to be competitive and to be sure, they weren't. They got swept by the New York Mets in their season-opening three-game series at Wrigley, and by the time they returned from a late April road trip they were a measly 6–14, including 0–8 at home.

Following the last game of the trip, Trebelhorn made a vow: "If we don't beat Colorado tomorrow, I'll be on the park bench in front of the [Waveland Avenue] fire station holding a fan conference after the game," he said. "I'll be taking all questions after the game. When we win, I'll be there to accept congratulations. Rain or shine, I'll be there."

A pretty nice show of confidence from a guy whose team just didn't have the horses. Aside from 25-year-old Sammy Sosa, who would finish this strike-shortened season with 25 homers and 70 RBIs, they had little offense. Ryne Sandberg was still a Cub, but his heart wasn't in it and he would retire a few weeks later.

The pitching staff, led by 23-year-old rookie Steve Trachsel, was too young and too ineffective. The only thing that could prevent this team from chugging along in last place was a work stoppage, but that relief was still 3½ months away.

When the Cubs lost to the Rockies for their ninth straight home loss, their worst start ever at Wrigley Field, Trebelhorn was on the hook to talk to some angry fans. Not that going 1–8 to start the season would have assuaged the 200 or so fans who came out to greet Trebelhorn about an hour after the game.

The mood was tense when he arrived flanked by a quartet of Cubs' security guards. Some fans, perhaps greased by a few Old Styles, were burning copies of the Tribune Co.-owned *Chicago Tribune* and chanting epithets.

Cubs players and coaches are public figures, so it's not rare to come across one of them in public and give them your two cents. That's something everybody is used to. What nobody had ever seen was a manager take it upon himself to face fed-up fans who for years lived with an absentee owner in Phil Wrigley and a faceless corporate owner in the Tribune Company.

Trebelhorn not only took it like a man but the former teacher won over the crowd. His opening line of, "Okay. Now what do you want to know?" didn't settle down the loose cannons right away, but after a few minutes he was engaging them with actual dialogue. Instead of screams and jeers, Trebelhorn took questions and answered them as honestly as he could, even saying, "The guy was a dumb [expletive]" to describe a recent bad decision by one of his players.

The entire episode lasted 30 minutes and ended with Trebelhorn getting applauded by the crowd for meeting them and then having a chicken dinner with the Engine Co. 78 firefighters.

If this had been the movies, Trebelhorn would have walked off to the sounds of up-tempo music with a quick cut to a montage of the Cubs winning game after game. Instead, they lost three more in a row at home and finished 49–64, the second-worst record in the National League, and Trebelhorn was fired.

But at least he survived.

77 As Bad As It Gets

There have been worse teams in Cubs history than the 1997 squad. Sadly enough, since then four teams have been worse if you go by record alone.

But no Cubs team, and no team in the history of the National League, ever got off to a worse start than the 1997 Cubs. They began their season, appropriately enough, on April Fool's Day and didn't win until April 20—a horrendous 0–14 start.

The schedule looked daunting having to face Florida and Atlanta's prized starting rotations in their first 10 games. It didn't help that free-agent signee Kevin Tapani was already on the disabled list and was expected to miss significant time with a finger injury.

Here's a closer look at how the worst start in NL history unfolded:

0–1: Florida 4, Cubs 2, Pro Player Stadium, April 1
What happened: Kevin Brown allowed one hit over seven innings, and rookie Cubs third baseman Kevin Orie tried to let a bunt by Edgar Renteria go foul. It didn't, and Renteria wound up on second base with a bunt double.
The quote: "We can play a lot better than that, and we will."—Cubs manager Jim Riggleman.

0–2: Florida 4, Cubs 3, Pro Player Stadium, April 2
What happened: The Cubs committed three errors, giving them five in two games, yet all four runs Cubs starter Steve Trachsel gave up were earned. Mark Grace homered and drove in all three runs.
The quote: "I don't know what's going on...we've got to get better. It's all concentration."—Mark Grace.

0–3: Florida 8, Cubs 2, Pro Player Stadium, April 3
What happened: Frank Castillo gave up five runs in the first inning, and the Cubs lost Grace to a hamstring injury.
The quote: "Hopefully it won't carry over into the next series, and we'll get a mulligan there."—Jim Riggleman.

0–4: Atlanta 5, Cubs 4, Turner Field, April 4
What happened: The Cubs took their first lead of the season but Terry Adams blew the save, giving up two unearned runs in the eighth.

The quote: "We knew it'd be a difficult two weeks, and we'd just try to deal with it."—Cubs General Manager Ed Lynch.

0–5: Atlanta 11, Cubs 5, Turner Field, April 5–6

What happened: Faulty lighting and rain caused the game to go deep into the night, and it was eventually suspended with Atlanta leading 8–5 in the bottom of the seventh. The Braves finished off the Cubs the following afternoon before their regularly scheduled game. Sammy Sosa went 1-for-5 to raise his average to .105.

0–6: Atlanta 4, Cubs 0, Turner Field, April 6

What happened: Greg Maddux toyed with the Cubs, allowing three hits over eight innings. Mel Rojas gave up a run in one inning to lower his ERA to 18.00

The quote: "At home, we'll play a little better...but we're not scared, and we won't panic."—Sammy Sosa.

0–7: Florida 5, Cubs 3, Wrigley Field, April 8

What happened: The wind chill was 1 above zero and the temperature was a balmy 29 degrees in the Cubs' home opener. Sammy Sosa hit his first homer, but Trachsel couldn't hold a 3–2 lead in the seventh.

The quote: "It hurts a lot. Anybody who says it doesn't hurt is lying."—Cubs catcher Scott Servais.

0–8: Florida 1, Cubs 0, Wrigley Field, April 10

What happened: Dave Hansen broke up Marlins pitcher Alex Fernandez's no-hit bid with one out in the ninth, but the Cubs set a team record for worst start ever. Afterward, team veterans called a players-only meeting.

The quote: "That was a good thing. They have some things they want to express to each other, and that's what they did."—Jim Riggleman.

0–9: Atlanta 2, Cubs 1, Wrigley Field, April 12

What happened: Again facing Maddux, the Cubs managed an unearned run but never held a lead. At this point, they had led in only five out of the season's 79 innings.

The quote: "Good thing it's not football where you've got to wait until next week [to play again]."—Cubs shortstop Shawon Dunston.

0–10: Atlanta 6, Cubs 4, Wrigley Field, April 13

What happened: The Braves broke a 4–4 tie with a pair of runs in the eighth. Brant Brown's line-drive foul ball into the Cubs' dugout hit Ryne Sandberg in the right ear. He left the game and needed stitches.

The quote: "The baseball gods aren't with the Cubs, and I don't know why."—Steve Trachsel.

0–11: Colorado 10, Cubs 7, Wrigley Field, April 15

What happened: Cubs pitchers gave up five homers, including Rockies pitcher Mark Thompson's first of his career, as the team set the NL record for most losses to start a season.

The quote: "We're 0–11. But it's going to change. That's all I can tell you."—Sammy Sosa.

0–12: Colorado 4, Cubs 0, Wrigley Field, April 16

What happened: Cubs catcher Tyler Houston dropped strike three and chased Larry Walker to first base, forgetting Quinton McCracken was on third base and he easily stole home. Someone named Roger Bailey shut out the

Cubs on five hits. He never pitched in the big leagues again after 1997.

The quote: "We are all embarrassed today."—Jim Riggleman.

0–13: New York Mets 6, Cubs 3, Shea Stadium, April 19
What happened: The 13th loss came when No. 13 Turk Wendell allowed the 13th unearned run of the season by the Cubs. Mark Grace returned from the disabled list and went 0-for-2 with two walks.

The quote: "This is a good ballclub. We're just not showing it on the field. We don't have any losers here."—Cubs outfielder Dave Clark.

0–14: New York Mets 8, Cubs 2, Shea Stadium, April 20
What happened: In the first game of a doubleheader, the Cubs moved past the 1904 Washington Senators and 1920 Detroit Tigers for the second-worst start in major league history, trailing only the 1988 Baltimore Orioles, who lost 21 straight.

1–14: Cubs 4, New York Mets 3, Shea Stadium, April 20
What happened: The Cubs led 4–1 after seven innings and hung on despite Turk Wendell giving up two in the ninth. He got Manny Alexander to ground out with the tying run on second base.

The quote: "Thank God. Something positive to talk about. We won a game. We're 1–14. That's atrocious, but I'm going to have a little fun tonight."—Mark Grace.

78 The Double No-Hitter

Jim "Hippo" Vaughn deserved better. His less-than-flattering nickname may be more memorable than what he should be best known for, which is his status as the best left-hander in Cubs history and a prominent role in arguably the best-pitched game in major league history.

The man wasn't a tiny thing like Greg Maddux, but at 6'4" and 215 pounds he wasn't exactly a hippo, either. When a nickname sticks there isn't much you can do about it and Hippo he was, and Hippo he'll stay.

He hadn't crafted much of a career when the Cubs picked him up in a minor-league deal near the end of the 1913 season, but from that point on he was among the most dominant pitchers in baseball. From 1914 through 1919 he went 124–77 with a 2.10 ERA and averaged 292 innings per season.

During the 1918 World Series, which the Cubs lost to the Boston Red Sox in six games, Vaughn threw three complete games and allowed only three earned runs in 27 innings. Vaughn won only one of the three games. Not surprising considering he had an established history of losing games in which he pitched brilliantly.

The best example of that took place on May 2, 1917, at Wrigley Field, then known as Weeghman Park, in a game commonly known as the "double no-hitter." That's actually an inaccurate description of the game in which Vaughn faced Cincinnati's Fred Toney. At least not by modern definitions of what constitutes a no-hitter.

It's true neither man allowed a hit through nine innings, but when Vaughn gave up a single with one out in the top of the 10th inning, his no-no was gone. The Reds got another hit as well as a

Near-Miss No-No's

The Cubs have had dozens of near no-hitters over the years, but a few stand out among the rest for their timing.

In April 1934, four years before Johnny Vander Meer threw back-to-back no-hitters, Cubs right-hander Lon Warneke tossed back-to-back one-hitters, including one on Opening Day in which he lost the no-no with one out in the ninth.

That feat hasn't been matched by any other Cub, but on May 24–25, 2001, they got another version of back-to-back near misses when Jon Lieber and Kerry Wood threw one-hitters on consecutive days against Cincinnati and Milwaukee.

The best timing for a one-hitter may have been on October 5, 1945. That's the day Cubs right-hander Claude Passeau gave up a second-inning single to Detroit's Rudy York and nothing else. What made that one-hitter so special? It came during Game 3 of the 1945 World Series. And 39 years earlier, on October 10, 1906, Ed Reulbach became the first player to throw a one-hitter in the World Series when he beat the White Sox in Game 2, a 7–1 Cubs win.

run in the 10th and Toney set down the Cubs to win the game 1–0 and finish off his no-hitter.

Vaughn, who faced the minimum 27 batters thanks to three double plays, was probably the more dominant pitcher that day as he struck out 10 while Toney only fanned three Cubs. The oddity of the event, which hasn't been repeated in the major leagues, is even more interesting when you take a look at the other players who figured in the pivotal 10th.

With one out, Cincinnati got its first hit from shortstop Larry Kopf, whose liner to right field fell just in front of a diving Fred Merkle. That's right, the same Fred Merkle whose infamous "boner" in 1908 helped the Cubs win the National League pennant.

With the no-hitter gone, Vaughn got the second out but center fielder Cy Williams dropped a ball for an error to put runners at the corners. The next batter up, Jim Thorpe, hit a swinging bunt that Vaughn fielded, but Kopf beat his throw to the plate.

That's right, the same Jim Thorpe who won Olympic medals, starred in the NFL, and many consider the greatest athlete of the 20th century. He had only 176 hits and 82 RBIs in his career but in this game had one of each that made the difference.

Vaughn, whose 151 victories with the Cubs are the most by any left-hander, ended up leaving the team and ending his major league career over bizarre circumstances. After the 1920 season, he was stabbed in the stomach by his father-in-law in an argument related to his pending divorce.

Although news reports at the time said the wound wouldn't threaten his career, he wasn't the same pitcher in 1921. He went 3–11 with a 6.01 ERA and after a dismal performance against New York decided he'd had enough and left the team.

Cubs manager Johnny Evers suspended Vaughn, who in turn signed a contract with a semi-pro team in Wisconsin. When Evers was fired a week into the suspension, Vaughn was going to be reinstated. However, baseball commissioner Kenesaw Mountain Landis viewed signing a contract with another league as practically treason and suspended him for the rest of the year.

Vaughn never returned to the majors.

79 Blame Norman Rockwell

If it's your thing to look to curses to explain the Cubs century of futility, then don't forget about artist Norman Rockwell, whose iconic 1948 *Saturday Evening Post* cover of four dejected players and a forlorn bat boy being jeered by fans seared the impression into the minds of Americans that the Cubs were a laughingstock.

There's no ambiguity in "The Dugout," which appeared on the cover of September 4, 1948, edition of the *Post*. The visiting Cubs, depicted in their road uniforms, are not only clearly losing and getting mercilessly mocked by fans but their faces and body language suggest they've also given up. It's quite damning, actually. The original watercolor painting is owned by the Brooklyn Museum and occasionally appears on display, most recently in a Rockwell retrospective in early 2011. Another version was auctioned off in 2009 and sold to an anonymous collector for $662,500, slightly less than what it was expected to go for.

The players depicted in the illustration were not figments of Rockwell's imagination but actual members of the Cubs organization who posed on May 23, 1948, before a doubleheader against the Boston Braves at Braves Field. The four players, from left to right, are pitcher Bob Rush, manager Charlie Grimm, catcher Al Walker, and pitcher Johnny Schmitz, according to the Norman Rockwell Museum in Stockbridge, Massachusetts.

The bat boy was the Braves' visiting team bat boy at the time, a 17-year-old named Frank McNulty who went on to become president of *Parade* magazine and mayor of the coastal South Carolina town of Seabrook Island. McNulty had a hard time looking sad and only achieved his glum expression after Rockwell told him to imagine his dog had died.

The history behind the cover is fairly well-documented, with one notable exception. There doesn't appear to be any rhyme or reason why Rockwell chose the Cubs. Living and working near Boston in Stockbridge, Mass., he could easily have visited Fenway Park, home to the American League's Boston Red Sox, to find a subject.

The late May date suggests he waited until the weather turned a bit warmer to head out to the ballpark, but that's just conjecture. The Cubs were one of six teams the Braves hosted on a 12-game homestand, the others being the Pittsburgh Pirates, St. Louis

Cardinals, Brooklyn Dodgers, Cincinnati Reds, and Philadelphia Phillies.

The Cardinals wouldn't have made sense, they were perennial contenders and had just come off a stretch in which they had won three World Series in five seasons. The Reds had been world champs as recently as 1940, and the Dodgers had lost the 1947 World Series. The Pirates were in a down period but had been above .500 most of the previous two decades.

The obvious choice should have been the Phillies. In 1948, they had only been to one World Series—which they had lost—and in the prior 30 seasons had finished above .500 just once while losing 100 games or more 12 different times. Yet the Cubs were immortalized by Rockwell despite having gone to the World Series five times since 1929, albeit losing all of them.

So why the Cubs? Well, possibly because they were the only team to agree to let Rockwell depict them in such a state. A letter from *Post* art editor Ken Stuart to the Rockwell Museum states that owner Phil Wrigley agreed to let his Cubs pose.

Nobody could have imagined the illustration would still have legs decades later, but if the outcome of that May 23, 1948, doubleheader was any indication, it shouldn't have come as a surprise. The Cubs got swept.

80 Visit Catalina Island

For three decades, the Cubs began their journey toward what they hoped would be baseball glory at Chicago's Dearborn Street Station. It was there they'd gather in front of reporters, photographers, and a multitude of fawning fans bearing gifts to board the

Santa Fe and head off on a three-day train ride toward spring training on Catalina Island.

"An hour before the train pulled out of Chicago there were a thousand bugs and bugettes in the station," wrote the *Chicago Tribune*'s Irving Vaughan in 1930. "All anxious to get one more closeup of men they have seen innumerable times before."

The train would arrive in Los Angeles, and the players, coaches, and popular trainer Andy Lotshaw would then board the S.S. *Catalina* and arrive in Avalon Bay to be greeted by their adoring fans on the West Coast, the few thousand residents of Catalina Island.

Located off the shore of Southern California, Catalina Island is undoubtedly the most idyllic spring base any baseball team ever had. It was home to the Cubs from 1921 until 1951, the only gap taking place during World War II.

What drew them there was the balmy weather, comfortable housing, training facilities, and the fact that in 1919 the island had been purchased by Cubs owner William Wrigley Jr.

The baseball diamond where the Cubs used to train on Catalina is gone, replaced by a soccer field. A fire station and city hall are where the outfield used to be. The spot is only marked by a single commemorative plaque that has moved around over the years.

A skip and a jump away is the old clubhouse, which years ago was renovated and turned into the Catalina Country Club, now a public golf club with a dining room that's lined with Cubs photographs and memorabilia. Phil Wrigley, who owned the Cubs from 1932 until his death in 1977, turned 88 percent of the island into a conservancy in the 1970s, while the rest of the island consists of the city of Avalon.

"It hasn't changed that much," said Jeannine Pedersen, curator of the Catalina Island Museum, which has Stan Hack's glove and a signed baseball from the 1932 team among its Cubs treasures. "The town is pretty much how it was. Still kind of a quaint small town just like when they were here."

Jim Vitti's book, *Baseball on Catalina Island*, is packed with wonderful pictures and tales of mischievous behavior, and it is a treasure in itself. The photos, which often made their way into Chicago's many daily newspapers, depict joyous players almost always in uniform whether they were at practice, playing golf, fishing, walking the beach, or hamming it up with the ostriches at the old Bird Park.

In one of the photos, 18-year-old Lolo Saldana and his buddies are wearing Cubs uniforms passed down to the kids over the years. Saldana, now 86, still lives on Catalina and regularly regales customers at his barber shop with stories from the Cubs years on the island.

He has many pieces of memorabilia, including his Hack Wilson uniform, a fungo bat used by Cubs manager Charlie Grimm, and many cherished memories, like the time Grimm gave him and one of his pals a tryout.

"Grimm says, 'I want to work you two guys out—be at the ballpark at 2:00 PM and see what you've got.' We went out, and he gave us a workout," Saldana recalled. "He made us feel real good."

The Cubs last spring on Catalina was in 1952, it was no longer practical to hold spring training on an island that had only one baseball field and was far removed from the other teams. So off to Arizona they went.

"It was kind of sad when they left," Saldana said. "They lit the whole island up."

81 Who Killed Sosa's Boom Box?

It's not on par with what happened to Amelia Earhart, the true identity of Deep Throat, or even who shot J.R., but in the annals of Cubs history, there may be no greater mystery in need of solving than the identity of who destroyed Sammy Sosa's boom box.

The background: Sosa's selfishness on the field extended to the clubhouse, where he would play the same loud music over and over again. Remember, this was Sosa's clubhouse, and nobody else had a say. Why would they? It was his house, as he liked to say, and he made the rules.

Doug Glanville, an outfielder with the Cubs in 1996 and 1997 and again in 2003, remembers giving Sosa a copy of "Killing Me Softly" by the Fugees. "I didn't realize he was going to play this song in a perpetual loop," Glanville told *Chicago Magazine*. "He'd get stuck on a song, and even if it was a good song, people were like, 'Okay, we kind of heard this 35 times today.'"

When Sosa deserted his teammates on the final day of the 2004 season, leaving Wrigley Field in the first inning and then lying about it later on, nobody knew it would be his last season with the Cubs. That decision wasn't final until just before spring training when he was traded to Baltimore.

So when a teammate exacted some retribution that day by taking some big-league swings to Sosa's boom box, it wasn't a cowardly act done with the knowledge Sosa wouldn't be returning. It was simply necessary and a wee bit cathartic.

There was intense interest in the culprit from the start, and an anti-Sosa website even started selling T-shirts that declared, "I smashed Sammy's boombox." Nobody has publicly admitted being the boom-box executioner, though there have been some attempts at outings that have always met with swift denials.

One of the immediate prime suspects was Kerry Wood, a veteran in the clubhouse whose hot temper some thought might lead to, you know, bashing a boom box. Shortly after the season ended, and before Sosa was traded, Wood was asked point-blank if it was him by *Chicago Tribune*'s Cubs beat writer Paul Sullivan.

"I don't have the balls to do that," said Wood, who added there were times when he felt like doing that.

In 2009, *Chicago Sun-Times* Cubs beat writer Gordon Wittenmyer spoke with Paul Bako, backup catcher with the 2004 Cubs and a suspect because of the proximity of his locker to Sosa's locker. Bako denied it was him.

"I shouldn't even say this much," Bako said. "But I can tell you it was not me."

There have been other suspects as well, notably former Cubs catcher Michael Barrett who had been guilty of engaging in two notorious fights, one with White Sox catcher A.J. Pierzynski and the other with teammate, pitcher Carlos Zambrano. Whether he's guilty of bludgeoning Sosa's boom box is just speculation.

In the spring of 2005, Sosa was asked about the incident and his response, as you might expect, did not help solve the mystery and even led to another.

"I don't really care," Sosa said. "You know why? Because when the man is not in the house, the chickens are jumping around."

The chickens are jumping around? What does that even mean? The world may never know.

82 Let's Play Two!

Forgive the misleading title, this isn't about Ernie Banks. It's just hard to resist getting a little silly when you're preparing to tell the story of one of the craziest plays in Cubs history.

On June 30, 1959, as the Cubs approached the first All-Star break (there were two midsummer classics played for several years), they were treading water. They were 36–36 and trailed the Milwaukee Braves by six games en route to a 74–80 record and a fifth-place finish.

The only exciting baseball to be found in Chicago came from the Go-Go White Sox, who were cruising to the American League pennant, and from Banks, who was cruising to his second straight National League MVP award.

Banks was so dominant and the rest of the team so mediocre that his 45 homers and 143 RBIs were 31 homers and 91 RBIs more than the next highest totals on the club. It was a rather quiet summer at Wrigley Field.

That is, except for the time a Laurel and Hardy routine broke out one Tuesday afternoon.

The Cubs trailed St. Louis 2–1 in the fourth inning when Cardinals legend Stan Musial came to the plate with one out against Bob Anderson. Musial ran the count to 3–1 and then took an inside pitch that also got past catcher Sammy Taylor.

According to the July 1, 1959, edition of the *Chicago Tribune*, instead of going after the ball, Taylor started arguing with home-plate umpire Vic Delmore over whether the ball had hit the bat of Musial, who in the meantime had drawn a walk and had jogged to first base.

The baseball, ignored for a time by every Cubs infielder, was picked up by bat boy Bob Schoenfeldt, who tried to toss it to long-time field announcer Pat Pieper, the man responsible for furnishing baseballs to the umpires.

Musial, meanwhile, realized nobody was paying attention to him and took off for second. Cubs third baseman Alvin Dark, who later managed the Oakland A's to the 1974 World Series title, grabbed the ball from the ground in front of Pieper and threw to second to try and get an advancing Musial. This is when hilarity began to ensue. Umpire Delmore, thinking a new ball was needed, gave one to Anderson, who also had the good sense to try and throw out Musial at second.

So to be clear, at this point there are two live balls in play. For those of you new to baseball, that's one too many.

The ball that Anderson threw sailed far over second baseman Tony Taylor's head and into center field as Musial pulled up safely at second. Meanwhile the ball Dark threw—the original live baseball—bounced into second base where Banks, playing shortstop, fielded it and put a tag on Musial, who had taken off for third after seeing a baseball land in center field.

The umpires gathered and after a discussion that took place with animated managers and players milling about, Musial was finally called out. The Cardinals played the game under protest, which was a moot point since they ended up winning the game 4–1. In the *Tribune* write-up the next morning, reporter Ed Prell relayed several accounts from the participants.

Musial: "I heard our bench yelling for me to run. When I slid into second base, I saw [Taylor] had the ball. I got up and started for third, never feeling a tag...the umpires finally told me to go back to first and later that I was out."

Schoenfeldt: "I saw Dark flying toward me, but I had already thrown the ball away."

Pieper: "I let the ball lie right there after the boy threw it toward me. Dark yelled at me, 'Give me the ball.' I told him to pick it up. I never touched it."

Umpire Al Barlick, the crew chief, had the final say: "When Dark charged in from third base I thought he was joining the argument. But he picked the ball up in front of Pieper. Musial was safe, but as he rounded the bag, Banks tagged him with the ball Dark had thrown. This was the ball that was in play. The other ball was not."

Got it?

83 Wild Thing

On Opening Day 1989, three days before *Major League* premiered around the country with Charlie Sheen portraying intense closer Ricky "Wild Thing" Vaughn, Mitch Williams made his Cubs debut. The timing was perfect, and by its imperfection so was Williams' execution in his initial outing.

Williams, a left-hander whose full-bodied delivery often ended with him flat on the ground, entered in the eighth inning with one out and the Cubs leading Philadelphia 5–4. Between a pair of fly outs, Williams walked a pair and committed a balk. That was a state of grace compared to what came in the ninth.

The first three hitters all singled, leaving the bases loaded for Mike Schmidt, a fearsome Cub killer who hit 50 homers at Wrigley Field during his career, tied for the second-most ever with Hank Aaron and trailing only the 54 hit by Willie Mays.

After going 2–0 to Schmidt, Williams struck him out on three pitches and proceeded to strike out Chris James on a 3–2 pitch and then fanned Mark Ryal to end the game. It was pure Williams, who would save 36 games but help Cubs fans become very familiar with the edge of their seats all season long.

At 24, Williams was far from a proven commodity. In three seasons with the Rangers he had just 32 saves, and though he averaged more than a strikeout an inning he had also walked 220 batters in 274⅔ innings. The connection to Sheen's "Wild Thing" character from *Major League*, which became a box office hit, was

Chicago Cubs pitcher Mitch Williams flies off the mound in the ninth inning during a game against the New York Mets at Chicago's Wrigley Field on July 29, 1989. Williams got the last four Mets out for his 26th save, tops in the major leagues. The Cubs defeated the Mets 6–5. (AP Photo/John Swart)

instantaneous and within a few days there was talk that Williams would also enter games to The Troggs' classic song.

"If it was that loud and people screaming, it would feel great," Williams told the *Chicago Tribune* on April 18. A few weeks later, on May 10, it became a reality. With "Wild Thing" blaring over the loudspeakers, Williams came on in the eighth inning with one on and the Cubs nursing a 3–2 lead against San Francisco, their eventual opponent in the 1989 National League Championship Series.

It was a disaster. Williams gave up two singles and then balked in what would be the winning run. But hey, at least a cool, albeit brief, tradition was started.

Mitch Williams came to the Cubs on December 5, 1988, in a multi-player deal that sent Rafael Palmeiro, Jamie Moyer, and Drew Hall to Texas for Steve Wilson, Curtis Wilkerson, Paul Kilgus, and two minor leaguers.

The Cubs were in dire need of a bullpen ace after a horrific trade the previous winter in which longtime closer Lee Smith went to Boston for Calvin Schiraldi and Al Nipper. Eight different pitchers saved games in 1988, including an aging Goose Gossage, who had a team-high 13 saves.

Williams gave Cubs manager Don Zimmer the closer he needed, not to mention an ulcer he didn't need. Williams was such a source of frustration that Cubs fans began to boo him when he had several untimely breakdowns during the heat of the divisional race. He walked at least one batter in 17 of his 36 saves and along the way blew 10 other save opportunities.

There haven't been many clinching moments in Cubs history, but Williams was on the mound for one of them. On September 26, he got the final two outs in a 3–2 victory over Montreal, striking out Mike Fitzgerald to end the game.

That was the last great moment Williams had in a Cubs uniform. He was a non-factor in the NLCS against the Giants until

Game 5 and the Cubs were facing elimination when he was called upon to face left-handed hitter Will Clark with the bases loaded in the eighth inning of a tie game. Clark, who hit an incredible .650 in the series, ripped a single up the middle to make it 3–1, and an inning later the series was over.

After a 1990 season in which he walked 50 in 66 ⅓ innings while saving only 16 games and missing a month to knee surgery, Williams was traded to Philadelphia for Chuck McElroy and Bob Scanlan.

Williams got his groove back with the Phillies and would later meet up with another ex-Cub, Joe Carter, in the 1993 World Series. But that's a tale for another book.

84 Carlos Zambrano's Neutral Site No-Hitter

With a fastball reaching the upper 90s and a right jab that once reached Michael Barrett's lip, Carlos Zambrano has been one of the most enigmatic Cubs in recent memory.

Even though he won at least 13 games for six straight seasons from 2003 through 2008, Zambrano has had to deal with the burden of high expectations and inadequate results. In 2007, a year he won a career-high 18 games, he signed a five-year, $91.5 million contract extension but never lived up to the fat contract.

On June 7, 2008, after giving up seven runs to the Los Angeles Dodgers, Zambrano assaulted not one but two Gatorade dispensers. He repeated the act a year later against Pittsburgh, destroying another defenseless dispenser after a close call at the plate set him off.

Zambrano's embarrassing fistfight with Barrett in 2007 during a Cubs–Atlanta Braves game at Wrigley Field was the main event in a career that has seen him, among other incidents, tussle with choirboy Derrek Lee, rip Cubs fans for being selfish, and throw Carlos Marmol under the bus after a blown save. Where some saw passion, others saw a selfish hothead.

During the 2010 season, Cubs manager Lou Piniella moved Zambrano to the bullpen after a rough April, and in late June he was suspended for more than a month and got professional help after his maniacal outburst with Lee during the Crosstown Classic.

On August 12, 2011, the final straw seemingly arrived. With the game still going on, Zambrano declared he was retiring and fled the Cubs' clubhouse in Atlanta after he had given up five homers to the Braves. Zambrano was placed on the disqualified list for 30 days, and Cubs chairman Tom Ricketts said he didn't see how Zambrano could ever wear a Cubs uniform again.

No, it hasn't been a dull career for Zambrano, who picked one of the most unusual games in Cubs history to have the greatest game of his career.

As the 2008 season entered its final month and the Cubs were battling for a second straight division title, Zambrano was struggling. In five starts from August 9 to September 2, he posted an 8.10 ERA, winning just once. During the start on September 2, which he made on six days of rest due to what he said was a "tired arm," he pulled himself after five innings. There was pain, and it was in his right shoulder.

Zambrano was shut down and underwent an MRI, which proved negative. The recommendation was to rest and wait. After years of watching Mark Prior and Kerry Wood go through this, nobody expected Zambrano to pitch—let alone pitch well—anytime soon.

Meanwhile, the Houston Astros, who were trying to catch the Cubs in the standings, had their own problems that had nothing to do with baseball. Hurricane Ike was moving through the Gulf

Coast and on Saturday, September 13, it began moving its way through Texas.

Astros owner Drayton McClane was stubbornly insisting a three-game series against the Cubs, that was supposed to start on Friday night, could still be played at Minute Maid Park, but finally Major League Baseball stepped in and forced actions. The series was moved to Milwaukee's Miller Park. Zambrano was now pain free and, with 11 days rest, was scheduled to start the Sunday night game. Whatever he and the Cubs expected, it wasn't what they got.

With mostly Cubs fans among the 23,441 in attendance, Zambrano was sending 98-mph fastballs into Geovany Soto's glove and looking like the Big Z of old. He walked a batter in the fourth but got a double play, and a hit batsman in the fifth didn't rattle him. Other than that, no Astro had reached base.

The possibility of a no-hitter was becoming apparent, and with Zambrano coming off shoulder trouble a pitch count, though not announced, seemed likely. But would anyone dare pull the combustible Carlos Zambrano during a no-hitter?

"We were talking before the ballgame about 90 pitches," Piniella said afterward. "But I told [Cubs bench coach] Alan [Trammell], 'If he's got to come out of the game, you go get him. I'm not.'"

Just 12 days after many Cubs fans thought his season was over, Zambrano needed 110 pitches to finish off the Astros in a remarkably easy 10-strikeout no-hitter, the first by a Cubs pitcher since Milt Pappas on September 2, 1972, and the first neutral-site no-hitter in major league history.

"Next stop will be the World Series," declared Zambrano afterward.

Well, nobody said he pitched a perfect game.

85 Who's On Third?

Ron Santo made 13 straight Opening Day starts at third base for the Cubs from 1961–73 and was a tremendous hitter and fielder. But by no means was he irreplaceable.

In fact, from the time he left the Cubs through the 2016 season, he was replaced 142 times.

That astronomical figure includes Santo's first replacement, Bill Madlock, who won a couple of batting titles before getting traded after three seasons, as well as Alfonso Soriano, who filled in at third base for ⅓ of an inning in 2009.

The search for a third baseman underscored Santo's talents, and even though the position was ably filled for a few seasons, it took nearly 30 years to find a long-term solution in Aramis Ramirez, who has hit more homers than anyone in Cubs history not named Sosa, Banks, Williams, Sandberg, or Santo.

Ramirez's critics will rightfully point to his often-abysmal defense, several prolonged slumps when the Cubs needed him most, and going 2-for-23 during the 2007 and 2008 playoffs, both three-game sweeps. However you view his tenure, you can't deny Ramirez's longevity ended the 30-year carousel at the hot corner. After coming over from Pittsburgh in a 2003 trade deadline deal, Ramirez made eight straight Opening Day starts.

Compare that to the previous 30 seasons when the Cubs tried 17 different players on Opening Day, some good, some bad, and some like Gary Scott.

Bill Madlock, 1974–76: A contract squabble got Madlock shipped to San Francisco after three brilliant seasons, and he went on to collect more than 2,000 hits and two more batting titles with Pittsburgh. His batting average (.3362) with the Cubs is the highest of all-time, slightly ahead of outfielder Riggs Stephenson (.3359), who played for the Cubs from 1926–34.

Steve Ontiveros, 1977–80: Managed to earn four straight Opening Day starts despite hitting a total of six homers during his last three seasons with the Cubs. He was released on June 24, 1980, at the age of 28 and never played in the big leagues again.

Ken Reitz, 1981: A decent hitter who came over from St. Louis with Leon Durham in the Bruce Sutter trade, Reitz hit .215 with two homers in 82 games and was released the following spring. He played in seven games with Pittsburgh in 1982 before retiring.

Ryne Sandberg, 1982: Ever heard of him? Sandberg had almost no experience at third base and went 1-for-32 to start the season. The Cubs stuck by him, and he committed 11 errors in 133 games before moving to second base in 1983.

Ron Cey, 1983–85: The Penguin hit 84 homers for the Cubs during four dependable seasons. He was actually the starter for

Ron Cey played third base for the Cubs from 1983–85. (AP Photo)

most of 1986, but manger Jim Frey used Manny Trillo on Opening Day in St. Louis that year because he felt Trillo performed better on artificial turf.

Manny Trillo, 1986: Was the Cubs starting second baseman from 1975–78, hit .281 as a utility infielder from 1986–88 during his second stint.

Keith Moreland, 1987: With nowhere else to play him, the Cubs moved Moreland to third base to keep his bat in the lineup, but he finished with more errors (28) than home runs (27).

Vance Law, 1988–89: Hit .303 with five homers and 41 RBIs during the first half of 1988 to make the National League All-Star team, but that was the high point. He got one more Opening Day start in 1989 but hit just .235 and was replaced by Luis Salazar before season's end.

Luis Salazar, 1990: Average hitter whose high point was hitting .325 down the stretch run in 1989 as the Cubs won the NL East.

Gary Scott, 1991–92: Even Ron Santo got caught up in the hype during spring training in 1991, calling Scott a "can't miss" prospect. Scott missed by as large a margin as any hyped prospect in Cubs history, hitting .160 with three homers and 16 RBIs in 67 career games.

Steve Buechele, 1993–95: After the Gary Scott experiment failed, the Cubs went back to finding fading players on their last legs. Buechele hit 31 homers with 147 RBIs over four seasons and was released on July 6, 1995, a few months after making his third straight Opening Day start.

Jose Hernandez, 1996: The Cubs traded for Jose Hernandez twice but only gave him one Opening Day start in 1996 when he hit .242 with 10 homers and 41 RBIs.

Kevin Orie, 1997–98: A slightly better version of Gary Scott, Orie was another overhyped prospect who actually produced respectable numbers his rookie season, hitting .275 with eight homers and 44 RBIs. But after getting his second straight Opening

Day start in 1998, he hit .219 and was traded to Florida as part of a deal for relief pitcher Felix Heredia. Orie had a second stint with the Cubs in 2002, hitting .281 in 13 games.

Gary Gaetti, 1999: Gaetti was a big reason why the Cubs won the 1998 NL Wild Card race, hitting .320 with eight homers and 27 RBIs in just 37 games after getting released by St. Louis. The mistake was thinking that, at 40, he could produce like that throughout a full season. Gaetti hit .164 in April 1999 and never recovered as the Cubs tried Tyler Houston, Shane Andrews, Jeff Blauser, and even Cole Liniak at third. Gaetti finished at .204 with nine homers and 46 RBIs.

Shane Andrews, 2000: Andrews emerged from the 1999 mess as the starter and, as he had done with Montreal, tantalized with some tape-measure homers but hit just .229 with 14 homers and 39 RBIs.

Bill Mueller, 2001: In his first season with the Cubs after arriving in an off-season trade with San Francisco, Mueller was hitting .317 with five homers when he fractured his left kneecap sliding into a wall while going after a foul ball at Busch Stadium in St. Louis. Would have been the 2002 Opening Day starter, but arthroscopic knee surgery kept him out until May. He was traded back to the Giants on September 4, 2002, for prospect Jeff Verplancke, who never reached the big leagues.

Chris Stynes, 2002: Another utility player masquerading as an Opening Day starting third baseman, the right-handed hitting Stynes won the start over Mark Bellhorn, a switch-hitter with more power from the left side. Bellhorn went on to get the bulk of the playing time, hitting 27 homers that year while Stynes hit .241 in 195 at-bats.

Mark Bellhorn, 2003: Bellhorn was hitting .209 when he was traded on June 20 for Jose Hernandez, who hit .188 in 23 games before getting shipped to Pittsburgh on July 23 as part of the deal for Ramirez.

86 Judging Jim Hendry

One day in the fall of 2003, as the Cubs were nearing their most thrilling playoff run in nearly a century, a woman gushingly approached Jim Hendry to thank him for the turnaround of the franchise.

"It's only just the beginning," Hendry assured her.

Well, no it wasn't. Within a few days, the Cubs were eliminated from the playoffs, and as the years went by Hendry's vision of a sustained period of excellence failed to materialize. Injuries that thwarted the careers of Kerry Wood and Mark Prior played a huge role in the direction the team took, but so did a series of misguided and expensive free-agent signings that hamstrung Hendry and gave him few options to improve the Cubs in his final seasons as GM.

Hendry, who joined the Cubs in November 1994 as director of player personnel, was named general manager on July 5, 2002, the same day the Cubs fired manager Don Baylor. Hendry was a tireless worker and nice guy whose Cubs teams finished last once, first three times, and at 9 years, 1 month, and 15 days his tenure as GM was the longest since John Holland ran the club from 1957 to 1975.

Those three division titles are nothing to be scoffed at for a franchise that had previously won only two division titles in its history. But Hendry's legacy will be how he finished, not how he started. He just didn't do enough with the resources and then oversaw a dramatic descent of the club in 2009 following the disastrous Milton Bradley signing.

The Tribune Company owned the Cubs during the first seven seasons Hendry ran the team and gave him enough money to win. He became a master at swiping young, talented players from small-market teams who weren't willing or able to pony up big bucks.

Chicago Cubs manager Lou Piniella, left, talks with Cubs general manager Jim Hendry during practice on Tuesday, October 2, 2007, at Chase Field in Phoenix. (AP Photo/Ross D. Franklin)

One of these trades came on July 23, 2003, when he acquired 25-year-old third baseman Aramis Ramirez and veteran center fielder Kenny Lofton from Pittsburgh for Jose Hernandez, Bobby Hill, and Matt Bruback. After the 2003 season, Hendry traded struggling young first baseman Hee Seop Choi and minor leaguer Mike Nannini to Florida for rising 28-year-old first baseman Derrek Lee. Give Hendry credit for getting those deals done, but it was like taking candy from a baby.

The 2003 trade in which he dumped Todd Hundley's contract on the Los Angeles Dodgers for Mark Grudzielanek and Eric Karros, two key pieces in their playoff run, was a bigger indication that he knew how to pull off a trade.

Ramirez and Lee became cornerstones for nearly seven seasons and were in their prime when Hendry got the okay—or perhaps the order—to open up the vault following a disastrous 2006 season in which the Cubs went 66–96.

Hendry brought in free agents Mark DeRosa, Ted Lilly, Jason Marquis, and Alfonso Soriano, whose eight-year, $136 million contract was ridiculous the moment he signed it. But at the time all that mattered was producing a winner and, with the exception of Marquis, they each produced for the Cubs, at least initially.

Back-to-back division titles in 2007 and 2008 produced no playoff wins and led to Hendry's defining decision to trade the right-handed hitting DeRosa and sign Milton Bradley, a switch-hitter, for $30 million for three years. It was, in every way, a disaster. Bradley imploded in September and thus began what became an annual event for Hendry—suspending his overpaid players in need of professional help.

Carlos Zambrano, signed by Hendry to a five-year, $91.5 million extension in 2007, was suspended in 2010 after fighting with Derrek Lee and then suspended again in 2011 after he announced his retirement and left the club after getting shelled in Atlanta.

It was fitting that two of Hendry's last acts as GM were to trade Kosuke Fukudome, a $48 million failure, and send Zambrano home. Banking on Fukudome's talent and Zambrano's brain were two of his biggest mistakes.

There was intense speculation about Hendry's fate, and it became a guessing game in the papers and on blogs as to whether he would return. On August 19, 2011, nearly a month after he had been informed by Cubs owner Tom Ricketts he was being fired, it was announced that Hendry was out as GM.

"Not a lot of guys get to be a GM for nine years without a world championship," Hendry told reporters at his farewell news conference. "I've gotten more than my fair chance to do that."

It was true, and it was time to move on.

87 The Streak

If you can't have fun being a Cubs fan, what's the point? With that in mind, late one night in June, 2012, I began something that has been more fun than I ever imagined.

To truly start at the beginning, let's go back to September 9, 1965. That's the day on which Los Angeles Dodgers Hall of Famer Sandy Koufax threw a Perfect Game against the Cubs. A memorable day for Dodgers fans, a rough day for Cubs fans. But the next day something better happened. The Cubs didn't get no-hit. And the day after that? The Cubs didn't get no-hit again. And on and on it went for years and decades until this streak of not getting no-hit became the longest of its kind in Major League history.

I didn't know if this was a streak other Cubs fans actually cared about, and I don't have any idea when I first noticed it existed, but for me it always just seemed kind of cool that no matter what happened on the field it provided at least a little bit of joy every time the Cubs played. They went 0–14 to start the 1997 season? Didn't get no-hit once. Finished in 5th place every year from 2010 to 2014? Painful, but they got a hit every game.   When this book was first published in 2012, this chapter was very different. It was a tongue-in-cheek look at how the streak—which stood at 7,339 games following the 2011 season—somehow compared to Babe Ruth's 714 home runs or Joe DiMaggio's 56-game hitting streak. Which, of course, it didn't. Writing that chapter led me to that aforementioned night in 2012.

I love Twitter and always appreciated fun accounts, such as @ CoachQsMustache and @OldHossRadbourn. Was there anything I could do with the Cubs? In fact, there was. On the night of June 1, 2012, the New York Mets' Johan Santana threw the first

The Streak—By The Numbers

Using Baseball-Reference.com, I created a database of every player who ever extended The Streak. Only five players ever did it in the 9th inning: Jim Qualls, Ken Rudolph, Joe Wallis, Dave Hansen, and Michael Barrett. Below are the top 10 Streak extenders of all-time, the inning in which it was extended, and the type of hit recorded over the 7,920 games.

Top 10 Streak Extenders

Ryne Sandberg	413
Don Kessinger	328
Mark Grace	276
Sammy Sosa	239
Glenn Beckert	238
Billy Williams	230
Bill Buckner	170
Ivan de Jesus	161
Alfonso Soriano	153
Starlin Castro	144

Type of Hit Recorded

Single	5488
Double	1451
Triple	192
Home run	789

Inning In Which Streak Was Extended

First	4791
Second	1804
Third	696
Fourth	390
Fifth	128
Sixth	73
Seventh	23
Eighth	9
Ninth	5

no-hitter in team history dating back 40 years. There was a Twitter account dedicated to the Mets streak called @NoNoHitters, which still exists to this day.

And that's when it hit me: Instead of announcing the extension of a form of futility as @NoNoHitters did, I'll celebrate a form of success and send out a tweet every time the Cubs get their first hit of the game. So at exactly 2:18 AM on the morning of June 2, I registered a Twitter account called @CubsNoHitStreak.

Two days later, I sent out this tweet: "The #Cubs have not been no-hit since September 9, 1965. That's a total of 7,392 games, the longest streak in baseball history." Later that day, this tweet went out: "No. 7,393: Bryan LaHair singles to left with one out in the second inning. The streak lives. #Cubs"

And thus began my life as the manager of the Twitter account @ CubsNoHitStreak. Over the next three years, covering 528 games, @CubsNoHitStreak announced the extension of The Streak with pomp and circumstance. For much of those three seasons, the Cubs were miserable. But we had The Streak, and to my great delight the account was discovered and embraced by thousands of Cubs fans.

With the help of my brother Bobby Greenfield and my friend Chris Malcolm, who occasionally pinch-hit for me when I couldn't be available to send the tweet, @CubsNoHitStreak didn't miss a game. No matter where I was—date with my wife, coaching first base at a Little League game, playing softball with my team The Lost Briskmen—I'd follow the game and when that first hit came...The Streak lives!

Until one day, it didn't. Philadelphia's Cole Hamels no-hit the Cubs at Wrigley Field on July 25, 2015, to end The Streak at 7,920 games. The tweet immediately after the end of the game: "No. 7,921: Cole Hamels has no-hit the Cubs. The Streak dies." was retweeted over 4,100 times. That will never cease to blow my mind.

Despite the end of The Streak, I've kept @CubsNoHitStreak going. That wasn't the plan at all, I announced the night of the

Hamels' no-hitter that I'd no longer be tweeting the first hit. But many Cubs fans who follow the account encouraged me to keep it going, so on July 26 I sent out this tweet:

"No. 1: Kyle Schwarber singles with no outs in the first for the @Cubs. Only 7,919 to go!"

See you on Twitter. And long live The Streak!

88 Arrange to Have Your Ashes Scattered at Wrigley Field

Other than watching the Cubs win the World Series, this might be the most difficult thing in this book to do. Certainly, it'll be the hardest to enjoy.

But here's the surprising truth. The Cubs actually do accept requests to have ashes of deceased fans scattered at Wrigley Field, and they even honor those requests from time to time. Not surprisingly, they don't make announcements over the public address system every time a former season-ticket holder gets mixed in with the infield dirt.

"It's something we can rarely accommodate but do take a look at on a case-by-case basis," said Peter Chase, Cubs Director of Media Relations. "It's also something we do not ever publicize, nor does the family publicize."

It's impossible to say how many people have chosen Wrigley Field as their final resting place and had their wishes carried out, but it's happened more than a few times. Cubs great Charlie "Jolly Cholly" Grimm died in 1983 and, according to Ray Sons of the *Chicago Sun-Times*, had it in his will that he was to be spread around Wrigley.

Not long after Grimm's death, his wife Marion, former Cubs executive Salty Saltwell, and former Cubs owner Bill Wrigley, who sold the team to Tribune Co., walked onto Wrigley Field and carried out his wish. When Marion died in 1997, her wish was to join Charlie and her ashes were also scattered at the Friendly Confines, according to a *Sun-Times* obituary.

Legendary Cubs fan and folk singer Steve Goodman, who died in 1984 from leukemia at the age of 36, famously sang about a long-suffering Cubs fan who wanted to have his ashes blown around Wrigley Field in "A Dying Cubs Fan's Last Request." He sang:

Let my ashes blow in a beautiful snow
From the prevailing thirty-mile-an-hour southwest wind
And when my last remains go flying over the left field wall
We'll bid the bleacher bums adieu
I will come to my final resting place
Out on Waveland Avenue

Al Bunetta, who was Goodman's friend and business partner, tried to get the Cubs to let him spread the ashes around Wrigley but he was denied. So he and Goodman's brother, David, found a connection to get them into Wrigley shortly before Opening Day in 1988.

According to a 2007 column by the *Chicago Tribune*'s Eric Zorn, David Goodman wrote about that day: "We stood along the wall, sang the song, and let his ashes flow in a beautiful snow. One problem, the wind was blowing in that day and instead of coming to rest on Waveland Avenue, Stevie landed jus' a little short, [on the] warning track under the 368 sign."

There are stories of regular fans either getting approval from the Cubs or taking matters into their own hands. In 1981, the family of Perry J. Goldberg asked the Cubs to grant his wish, and team president William J. Hagenah Jr. said in a *Tribune* article that they would.

"This is not the first time we have had such a request. It would not be the first time we have granted such a request," Hagenah said. "But the ceremony, if it takes place, will be conducted in complete privacy. There will be no fanfare, no media coverage. And we certainly won't permit it while people are in the stands."

No, the Cubs won't permit it, but at least one fan didn't care. On May 2, 1995, a man in left field was spotted pouring something onto the warning track. It turned out to be his father's remains.

"I thought it was flour or white chalk or powder or something," Houston Astros left fielder Luis Gonzalez said after the game. "Man, there were a lot of ashes."

The man was ejected and a few days later the Cubs, concerned about a repeat performance, made it clear this would not be tolerated.

"I understand these are dying wishes, especially if they were Cub fans," Cubs general manager Ed Lynch said. "But we can't have that sort of thing."

So there you have it. Ed Lynch, who once traded Jon Garland for Matt Karchner, said you can't scatter your ashes at Wrigley Field.

Your move, Cubs fans.

89 Start Your Own Cubs Blog

One of the best reasons to start a Cubs blog can be summed up in a single word: TOOTBLAN.

Well, that's not exactly a word—it's an acronym that stands for Thrown Out On The Bases Like A Nincompoop, and it was invented in a May 7, 2008, post published by Tony Jewell on his Cubs blog, *Wrigleyville23*.

TOOTBLAN is actually one portion of a larger statistical term he dubbed "The Ryan Theriot Adjusted On-Base Percentage," which he created to help determine how much Theriot's value as a leadoff man was being eroded by being a nincompoop on the basepaths.

Here's how the first post began:

"To cement our legacy, Wrigleyville23 is introducing a new stat to the baseball world—The Ryan Theriot Adjusted On-Base Percentage. It is calculated as such: RTAOBP = (Hits+Walks+HBP-CS-Thrown Out On The Basepaths Like A Nincompoop)/Plate Appearances (AB+BB+HBP+SF)."

Here's how Jewell later defined TOOTBLAN on his blog:

In short, it is any out a runner makes on the basepaths while attempting to take an extra base—whether advancing from second to third on a ground out (with no runner on first); attempting to stretch a single into a double, a double into a triple, and so on; or getting thrown out while advancing on a flyball. It also applies to base runners who are picked off or who are doubled out on a line drive.

And here's what Jewell wrote in an email after helping me understand exactly how the term was derived:

"That was the genesis," wrote Jewell, who lives in Philadelphia and no longer updates Wrigleyville23. "And yes, I had a lot of time on my hands in the evenings."

Google "TOOTBLAN" and you'll see it appear on countless blogs, particularly ones about teams for which Theriot has played and whose fans' patience he has tested. You'll also see the power one creative blogger can have on highly engaged communities.

Creating and giving rise to your own statistic couldn't have happened before the age of blogging, which has enabled any Cubs fan to be their own publisher and show they can be every bit as witty, dumb, arrogant, and brilliant as those in traditional media. If you decide to start your own blog, here are a few tips that will help you get underway.

- Don't worry about the title. Pick something you're happy with and get to the important stuff.

- Post a lot, and during the baseball season post every day. If you're having a hard time coming up with something to write when there are about a million storylines, then you're just not paying attention.

- With wire stories and game casts, there is never any reason for you to write your own game story. Ever. Instead, you should focus on breaking down managerial blunders or ripping somebody who TOOTBLAN'd the Cubs into a loss. Your personality and opinion is your most valuable commodity, not your ability to relay what happened from reading a box score.

- Read up on the Cubs' minor leaguers at baseballamerica. com, minorleaguebaseball.com, or on blogs and news sites in the cities where the Cubs' farm teams play. There's a voracious appetite for minor league news and analysis. And there's nothing wrong with doing your own Top 10 Cubs Prospects list.

- Pick out a whole bunch of Cubs blogs, figure out which ones you like, and start commenting on them. Share their posts on your blog; if you start to send traffic their way, it won't go unnoticed and maybe the favor will be returned. In short, be a good neighbor.

- Invite your Cub fan friends to start commenting and even contribute their own posts, there's nothing wrong with having more than one writer on a blog. When somebody new leaves a comment, be sure to respond whether it's positive or negative. You want to be present and make your blog a place where other Cubs fans want to hang out.

Since 2009, I've been the Community Manager at ChicagoNow, the *Tribune*'s blog network, and an avid reader and lover of blogs. If you're just starting to explore, here are three suggestions:

- John Arguello's Cubs Den at chicagonow.com/cubs-den
- Brett Taylor's Bleacher Nation at bleachernation.com
- SB Nation's Bleed Cubbie Blue at bleedcubbieblue.com

They're all great in their own ways with smart writers who can be wickedly funny. And if you're interested in starting a Cubs blog on ChicagoNow, email me at jgreenfield@chicagonow.com.

90 Jerome Walton Streaks In and Out

The short, ultimately unsuccessful major league career of Jerome Walton had such promise when it started it's still remarkable he's known more for what went wrong than for what went right.

And to be sure, when his career started, almost everything went right.

Walton was drafted in the second round out of Enterprise State Junior College in 1986 and quickly soared to the upper echelon of the Cubs' minor league system at a time when they were producing prospects like Joe Carter, Mark Grace, Rafael Palmeiro, and Greg Maddux.

After hitting .331 at Double-A Pittsfield in 1988, Walton went to camp poised to make the club with a great supporter in Cubs manager Don Zimmer, who said Walton, 23 at the time, only needed to prove he could hit .260 to be named his Opening Day center fielder.

Walton hit just about .260, proved humble in saying all the right things during camp, and on April 4, 1989, made his major league debut by going 2-for-4 with an RBI in a 5–4 Opening Day win over Philadelphia. It was a sign of things to come.

During the Cubs drive to win the NL East, their second division title in six years, Walton provided remarkable consistency at the top of the lineup. He hit safely in 91 of 116 games and never went more than three games all season without a base hit despite the threat of rustiness from losing a month in the first half to a hamstring tear.

On July 21, Walton got a single off of San Francisco's Scott Garrelts. The next day he got another hit and the next day another, and by the time he finally went hitless a month later on August 21, he had compiled a 30-game hitting streak, the longest in Cubs history.

The dream season extended into the postseason when Walton hit .364 in a five-game loss to San Francisco in the National League Championship Series. Not long afterward, with a .293 average, 24 stolen bases, and a headline-inducing hitting streak, he was named the NL Rookie of the Year, the first Cub to win the award since Ken Hubbs in 1962.

And thus ended the glory days for Jerome Walton.

A rancorous off-season contract negotiation ended with the Cubs renewing Walton's salary at $185,000, far less than the $270,000 he had been seeking. He told the *Tribune* the negotiations were "behind me" but they weren't.

The 1990 season wasn't a terrible one for Walton; it was actually not that far off from his rookie year. He hit .263 with 14 stolen bases and once again lost a big chunk of time—this time 60 games—to injuries. In the off-season, the Cubs again renewed his contract at Walton's displeasure, but the point was moot because he never had a leg to stand on during negotiations.

Walton hit .219 in 1991 and then plummeted to .127 in just 30 games in 1992. He was sent down to Triple-A Iowa on June 19 and never returned. He signed with the California Angels in 1993 and actually hit .302 over the next six seasons with five different clubs but during that span only had 381 at-bats.

Less than three years after being named the NL's top rookie, Walton was released by the Cubs and during his exit interview with the media said his first contract after winning Rookie of the Year distracted and disturbed him. "I felt I was treated unfairly on my contract," he told the *Tribune*. "From then on, I just kind of had a grudge. I didn't really clear my head and say, 'Just forget it and go out and do what you've got to do.'"

Jerome Walton has a place in the Cubs' record book and will always have an indelible spot in the hearts of Cubs fans for his contributions to a magical 1989 season. He'll also go down as something of a mystery for the way his seemingly golden future turned into just another link to the Cubs disappointing past.

91 Smilin' Stan Hack

There may not have been a more joyous, pleasant man to be around in Cubs history than Stanley Camfield Hack, a leadoff man extraordinaire who patrolled third base at Wrigley Field for a generation.

Hack lived with two nicknames over the course of his long, productive career—one that seemed true but wasn't, and another that made sense the moment you gazed at his face. Charlie Grimm dubbed him "Stanislaus," and for many a teammate that's what he was called.

But he's remembered best as Smilin' Stan, who wore a permanent grin on his face in the same way that Dave Kingman wore a scowl.

"I enjoy playing baseball," Hack once said. "And this is my way of showing it."

During his 16 seasons with the Cubs—the only team he ever played for—Hack had plenty to smile about. The Cubs made it to four World Series from 1932 to 1945—they also went in 1935 and 1938—and Hack was the only player to appear in all four, though his entire line in the '32 Series was a single appearance as a pinch-runner.

Fast, smart, and possessing one of the best batting eyes in the game, Hack was the quintessential leadoff man in an era that rewarded station-to-station baseball. In 8,506 career plate appearances, he only struck out 466 times while drawing 1,092 walks, still the most ever by a Cub.

Between 1938 and 1945 he finished in the top 20 in MVP voting seven times, and the only time he didn't crack that barrier was in 1944 when he had quit baseball for the first two months of the season. Some alleged it was because he disliked Cubs manager Jimmie Wilson, but Hack's version was that he needed to tend to an Oregon farm he had recently purchased.

Wilson only lasted 10 games into the 1944 season before getting fired following a 1–9 start and was replaced by Hack's old buddy Grimm. Within a few weeks Hack was indeed making plans to return to the Cubs, and in 1945 he led them to the World Series again.

Hack's play in his first two World Series where he was a starter were mixed. In 1935 against Detroit, he only hit .227 with two runs scored and in the decisive Game 6, he was involved in two plays that could have altered the outcome. In the top of the sixth with the Cubs up 3–2, Hack hit a two-out double and went for third on Billy Jurges' grounder to Tigers third baseman Flea Clifton. Hack was able to elude the tag, but he was called out for leaving the base line.

In the ninth, Hack again got an extra-base hit, this time a leadoff triple in what was now a tie ballgame. After Jurges struck out, Grimm was expected to use a pinch-hitter for starting pitcher

Larry French. But Grimm went with French, who tapped out to the pitcher, and Augie Galan flew out to end the inning. The Series ended when the Tigers pushed across a run in the bottom of the inning.

In the 1938 and 1945 World Series, Hack was one of the best players on the field. He hit .471 in a four-game sweep at the hands of the New York Yankees in '38 and in 1945 had a team-high 11 hits while batting .367.

Hack's last hurrah with the Cubs wasn't as a player but as a manager. He took over for Phil Cavarretta just before the start of the 1954 season and skippered the club through three miserable seasons before turning over the reins to Bob Scheffing, who would fare no better.

Smilin' Stan also played a role in one of Bill Veeck Jr.'s ingenious promotions. In 1935, Veeck had some small mirrors with Stan's face on the back put up for sale in the Wrigley Field bleachers. The promotion—dubbed "Smile with Stan Hack"—ended when umpires realized bleacherites were using the mirrors to blind opposing hitters.

"I've always hoped Stan saved one of those mirrors so he could occasionally look at it and enjoy his own smile," Veeck told the *Chicago Tribune* after Hack passed away in 1979. "As so many of us did."

92 Attend Randy Hundley's Cubs Fantasy Camp

You look to your left, and there's Ryne Sandberg spitting out batting tips. Then you look out at the mound and you see Fergie Jenkins, leg kicked high, ready to throw high heat your way.

And just when you think it's time to wake up, you remember that you're not dreaming. The fantasy of playing for the Cubs is real. Well, sort of.

In 1982, former Cubs catcher Randy Hundley stumbled upon a ridiculously brilliant idea that has been copied by practically every major league team whose starry-eyed fans happen to have a few thousand dollars lying around.

Hundley, the gritty West Virginian who served as the Cubs catcher on Leo Durocher's star-crossed teams, was instructing little kids at a baseball camp when innovative Chicago *restaurateur* Rich Melman suggested he have a camp for men who were still little kids at heart. And that's how an industry was spawned.

By January 1983, Hundley had organized the first Cubs Fantasy Camp in Scottsdale, Arizona, where 63 men who were 35 or older (the age limit has since been lowered to 30) brought their wrinkled gloves, worn hats, and tender hamstrings to pretend to be Cubs for a week.

Scott Mermel, then 35, attended that first camp and spent the week before trying to get in shape with a friend, former Cubs pitcher Rich Nye, a reliever and spot starter on the '69 team who was working at the camp as one of the instructors.

Mermel remembers walking into the clubhouse and immediately being in awe to see he had his own locker and his own uniform with his name on the back. Then he noticed his locker mate was Billy Williams, good ol' No. 26. Between the two of them, Mermel and Williams hit 426 career home runs.

One of Hundley's not-so-hidden reasons for having that first camp was so his old pals from the '69 club could get together again, and almost without exception they all showed up. Even the crusty old Durocher came out toward the end of the week and got emotional talking about the old club during a speech at a banquet held at the camp.

The failure of 1969 was still fresh on the minds of anybody who loved that most memorable of Cubs teams, and it was so recent that Jenkins was still an active player. Durocher, who was 77, tried to use the opportunity to mend some old wounds.

"He apologized to the guys for not being a better manager," Mermel recalled. "And maybe working them too hard. We just got the feeling there was a lot going on between the lines."

There is certainly a ton of baseball played at camp. The campers break up into teams, and the coaches—whether it's Lee Smith, Don Kessinger, Rick Reuschel, or Bobby Dernier—easily fall back into the same competitiveness that surely helped them to the big leagues.

Playing baseball with a Cubs uniform on isn't the real fantasy; it's being just one of the guys recalled Tom Levy, who attended the 2003 camp. One of his favorite memories is seeing Jose Cardenal waltz into the locker room casually holding Joe Pepitone's hairpiece. But even more than the hijinks was hearing the stories and getting to know his boyhood idols as real people, not just some face on a baseball card.

"You're allowed in their world for that short period of time," said Levy, a budding seven-year-old Cubs fan in 1969. "I left with a better understanding of who they are and what they were like. When I see stuff about the '69 club, it makes my heart ache even more because I heard them talk about it."

More heartache? That's all too real.

93 Throw It Back! Throw It Back! Throw It Back!

You spend your whole life waiting to catch a home run ball, always trying to find the seat most likely to give you a chance, and when that glorious moment finally comes and the Baseball Gods have smiled upon you, thousands of strangers start a chant telling you what to do with your treasure.

"Throw it back!" they yell. "Throw it back!"

So you take a deep sigh, wind up, and heave the demon ball as far as you possibly can to great cheers from your fellow bleacher mates. And immediately you know it was the right thing to do.

It's generally accepted that this grand, irreverent tradition of throwing back visitor's home run balls was started at Wrigley Field, but exactly when and by whom isn't clear. Longtime sports radio broadcaster Mike Murphy claimed in author Dan Helpingstine's *The Cubs and the White Sox: A Baseball Rivalry, 1900 to the Present* that the first to throw it back was Ron Grousl, one of the original Bleacher Bums.

"It was totally unplanned," Murphy told Helpingstine. "I was standing next to Ron when it first occurred. Hank Aaron hit a home run into the left-field bleachers, which Ron caught on the fly. He looked at the ball and said, 'We don't want this stinking ball… it's an enemy homer!' With that he wound up and flipped it on the fly behind second base.

"There was a stunned silence for a moment—no one had ever seen anything like this before. Then the crowd went nuts. Cheering, laughing, jeering the great Hank Aaron…from then on, enemy home runs hit into the Wrigley Field bleachers were expected to be thrown back."

That first incident allegedly took place on June 1, 1969, when Aaron did, indeed, hit his 521st home run. But Helpingstine points out some inconsistencies in Murphy's story so take it with a grain of salt.

However, if that was the first time an opposing ball was thrown back the tradition seemed to have taken hold a week later. A *Chicago Tribune* story from June 7, 1969, about the emergence of the Bums began, "A strange thing happened yesterday in Wrigley Field. A fan in the left-field bleachers caught a home run ball and immediately threw it back on the field—scornfully."

Whatever the origin, the truth is that if you go to Wrigley Field and catch a visitor's home run ball, you're going to have to cough it up. Unless, of course, you came ready for such a possibility and throw back a fake one while pocketing the real one for yourself.

But you would never do such a thing, would you?

94 The John Baker Game

OK, maybe John Baker doesn't quite deserve to have a game named in his honor like Cubs legend Ryne Sandberg does but Baker's feat was no less historic. After all, what he accomplished had never happened in Cubs history and may never happen again.

As the evening of July 29, 2014 began the Cubs were enduring their fifth consecutive losing season and their annual selloff of talent to playoff contenders was well underway. Jeff Samardzija and Jason Hammel had been shipped to Oakland, Darwin Barney went to the Los Angeles Dodgers while Emilio Bonifacio and James Russell would soon be off to Atlanta.

John Baker? He wasn't going anywhere. He wasn't even in the starting lineup when the Cubs hosted Colorado at Wrigley Field.

A backup catcher with 14 career homers, none since 2009, Baker had endeared himself to Cubs fans with a happy-go-lucky demeanor that was sorely needed during this dire period in Cubs history. How many players besides Baker have sat in the Cubs dugout strumming a guitar to while away the time?

There was little to suggest history would be made as the Cubs and Rockies got underway, neither Cubs starter Edwin Jackson nor Rockies starter Jorge De La Rosa were spectacular. They each gave up three runs before departing, which is when things started to get interesting.

The bullpens were brilliant with each team using seven relievers to get the game into the 16th inning still knotted 3-3. And where was backup catcher John Baker when the 16th inning began? Why, on the pitcher's mound of course.

Cubs manager Rick Renteria had decided not to have Baker pinch-hit during the 13th inning with two runners on, electing to go with a pitcher—Jake Arrieta—since Baker was the last position player remaining on the bench.

Turns out the move was prescient, because when the 16th inning began the Cubs were out of available relief pitchers as well, Hecton Rondon had pitched the previous two games and couldn't go. Baker hadn't pitched since the Cape Cod League during a summer break from college, and true to his personality enjoyed every minute of it. He later said he could barely suppress a smile while standing on the mound.

Baker's fastball, topping out in the high 70's, didn't exactly fool Rockies hitters but after retiring Charlie Culberson on a foul ball and walking Drew Stubbs he got Cristhian Adames to hit into an inning-ending double play. It wasn't quite like facing the 1927 Yankees—Adames still only has 63 career hits in the majors through the end of the 2016 season—but it was still a hitless and scoreless inning when the Cubs needed it.

As fate would have it, Baker found himself leading off when the bottom of the 16th commenced and drew a walk. Bonifacio sacrificed Baker to second, he took third on an Anthony Rizzo single and raced home to score on a Starlin Castro sacrifice.

Baker's face lit up as he scored at 1:33 AM to end the longest game by time in Cubs history and make him the first Cubs' position player to ever record a win as a pitcher.

The John Baker Game? Sounds about right.

95 Be a Guest Conductor of the Seventh-Inning Stretch

Hey, if Ozzy Osbourne can butcher it, so can you.

After Harry Caray died a few weeks before the start of the 1998 season, how the Cubs would handle the singing of "Take Me Out to the Ballgame" in the post-Harry era became a hot topic of discussion.

The first choice was perfect. Dutchie Caray, Harry's widow, led the Wrigley Field faithful in an emotional rendition and after she was done, as she hugged Harry's grandson, Cubs broadcaster Chip Caray, "Amazing Grace" was performed by bagpipers. "I'm sure he was watching me," Dutchie said afterward. "And guiding me waving that microphone."

That first season was generally well-received as 85 different people or groups ranging from Cardinal Francis George to Bill Murray to Mike Ditka, whose rushed, off-key rendition on July 4 became the standard by which future awful renditions would be measured.

Sing the National Anthem at Wrigley Field

While there's no application process to become a guest conductor for the seventh-inning stretch, the Cubs are looking for people who would like to sing the National Anthem.

According to cubs.com, here's what you need to do in order to get your shot at singing before 40,000 at Wrigley Field:

"Any person(s) wanting to perform the National Anthem prior to a Cubs game must submit an audio file or video link of the musician(s) performing an "a cappella" version of the National Anthem. To be considered for the upcoming season, auditions should be emailed to NationalAnthem@cubs.com before March 1 each year.

It's accepted now that the celebrity-laden singing of the stretch will endure, but after that first year the Cubs went so far as to announce it would return. "One of the many things that Harry Caray left behind was this legacy of the Seventh Inning Stretch and we would just like to keep it alive and have some fun with it," Cubs vice president of marketing John McDonough told the *Chicago Tribune.*

You'd think having to come up with singers for 81 games would be difficult and well, it is. If having to come up with people who can sing is the goal. But the Cubs have had no shortage of willing celebrities looking to promote themselves or their projects even if they didn't seem to mind embarrassing themselves.

Just being bad isn't an issue. Being bad and showing your ignorance is. Osbourne's unintelligible version is an all-time great. NASCAR driver Jeff Gordon famously called it "Wrigley Stadium" before launching into an awful version that led to merciless booing throughout. *American Idol* reject Kellie Pickler sang about "popcorn and cracker jacks."

There has been one ejection in guest conductor history. On August 7, 2001, former Bears defensive lineman Steve McMichael entered the booth an inning after umpire Angel Hernandez had made a controversial call in a game against Colorado. McMichael looked menacingly down to the field and threatened that he was "going to have some speaks" with Hernandez after the game. Hernandez stared back at the booth then told the Cubs McMichael had to go, and they complied.

Since guest conductors began they have been invited to stay for a post-stretch interview that encompasses the bottom of the seventh inning. Whoever sings the stretch joins current Cubs broadcasters Len Kasper and Jim Deshaies, who simultaneously conduct an interview while attempting to broadcast an actual game.

For those of us who just want to watch a Cubs game nearing its conclusion, that's more painful than listening to Ozzy Osbourne.

96 The Emil Verban Memorial Society

On January 1, 2010, Bruce Ladd Jr., a retired Washington D.C. lobbyist, mailed out a newsletter to the 700 members of the world's most renowned Cubs fan club. The purpose was to let the members know he was shutting it down.

And so the Emil Verban Memorial Society ended just as it began, on the sole whim of its founder.

Retired and living in North Carolina, Ladd said he dreamed up the Verban Society in 1975 as a way to gain access to politicians and members of the media, many of whom he knew to be rabid Cubs fans. Among the first to join was former Vice President Dick Cheney, also known as Society member No. 4.

There were never any rules, responsibilities or, perhaps most importantly, dues to be paid. At first, you had to live in the D.C. area, but as the club grew in notoriety, its borders were expanded.

Before he knew it, the Emil Verban Memorial Society took on a life of its own. Ladd cut off membership at 700 in the mid–1980s after President Reagan, a former Cubs broadcaster, gave the Emil Verban Society—and Ladd—the kind of publicity one can only dream about.

"You're looking for an edge," Ladd said. "This was an edge. It always amazed [me that] nobody else did it."

By 1980, after five years of doing nothing but existing, Ladd decided to hold what became a Verban Society biennial lunch, and some awards were even given out from time to time. For example, the Ernie Banks Positivism Trophy was once won by Reagan.

On the other side, the Brock-for-Broglio Judgment Award—given to a person who shows the lousiest judgment—was awarded to the CEO of Coca-Cola for creating New Coke and to Rafael Palmeiro for having taken steroids.

Over the years, Democrats joined, as well. Hillary Clinton became a proud member, and White Sox fan Barack Obama became a not-so-proud member who joined against his will shortly after becoming president.

Obama had been nominated by another member, which was the only criteria for entrance. Once you're in, it's impossible to quit, unless of course Ladd decides it's time for you to go.

Disgraced Illinois governors George Ryan and Rod Blagojevich both were Verban members, although Ryan was able to stay in good standing despite going to prison while Blagojevich was given the boot after being kicked out of office.

"There's a difference between regular, normal Illinois graft and being an idiot," Ladd explained.

So who the heck was Emil Verban? As far as baseball historians are concerned, he was a hard-working yet weak-hitting second baseman whose seven-year career, which ended in 1950, is most notable for the lone home run he hit in 2,911 career at-bats.

Verban only played 199 games with the Cubs during three seasons, but when Ladd was thinking about who to name his Society after, he knew he'd found his man. He felt Verban's lunch-pail demeanor and Midwestern-style personality perfectly epitomized Cubs fans.

When Verban, who died in 1989, first heard about the Society, he thought he was being ridiculed and being made the butt of a joke. Ladd reached out to him and put an end to that notion and soon Verban grew to embrace the Society, often joining members for their biennial luncheon.

Verban became a mini-celebrity thanks to Ladd, who used his contacts to get Verban into old-timers games in Washington and even earned him an audience with President Reagan in the oval office. That's why Ladd decided it had to end rather than let the Verban name be misused.

"It was an interesting life experience, and I'm glad it happened," Ladd said. "And I'm glad I don't have to spend any time on it anymore."

97 Don Cardwell's No-Hit Debut

Don Cardwell wasn't happy at all, not one little bit. The 24-year-old right-handed pitcher had just been traded from the Philadelphia Phillies to the Chicago Cubs, and he wasn't feeling the love.

"Being traded makes you feel as if you aren't wanted," he lamented to reporters.

Less than 48 hours later, Cardwell made Cubs history and felt wanted. Maybe too wanted.

With the help of several defensive gems, including a miraculous shoestring catch by left fielder Walt Moryn to secure the final out, Cardwell thrilled a Wrigley Field crowd of 33,543 by throwing a no-hitter against the St. Louis Cardinals in his Cubs debut on May 15, 1960.

Moryn's grab ended a contest that only lasted one hour and 46 minutes, but being the back end of a doubleheader, restless fans immediately began pouring onto the field, clamoring for a piece of Cardwell. The ushers tried in vain to maintain order, but it was hopeless. Fans besieged Cardwell, who would later need a police escort to get back to his hotel, still carrying a Phillies bag with his clothes stuffed inside.

Afterward, he told the *Chicago Tribune*: "While all the fans were crowding around me, they kept beating my shoulder and pulling on my arm like they wanted a souvenir…me!"

Cardwell didn't have much of a track record when the Cubs got him. In four seasons with the Phillies he went 17–26 with a 4.46 ERA while mainly working as a starter. However, Cubs General Manager John Holland said Cardwell was the key to the four-player deal that also brought over first baseman Ed Bouchee and sent backup catcher Cal Neeman and second baseman Tony Taylor to the Phillies.

Cardwell had been pitching well of late and in his previous start against the Los Angeles Dodgers had a no-hitter going through six innings. But he also walked six and didn't factor in the decision. Against the Cardinals, he was a little wild at the outset. He walked the second batter he faced, shortstop Alex Grammas, before getting out of the first inning. Grammas was the final hitter Cardwell allowed to reach base.

He blew through the next six innings and arrived at the top of the eighth with history beckoning. Cardwell was well aware he had a no-hitter going, not because his teammates mentioned it to him or because he was scoreboard watching but because some excited kids apparently didn't know the unwritten rule that you don't talk to a pitcher in the midst of a no-hitter.

"A couple of kids [at the] back of the dugout kept telling me how many men I had retired in a row and how many I had to go," he said.

So much for jinxes.

A couple of nice defensive plays in the eighth inning by Jerry Kindall and Bouchee, who also came over from the Phillies with Cardwell and went a quiet 0-for-4 in his Cubs debut, preceded Cardinals legend Stan Musial coming to the plate as a pinch-hitter. A little over a year earlier, Musial had broken up Glen Hobbie's no-hitter in the seventh inning, the only hit the Cardinals would get in a 1–0 Cubs victory. This time he struck out on four pitches.

In the ninth, Joe Cunningham's line drive to Moryn nearly gave WGN's Jack Brickhouse a heart attack. Brickhouse, who was always part fan and part broadcaster, screamed out, "Come on, Moose!" as the ball hovered above the outfield grass.

Moose got it, Brickhouse survived, and Cardwell got his no-hitter as well as a $2,000 raise a few days later from Cubs owner P.K. Wrigley.

And Cubs fans? They got their money's worth for just about the only time all season. This was a terrible team already well below .500, and the no-hitter turned out to be one of the few bright spots. The Cubs drew only 809,770 fans and ended up in seventh place with a 60–94 record.

Cardwell, who was 1–2 at the time of the trade, finished the season with an 8–14 mark in a Cubs uniform. Two years later, on October 17, 1962, he was traded to the Cardinals in a deal that brought the Cubs pitcher Lindy McDaniel, who also happened to be the pitcher on the losing end of Cardwell's no-no.

98 Keep Loving Buck O'Neil

If there's an unsung hero in Cubs history it's Buck O'Neil, the great baseball man who had a hand in signing, nurturing, and coaching everyone from Ernie Banks to Billy Williams to Lou Brock to Lee Smith to Joe Carter.

O'Neil belongs to all of baseball, not just the Cubs. His support and passion for the Negro Leagues Baseball Museum endeared him to generations of fans, and his passing in 2006 at the ripe old age of 94 came far too soon.

There's little doubt O'Neil would have been a big-league skipper if racism hadn't kept baseball's managerial ranks segregated until Frank Robinson became Cleveland's manager in 1975. Still, he found a way to make his mark on baseball and Cubs in many ways.

It took six years after Jackie Robinson broke the color barrier in 1947 for the Cubs to bring an African American player to Wrigley Field, and both of them—Ernie Banks and Gene Baker—played for O'Neil when he managed the Kansas City Monarchs of the Negro Leagues.

In late 1955, with the big leagues having driven the Negro Leagues out of business thanks to integration, the Cubs hired O'Neil as a scout and he remained employed by the club for more than two decades.

A short time after signing Williams, O'Neil got a call from the Cubs that the very promising young player had gone back home to Alabama, fed up and disgusted with being called "nigger" every time he took the field.

Buck O'Neil talks about the Negro League on Sunday, July 30, 2006, at the Baseball Hall of Fame Induction in Cooperstown, New York. (AP Photo/ Jim McKnight)

O'Neil arrived in Williams' hometown of Whistler and sized up the situation. Instead of lecturing Williams to consider his future or how he needed to dismiss the bigots, the pair instead went out for some dinner and O'Neil didn't once mention returning to his minor league club.

After dinner O'Neil took Williams out to a semi-pro game where other kids were playing, laughing, and enjoying the game of baseball. How they wished they could trade places with Williams. A day later, Williams went back to Texas to join his teammates. And 426 homers later, he entered the Baseball Hall of Fame.

Of course, O'Neil was no stranger to racism in baseball. The Cubs helped temper that somewhat in 1962 when they made O'Neil the first African American coach in baseball history, a milestone that opened doors but also led to one enormous wasted opportunity.

When O'Neil was hired the Cubs were using the absurd College of Coaches system in which a rotating group of coaches would take turns running the club as the head coach. Despite being on staff, O'Neil wasn't offered the same opportunity. Cubs general manager John Holland said O'Neil would not be part of the rotation, and his title would be "instructor."

One day when the Cubs were playing Houston, head coach Charlie Metro was ejected and third-base coach Elvin Tappe soon followed. The Cubs needed a new third-base coach, and the only option in the dugout was O'Neil.

"All of the guys, they thought, 'Buck's going to coach at third base now.'" O'Neil told Carrie Muskat in *Banks to Sandberg to Grace*. "But I was there on the bench. They got Fred Martin, who was the pitching coach, and brought him from the bullpen to coach, which left nobody down in the bullpen. All that just to keep me from coaching at third base, which was stupid."

Williams also recalled that moment.

"I think it kind of made him feel bad, and of course the black players on the ballclub, they sensed that. It made you uncomfortable. It was a thing you couldn't do anything about."

But O'Neil didn't dwell on disappointment, just like he didn't dwell on not being elected to the Baseball Hall of Fame with other Negro League stars a few months before he died.

"Shed no tears for Buck," he said. "No, no. Ol' God's been good to me. You can see that, don't you? If I'm a Hall of Famer for you, that's all I need. Just keep loving ol' Buck."

99 The Veeck Boys

There's something missing from Bill Veeck Jr.'s Hall of Fame plaque. It fails to mention the Cubs a single time, a grave oversight for a man who was fond of saying, "I am the only human being ever raised in a ballpark."

That ballpark was Wrigley Field, and the man who raised him was responsible for some of the greatest Cubs teams ever.

William Veeck Sr. was a well-liked sports columnist who wrote for the *Chicago American* under the pen name Bill Bailey. In 1917, after writing a series of pieces explaining what he would do if he ran the Cubs, owner William Wrigley offered him the chance to put his money where his mouth was and run the team. Veeck Sr. accepted.

The following season, the Cubs won the National League pennant, and before Veeck Sr.'s death in 1933 they had won pennants in 1929 and 1932. The Cubs also won in 1935 with a roster largely comprised of Veeck Sr.'s players, not to mention a manager, Charlie Grimm, whom he had hired.

During these years, Veeck Jr. began his lifelong love affair with not just baseball but baseball fans. By the time he was 10, Veeck Jr. was going to Wrigley Field on a daily basis with his father, and by 15 he was working in the ticket office and moved on to being a vendor, concession stand salesman, and member of the grounds crew.

The elder Veeck was beloved by his son and taught him to treat customers as you would someone you'd invite into your own home, a lesson he never forgot while owning the St. Louis Browns, Cleveland Indians and, on two separate occasions, the Chicago White Sox.

When his father died of leukemia in 1933, Veeck Jr. was on his own and went to Cubs owner P.K. Wrigley, who had just inherited the team from his father, and asked for a job. He was hired for $18 a week as an office boy.

"My father left me a far more valuable and lasting legacy than money," Veeck Jr. wrote in his autobiography *Veeck—As In Wreck*. "He left me a good name. All my life I have run across old friends of his eager to show their affection for him by helping his son."

Within a few years, Veeck was named treasurer of the Cubs, and he began to have a hand in projects that still define the franchise. In 1937, he oversaw the building of the bleachers, designed the current scoreboard, and even planted the ivy that grows each spring on the outfield walls.

Veeck Jr. was always ahead of his time. He tried and failed to get Wrigley to install lights at Wrigley Field, and a few years before the "W" or "L" flags started waving atop the scoreboard to alert residents and passengers on the "L" riding by, Veeck was permitted to install lights that would serve the same purpose the flags later would. Those lights were originally green for a win and red for a loss, but they're now white for a win and blue if the Cubs go down to defeat.

Years after he last drew a paycheck from the Cubs, Bill Veeck Jr. could still be found with his wife and companion, Mary Frances, enjoying the sunshine in the bleachers he helped build and surrounded by the bittersweet ivy he helped plant.

There will never be another quite like Bill Veeck. Either one of them.

100 Talk to an Old-Timer about the Cubs

Everybody has a Gus, or at least everybody should have one.

The one in my family—or at least the family I was lucky enough to marry into—is Gus Kapellas, whose life story blends many elements of the American dream, nearly all of it intertwined with his beloved Chicago Cubs.

Gus, who was born in Joliet, Illinois, on April 29, 1920, truly has lived the American dream, and falling in love with the Cubs and baseball weren't the only reasons why. In 1952 he met an enterprising restaurateur named Ray Kroc, who convinced Gus to join him in his new enterprise: McDonald's.

Over the years, Gus built up dozens of McDonald's restaurants in Chicago and then Arizona, where he moved in 1983. That was only fitting, since Mesa has been home to Cubs' spring training since 1952.

"One time, my first wife, we were at the ballpark, and it was the 9th inning and the Cubs were losing 10–1," Gus told my wife and I one night at dinner. "She said 'Let's go.' I said 'No, no. They may win this game.'

"She said, 'You're really sick.' They lost 10–1. We stayed until the last man was out. I've never left that ballpark until the game was over. I loved the Cubs."

That story, and many others like it, came out on a warm evening in April 2011 near Gus' home in Scottsdale, Arizona. It's not hard to get Gus to talk about the Cubs, but on this night it was particularly easy because that's what my wife and I asked him to talk about. The stories, some dating back more than 70 years, came to him in an instant as if they had happened yesterday.

Gus told us about the days of his youth spent toiling on the vegetable farm his family owned in Joliet, Illinois. The youngest of 11 kids, Gus would work the field while his sister listened to Cubs broadcaster Pat Flanagan on their $19 transistor radio.

"Every so often I would go get a drink of water, and she'd have the scorecard all ready for me," said Gus, whose favorite ballplayers over the years included Phil Cavarretta, Stan Hack, Guy Bush, Lon Warneke and, among the modern ballplayers, Andre Dawson. "And I knew what was going on."

He told the story about the day in 1929 when he first saw Wrigley Field. He was nine years old, and the bleachers had not yet been built. He remembers the outfield being roped off so any ball hit into it was a ground-rule double.

What he doesn't remember is how his brother, somehow, got them tickets.

"I was so amazed to see so many people at a ballgame," he said. "That made me a Cub fan. As time went on I would do anything and everything in order to go to Cubs park.

Gus worked at the Joliet brickyards, and every once in a while he and his pals would knock off a little early, grab a quick shower, and take a two-hour journey on the train, then the "L", before arriving at Wrigley Field.

Gus told us about the time in 1945 when he was stationed in Dutch Guyana and the Cubs were about to play Game 7 of the World Series against Detroit. Somehow they configured some wires on a telephone pole and were able to pick up a radio broadcast.

Their ingenuity brought them baseball but also a quicker disappointment as the Cubs lost that World Series and haven't been back since.

"That was the biggest disappointment of my life," he said. "I couldn't believe it. I thought it was in the bag." Spoken like a true Cubs fan.

Gus passed away at the age of 95 in 2015. I'm so grateful for so many of our conversations, but particularly the time I sat him down to talk about the Cubs.

Everybody has a Gus. Take the time to talk to yours and get the stories down on paper or video because, like all of us, we won't be here forever.

But our stories can be.

Acknowledgments

This book may never have been written if the 2011 Cubs weren't a pretty awful team. Their consistently lousy play saved me from the distraction of paying too much attention to their games during the four months I wrote this book. So to Tyler Colvin, Kosuke Fukudome, Carlos Zambrano, Doug Davis, among many deserving others, I thank you.

It would be great to hear from all the other authors of this wonderful series about how it went for them, but for me coming up with the first 60–70 "things" came fairly easily. For the last 30–40, I want to thank Ed Hartig, Teddy Greenstein, Phil Rogers, Carrie Muskat, and Julie DiCaro for sharing their vast knowledge. And very special thanks to Dan McGrath, who I can't thank enough for helping make this a vastly better book. In addition to their advice, I immersed myself in hundreds of books, newspaper articles, and blog posts that span Cubs history. For a baseball junkie, there wasn't a better way to spend a day.

This opportunity would never have come my way if not for Chris Malcolm, whose creativity and friendship I'll always admire and treasure. Many thanks to Tab Bamford, author of *100 Things Hawks Fans Should Know & Do Before They Die* for putting up with my DM's. You don't know how helpful it was to go through this at the same time as you. Beth Arthur saved me hundreds of hours with her suggestion to stop bothering with microfilm and use Proquest. Beth, thanks for introducing me to the 21st century.

I want to thank several people at Triumph Books, including Scott Rowan for hiring me to write this book, Adam Motin for creating this series, and Karen O'Brien for her careful editing and patience.

To Granny Franny, who always told me I'd find my niche, I miss and love you. To my dad, Michael, and my mom, Rochelle, who are probably smiling at each other and whispering "kvell, kvell, kvell" as they read this, the best part of covering the Cubs and White Sox was calling you from the press box to share those moments. Every son should get to share a dream come true with his parents.

My own sons, Casey and Eli, went without their dad on countless weeknights and a summer of Sundays when we could have been playing catch. It was all the more painful because they both fell in love with baseball during the summer I wrote this book. Future summers will be different, if not with the Cubs at least with my availability.

Finally, if I had realized beforehand how much time this book would have taken to write, my wife, Jill, would still have told me to go ahead and do it. While I got to immerse myself in Cubs lore, Jill essentially became a single parent for an entire summer. Everyone who knows Jill loves her, but I get to spend my life with her and that amazes me every day. Jill, I love you and look forward to us watching a lifetime's worth of gymnastics and figure skating for years to come.

Not to mention a little baseball.

Sources

There weren't many mornings during the summer this book was written that I wasn't lugging a backpack loaded with some tremendous books by authors who I came to respect and depend on. As much as my back was in danger of going out, the greater danger was getting sucked into these wonderful resources and reading when I should have been writing.

This book couldn't have been written without the first drafts of history put forth by the remarkable beat writers, reporters, and columnists from the *Chicago Tribune, Chicago Sun-Times, Chicago Daily News, Daily Herald, New York Times, Washington Post,* and *Pittsburgh Tribune-Review.* I spent many hours poring over *Sports Illustrated, Baseball Digest,* ESPN.com, and SB Nation's Bleed Cubbie Blue both to inform the creation of the 100 Things and help guide my research. Just how baseball books were written before the existence of Baseball-Reference.com I'm not sure, it's an essential resource for any writer or fan.

Here are the books that served as invaluable resources and for which I hope you'll take the time to indulge yourself.

Ahrens, Art. *Chicago Cubs: Tinker to Evers to Chance* (Charleston, S.C.: Arcadia Publishing, 2007).

Billington, Charles N. *Wrigley Field's Last World Series: The Wartime Chicago Cubs and the Pennant of 1945* (Lake Claremont Press, 2005).

Brown, Warren. *The Chicago Cubs* (Carbondale, IL: Southern Illinois University Press, 1946).

Caray, Harry with Bob Verdi. *Holy Cow!* (New York, NY: Villard Books, 1989).

Carmichael, John. *My Greatest Day In Baseball* (A.S. Barnes & Company, 1945).

Durocher, Leo with Ed Linn. *Nice Guys Finish Last* (New York, NY: Simon and Schuster, 1975).

Feldmann, Doug. *Miracle Collapse: The 1969 Chicago Cubs* (Lincoln, NE: University of Nebraska Press, 2006).

Freedman, Lew. *Cubs Essential* (Chicago, IL: Triumph Books, 2006).

Grimm, Charlie with Ed Prell. *Jolly Cholly's Story: Baseball, I Love You!* (Chicago, IL: Henry Regnery Company, 1968).

Golenbock, Peter. *Wrigleyville: A Magical History Tour of the Chicago Cubs* (New York, NY: St. Martins Press, 1996).

Helpingstine, Dan. *The Cubs and the White Sox: A Baseball Rivalry, 1900 to the Present* (Jefferson, NC: McFarland & Co., 2010).

Hughes, Pat and Rich Wolfe. *Ron Santo: A Perfect 10* (Lone Wolfe Press, 2011).

Jenkins, Ferguson with Lew Freedman. *Fergie: My Life from the Cubs to Cooperstown* (Chicago, IL: Triumph Books, 2009).

Kogan, Rick. *A Chicago Tavern: A Goat, a Curse and the American Dream* (Chicago, IL: Lake Claremont Press, 2006).

Langford, Jim. *Runs, Hits & Errors* (South Bend, IN: Diamond Communications, 1987).

Matthews, George R. *When the Cubs Won It All: The 1908 Championship Season,* (Jefferson, NC: McFarland & Co., 2009).

Muskat, Carrie. *Banks to Sandberg to Grace* (Lincolnwood, IL: Contemporary Books, 2001).

Rogers, Phil. *Ernie Banks: Mr. Cub and the Summer of '69* (Chicago, IL: Triumph Books, 2011).

Shea, Stuart. *Wrigley Field: The Unauthorized Biography* (Dulles, VA: Brassey's Inc., 2004).

Snell, Roger. *Root for the Cubs: Charlie Root & the 1929 Chicago Cubs* (Nicholasville, KY: Wind Publications, 2009).

Stout, Glenn. *The Cubs: The Complete Story of Chicago Cubs Baseball* (Boston, MA: Houghton Mifflin, 2007).

Talley, Rick. The Cubs of '69: Recollections of the Team That Should Have Been (Chicago, IL: Contemporary Books, 1989).

Thomson, Cindy and Scott Brown. Lincoln, *Three Finger: The Mordecai Brown Story* (Lincoln, NE: University of Nebraska Press, 2008).

Veeck, Bill. *Veeck—As In Wreck* (New York, NY: Putnam, 1962).

Vitti, Jim. *Chicago Cubs: Baseball on Catalina Island* (Charleston, S.C.: Arcadia Publishing, 2010).

Vorwald, Bob. *What It Means To Be a Cub* (Chicago, IL: Triumph Books, 2010).

Williams, Billy with Fred Mitchell. *Billy Williams: My Sweet-Swinging Lifetime with the Cubs* (Chicago, IL: Triumph Books, 2008).